OXFORD ISLAMIC LEGAL STUDIES

Series Editors:
Anver M. Emon, Clark Lombardi, and Lynn Welchman

NARRATIVES OF ISLAMIC LEGAL THEORY

OXFORD ISLAMIC LEGAL STUDIES

Series Editors:
Anver M. Emon, Clark Lombardi, and Lynn Welchman

Satisfying the growing interest in Islam and Islamic law, the *Oxford Islamic Legal Studies* series speaks to both specialists and those interested in the study of a legal tradition that shapes lives and societies across the globe. Islamic law operates at several levels. It shapes private decision making, binds communities, and it is also imposed by states as domestic positive law. The series features innovative and interdisciplinary studies that explore Islamic law as it operates at each of these levels. The series also sheds new light on the history and jurisprudence of Islamic law and provides for a richer understanding of the state of Islamic law in the contemporary Muslim world, including parts of the world where Muslims are minorities.

Narratives of Islamic Legal Theory

RUMEE AHMED

OXFORD
UNIVERSITY PRESS

OXFORD
UNIVERSITY PRESS

Great Clarendon Street, Oxford, OX2 6DP,
United Kingdom

Oxford University Press is a department of the University of Oxford.
It furthers the University's objective of excellence in research, scholarship,
and education by publishing worldwide. Oxford is a registered trade mark of
Oxford University Press in the UK and in certain other countries

First Edition published in 2012

Published in the United States of America by Oxford University Press
198 Madison Avenue, New York, NY 10016, United States of America

British Library Cataloguing in Publication Data
Data available

Library of Congress Control Number: 2012931996

ISBN 978–0–19–964017–1

For Ayesha,
Your love gives me meaning,
Your faith gives me purpose,
Your smile gives me peace.

Series Editors' Preface

In this inaugural volume in the *Oxford Islamic Legal Studies* series, Rumee Ahmed challenges his readers to rethink how and why pre-modern scholars devoted so much energy to the production of sophisticated manuals of legal theory (*uṣūl al-fiqh*). Some scholars have suggested that they wrote these manuals as post-hoc justifications of legal rulings that had already become authoritative. According to such scholars, the legal theory genre had little practical effect in the initial development of law or the further elaboration of it. Although Ahmed recognizes this important historical-critical research on Islamic law, he suggests that there is more to the story. His study offers a close analysis and interrogation of the underlying arguments that pre-modern jurists presented in their legal texts. The monograph focuses on two pre-modern Ḥanafī jurists, al-Sarakhsī and al-Dabūsī, who might otherwise seem quite similar to one another. Through close analysis, however, Ahmed shows that these two jurists went beyond the theoretical justification of existing rules. Studying and writing about legal theory thus offered jurists an arena in which to engage in a discourse that both explored and even challenged politically sensitive theological ideas.

Ahmed situates his study at the intersection of law, theology, and philosophy. His research is characterized by an innovative use of semiotic theory and narrative theology to re-conceive the genre of legal theory as one that provided legal, theological, social, and political meaning to communities of jurists. Significantly, he demonstrates that pre-modern jurists used the genre of legal theory as a medium through which to address the relationships between God, humanity, and the natural order of the universe. Indeed, his monograph shows that the jurists' theoretical arguments transcended formal jurisprudence. Ahmed explains how legal theorists appropriated existing legal principles and used them to construct worlds ordered by higher ethical and cosmological ideals.

Anver M. Emon
Clark Lombardi
Lynn Welchman

Acknowledgments

There are many people to whom I owe thanks for the publication of this book, foremost being my wife. Her unwavering belief and support made this possible, and her personality kept us both sane as the project evolved. In the writing of this book, she played the role of editor, nursemaid, critic, psychologist, colleague, administrative assistant, best friend, and cheerleader, all at the same time. My gratitude to her is unending, and my wonder at my good fortune unceasing.

For this project I am deeply grateful for the leadership and guidance of the editor of this series, Anver Emon. He embodies the belief that criticism need not be destructive to be constructive, and I cannot imagine a more dedicated and supportive editor. His comments made this manuscript immeasurably better, and any errors found herein are my own. I was also fortunate to have wonderful advisors on this project. In Peter Ochs I had a wise and patient teacher, whose ability to help students understand and feel ownership over complex philosophical concepts is inspiring. Now a professor myself, I marvel at his repeated, often fruitless attempts to teach me the intricacies of historical philosophical debates, most memorably his weeks of trying to teach me the pragmaticist critique of Kant's transcendental dialectic. These attempts often took us into the night, resulting in epiphanies that were sure to be forgotten a few days later, at which point he would try yet again. Abdulaziz Sachedina gave me the space and the tools to cultivate my own relationship with medieval texts and the Islamic legal tradition, and pushed me to question all my assumptions. I am grateful to Timothy Gianotti and Jorge Secada for their comments on an early draft, which resulted in significant revisions.

The academy has provided me with colleagues who have also been both friends and mentors, and who made the writing process enjoyable. These include Kecia Ali, Aryeh Cohen, Elliott Colla, Farid Esack, Bob Gibbs, Tom Greggs, Steven Kepnes, Mahan Mirza, Randi Rashkover, Mohammed Rustom, and Laurie Zoloth. I have many people to thank for their continued friendship despite my best efforts; especially Sarah

Abdallah, Imran Baig, Charlie Bergstrom, Susan Hardy, Haqnawaz Khan, Omar Nawaz Khan, Krisjon Olson, Maher Samra, Bill Twaddell, Amer Tobing, and Michael Townes.

My family has been a source of strength and support, for which I am truly grateful. My in-laws accord me an outmoded level of love and respect that stretches the boundaries of hospitality. Special thanks go to Tayyab for showing me the humor in all things, to Maryum for humoring my many phases, and to Khadijah for challenging my notions of sense and sensibility. My parents and my brothers remind me that my universe is of my own creation and that taking yourself too seriously is vastly overrated. Special thanks to my Dad, Iqbal Ahmed, whose pride in my achievements warms the depths of my soul.

Contents

Introduction

This is a book about the logic of medieval Islamic legal theory (*uṣūl al-fiqh*), a yawn-inducing subject even for seasoned scholars of Islamic Studies. Indeed, legal theory manuals lend themselves to a study that is, in a word, boring. This is unfortunate, because as recent studies demonstrate,[1] legal theory manuals are the sites of some of the most wildly creative, deeply personal, and intensely ideological Islamic legal thought in the medieval period. These exciting aspects of legal theory, however, are buried deep within abstruse discourses on hermeneutics, defenses of historical juridical opinions and attacks on competing legal schools. So deeply are they buried that most scholars assume that legal theory manuals have little to offer in the way of creative articulations of Islamic law (*sharīʿa*). As a result, medieval legal theory is usually written off as nothing more than a self-consciously reified regurgitation of sectarian rules set down

[1] Such studies include Anver Emon, *Islamic Natural Law Theories* (Oxford University Press 2010); David Vishanoff, *The Formation of Islamic Hermeneutics: How Sunni Legal Theorists Imagined a Revealed Law* (American Oriental Society 2011); Bernard Weiss, *The Spirit of Islam* (University of Georgia Press 1998); and many of the essays in Bernard Weiss (ed), *Studies in Islamic Legal Theory* (Brill 2002). The heterogeneity amongst assumed uniformity was noticed earlier in Wael B Hallaq, 'The Primacy of the Qur'ān in Shāṭibī's Legal Theory' in *Islamic Studies Presented to Charles J. Adams* (Brill 1991) 69ff; but works dedicated to the re-evaluation of *uṣūl al-fiqh* emerged only recently; Wolfhart Heinrichs, '*Qawāʿid* as a Genre of Legal Literature' in *Studies in Islamic Legal Theory* (Brill 2002) 365. A similar genre re-evaluation has already taken place with regard to other Islamic sciences, most notably in *fiqh* studies. Baber Johansen, writing in the context of *fiqh* wrote, '... contrary to the received wisdom in this field, Islamic law retained its vitality and continued to evolve and change throughout its history. This position differs fundamentally from the views set forth by such eminent authorities as Schacht, Coulson, and Chehata, who hold that by the 10th century the essentials of Islamic legal doctrine (in particular that of the Hanafi school) were already fully formulated and that, with the exception of some minor points, this doctrine remained fixed forever.' Baber Johansen, 'A Response to Ann Elizabeth Mayer's Review of *The Islamic Law on Land Tax and Rent: The Peasant's Loss of Property Rights as Interpreted in the Hanafite Legal Literature of the Mamluk and Ottoman Periods*' (1992) 24 *International Journal of Middle East Studies* 553.

by ancient legal thinkers, never to be challenged or changed, and wholly disconnected from any lived reality.

Part of this impatience with legal theory is certainly borne of disappointment from a genre that sounds so intriguing yet appears so moribund. Legal theory, one might think, should be a thought-provoking, creative enterprise. Even the name of the genre, *uṣūl al-fiqh*, literally 'the foundations of jurisprudence,'[2] suggests a forum for enumerating the higher ethical ideals to which jurisprudence should adhere. Legal theory works could theoretically establish procedural principles that would serve as a check on Islamic jurisprudence (*fiqh*), so that any derived injunction could be examined to see whether or not it violates a foundational ethical concern. But legal theory works do not function in any such way. In fact, they encourage a cynical reading by virtue of their very arrangement.[3]

A brief glance at any medieval legal theory text written after the 9th century would surely encourage intrepid researchers looking for creative articulations of Islamic doctrine and law to look elsewhere. To begin with, most legal theory manuals look exactly the same in terms of their structure. Within any given legal school, scholars typically address the exact same subjects under the same topic-headings. Furthermore, they generally come to the same conclusions about those subjects; so that a 16th-century jurist from the Shāfiʿī legal school writing in Baghdad will

[2] Islamicists have translated '*uṣūl al-fiqh*' into English in multiple ways, including 'the roots of law,' 'the principles of jurisprudence,' and 'source methodology.' I believe that Joseph Lowry's translation of 'legal hermeneutics' is the most accurate given the use of technical terms within *uṣūl al-fiqh* works to interpret revealed texts for the purpose of arguing for legal norms; Joseph Lowry, *Early Islamic Legal Theory: The Risāla of Muḥammad ibn Idrīs al-Shāfiʿī* (Brill 2007) 1. Nevertheless, I have chosen to use the term 'legal theory' for two reasons. First, 'legal theory' is utilized in modern secular debates about the function of norms in the articulation of law. Second, 'legal theory' is regularly used by Islamicists to refer to *uṣūl al-fiqh*; Lowry himself uses 'legal theory' in the title of his own work on Shāfiʿī's *uṣūl*. 'Legal theory' appears to be the standard translation for '*uṣūl al-fiqh*' and I see no compelling reason to divert from it.

[3] Indeed, such a cynical reading has dominated much of both the historical and modern discussions surrounding *uṣūl al-fiqh*; see Muḥammad Abū Zahra, *Uṣūl al-Fiqh* (Dār al-Thiqāfat al-ʿArabiyya 1957) 18–20; George Makdisi, 'The Juridical Theology of Shāfiʿī: Origins and Significance of Uṣūl al-Fiqh' (1984) 59 *Studia Islamica* 5, 35–6; Brannon Wheeler, *Applying the Canon in Islam: the Authorization and Maintenance of Interpretive Reasoning in Ḥanafī Scholarship* (SUNY Press 1996) 113ff; Sherman Jackson, 'Fiction and Formalism: Toward a Functional Analysis of Uṣūl al-Fiqh' in *Studies in Islamic Legal Theory* (Brill 2002) 178–81.

come to the same conclusion about the inability of prophetic practice to abrogate the Qur'ān as an 11th-century Shāfiʿī jurist writing in Cairo. At first blush, legal theorists appear to simply copy and perpetuate the works and ideas of their predecessors. Modern scholars have taken note of this mimesis in legal theory manuals and concluded that legal theory was a way for a legal school to establish and defend its particular doctrines while simultaneously attacking competitors. It was assumed, therefore, that legal theory had nothing to do with the lived practice of the community; rather, it was basically a forum for erudite scholars to prove, at the highest intellectual level, the superiority of their legal school.

For the legal theory genre to be, in essence, a glorified chat room for scholars to push their agendas casts doubt on the ethical integrity of the entire Islamic juridical enterprise; not least because of the missed opportunity to formulate innovative principles upon which Islamic jurisprudence could be founded. If it is true that legal theory manuals did not enumerate ethical principles to which jurisprudence should adhere, then jurists were theoretically free to derive jurisprudence without concern for higher ethical ideals. Certainly, jurists may have used their own, personal ideals according to which they derived jurisprudence, but those ideals were not explicitly captured and enumerated in any corresponding work of legal theory.

Some modern scholars have argued that a lack of a functional legal theory was actually of great benefit to Islamic jurisprudence. Freedom from theoretical constraints would allow Islamic jurisprudence to respond to changing times and places without needing to conform to ethical postulates which may themselves be context-specific.[4] This may well be an accurate description of Islamic jurisprudence, but such depictions of Islamic law paint legal theory manuals in an unflattering light. What was the point of writing a work of legal theory if it neither argued for ethical standards in the derivation of

[4] Mawil Izzi Dien, *Islamic Law: From Historical Foundations to Contemporary Practice* (Edinburgh University Press 2004) 114; William J Donaldson, *Sharecropping in the Yemen: A Study of Islamic Theory, Custom and Pragmatism* (Brill 2000) 49; Frank Vogel, *Islamic Law and Legal System: Studies of Saudi Arabia* (Brill 2000) 327.

jurisprudence nor functioned in any meaningful way for jurists when articulating jurisprudence in their own milieu? If they were merely perpetuating the traditions of their legal school, then that suggests a willful hypocrisy on the part of the legal theorists. It would seem that legal theorists were writing under the guise of a genre that binds jurisprudence to moral principles, knowing that it would practically never do so, to provide a moral façade to what is essentially evangelism and polemics.

However, this indictment of legal theorists rests on certain assumptions about how legal theory manuals were meant to function. These assumptions, despite being inaccurate, were perpetuated by jurists themselves, especially in their introductions, in an attempt to summarize the methodology of their legal school in rational terms. Presenting one's legal school as dispassionate and calculating gives the particular injunctions promoted by that school an air of sagacity, as though all their injunctions necessarily followed from the dictates of basic logic. Hence, the common assumptions that jurists perpetuated about how legal theory and legal theory manuals were 'supposed' to work served a rhetorical function. It was in the interest of jurists to assert that legal theory was supposed to function in a way that connected individual injunctions to higher ethical principles, even if legal theory manuals did not function, and were not intended to function, in such a manner.

Jurists regularly suggested that legal theory manuals demonstrated the logical connections between the particular principles and injunctions promoted by their legal school. These rhetorical, though mythical, connections were usually presented as rational syllogisms. Legal theorists supposedly utilized these syllogisms in one of two ways. The first way, ascribed to the Ḥanafī school of law, holds that inherited legal injunctions conform to a certain logic and that that logic can be ascertained through a careful study of jurisprudence. That is, an astute jurist can *induce* a principle by analyzing inherited jurisprudence. For example, grape wine is categorically forbidden in almost all Islamic jurisprudential works. This inherited jurisprudence, then, forms the foundation of the syllogism that leads to the principle. Once induced, the resulting principle can be used in novel circumstances to derive new injunctions. The syllogisms that move from injunction to principle conform to the following format,

Grape wine is forbidden (Injunction)
Grape wine is an Intoxicant (Case)

Intoxication is forbidden (Principle)

From the injunction prohibiting the consumption of wine made from grapes, the Ḥanafī jurist is, theoretically, able to induce a principle that explains the injunction, which can then be used as a principle in other circumstances involving other types of intoxicants. Ḥanafī legal theory manuals are presumed to describe the precise procedures through which principles can be accurately induced from injunctions. In practice, these manuals do not serve this function, despite rhetoric—often propagated by Ḥanafī scholars themselves—to the contrary.

The second way that legal theorists purportedly used syllogisms is ascribed to the Shāfiʿī school of law and involves *deducing* injunctions from principles. In this model, early Shāfiʿīs determined the principles that underlay Islamic jurisprudence and used those principles to derive their law. In our example of grape wine, they would start with the principle, 'intoxication is forbidden' to formulate the following syllogism:

Intoxication is forbidden (Principle)
Grape Wine is an Intoxicant (Case)

Grape wine is forbidden (Injunction)

Theoretically, one could substitute the term 'grape wine' in the case with any similar intoxicant, such as 'apple wine' or 'heroin' to derive an injunction that would similarly judge that intoxicant to be illicit. Once again, Shāfiʿī works of legal theory do not actually describe how a jurist should deduce injunctions from principles. Rather, both Ḥanafī and Shāfiʿī legal theory manuals discuss broad ideas in light of the principles and injunctions already laid down by seminal historical figures in their respective legal schools.[5] What one quickly finds is that legal theory manuals are dedicated neither to the induction of principles nor the deduction of injunctions, for both are considered already resolved. What is actually happening in legal theory manuals is far more exciting and has greater ramifications for the way Islamic law is conceptualized.

To engage the logic of legal theory manuals, one must first be disabused of the notion that legal theory is about 'discovering' either the principles or injunctions of one's legal school. By the time legal theory coalesced as a genre, legal schools had already achieved a level of fixity regarding central principles and injunctions. To work within a legal school, indeed to maintain a standard criterion by which laws are deemed valid, requires a jurist to adhere to established tenets of a legal school, not to contravene them. In the words of a modern scholar of legal theory, jurists needed to abide by the maxim: 'Thou shalt not controvert established and binding rules of law.'[6] In works of legal theory, then, jurists were less concerned about *discovery* and more concerned about *justification*.

Legal theorists used the genre of legal theory to justify inherited principles and injunctions; and here we must be careful not to confuse justification with apologia. To apologize for the law is to explain the

[5] It is understandable that Ḥanafī and Shāfiʿī legal theories are presumed to work according to inductive and deductive syllogisms, rhetoric aside. If one breaks down their argument into their constituent parts, Ḥanafīs seem to argue from injunctions and Shāfiʿīs appear to argue from principles. It is a bit difficult to explain without using technical terms, but after reading chapter 4, the following should be intelligible. In the example of grape wine, Shāfiʿīs argued that the *waṣf* that characterized the *ʿilla* of wine's impermissibility was intoxication. The practical effect (*ta'thīr*) of the *waṣf* was that wine adversely affects an individual's ability to use his intellect. Thus, the transitivity of the *waṣf* extends the prohibition to all other drinks that impede the intellect. Ḥanafīs, on the other hand, note that in the juridical texts, grape wine is considered unclean, whereas other drinks that may cause intoxication are not similarly unclean. Therefore, the *waṣf* of intoxication is not transitive to all other cases. Since the *ʿilla* is not transitive, it cannot be the actual *ʿilla* intended by the texts. Ḥanafīs therefore argue that grape wine is specifically forbidden by the definitive texts, though other types of intoxicants are forbidden by more speculative texts; ʿAbd al-ʿAzīz al-Bukhārī, *Kashf al-Asrār ʿan Fakhr al-Islām al-Bazdawī* (Muḥammad Baghdādī ed, Dār al-Kitāb al-ʿArabī 1997) 3:542–3. See also Kathryn Keuny, *The Rhetoric of Sobriety: Wine in Early Islam* (SUNY Press 2001), 126, endnote 23. In the above arguments, the disagreement is not about how to reason—whether from principles or injunctions, though at first glance one might think so—but it is about transitivity and the identification of a correct *ʿilla*.

[6] Neil MacCormick, *Legal Reasoning and Legal Theory* (Oxford University Press 1978) 195. The dichotomy I posited above between discovery and justification was inspired by MacCormick (n 5) 15–18 and 62–5.

reason for its existence in the canon. To justify law is to argue for its proper definition, application, and continued relevance. Apologia is a defense of validity; justification is a contention about the proper application of law.[7] In essence, to justify a law is to explain not why that law exists, but why it is to be applied. Each jurist has his own particular justifications for why laws are to be applied, and those justifications speak to how the jurist conceives of Islamic law as a whole. The jurist, however, must engage in a sort of balancing act, because though he may justify law in a unique manner, he must be sure to uphold central inherited principles and injunctions; else he would undermine the very foundations of his legal school.

The process of justification in Islamic legal theory follows a type of logic that involved neither the induction of principles nor the deduction of injunctions. Rather, legal theory's logic is most accurately described by the term 'abduction' coined by CS Peirce. Abduction, in its simplest form, involves 'studying facts and devising a theory to explain them.'[8] In the process of abduction, facts are neither created nor posited; they are accepted, explained, and justified. In the same way, legal theorists did not question or innovate principles or injunctions; they were 'facts' and part of the inherited legacy of their legal school. To question these facts or to abandon them would defeat the purpose of being in a legal school in the first place. In legal theory manuals, jurists analyzed previously established principles and injunctions—the 'facts' that were practically

[7] There is an instructive parallel here between my use of apology and justification and Martti Koskenniemi's idea of 'apology and utopia.' In Koskenniemi's conception, law can become an apology for politics if it demonstrates a close connection (a 'concreteness') between normative legal texts and State behavior. When texts retained their normativity they moved closer to a vision of utopia. As we will see in the Conclusion of this text, in medieval Islamic societies there tended to be a strong distinction between normative legal texts and social praxis. Thus, my use of the term 'justification' is closer to what Koskenniemi intends with the term 'utopia'; Martti Koskenniemi, *From Apology to Utopia: The Structure of International Legal Argument* (Cambridge University Press 2005) 17, 58. Wael Hallaq argues that legal theory served the dual purpose of discovery and justification; *A History of Islamic Legal Theories* (Cambridge University Press 1997) ix. Hallaq, however, uses the term 'justification' in the sense of 'apologia.' My use of the same term is intended in a different manner.

[8] Charles Sanders Peirce, *Pragmatism as a Principle and Method of Right Thinking* (SUNY Press 1997) 218.

unchangeable—and justified them to help jurists abduce cases.[9] The justifications that lead to such abductions, when taken together, represent a theoretical approach to Islamic law that determines the appropriate application of inherited principles and injunctions in a legal theorist's legal school.

In our earlier example, the forbidding of both grape wine and of intoxicants are settled matters in the Ḥanafī and Shāfiʿī schools of jurisprudence. Whether one goes from principle to injunction or vice versa seems to make no difference. What is not immediately clear, however, is *why* they are to be forbidden. The justification that occurs in works of legal theory is an attempt to explain why the principles and injunctions of one's legal school are to be applied. To suggest that this is mere defense of a legal school is to miss the point of Islamic jurisprudence as a project. Islamic jurisprudence claims to represent the divine will and touches all aspects of individual and communal life, from ritual purification to governmental regulations. To explain the 'why' of Islamic jurisprudence is to attempt nothing short of explaining why God speaks to humans and what God expects of them.

Interestingly, the 'why' that is hypothesized on the basis of inherited principles and injunctions is unique to each individual legal theorist. The 'why's do not conform to any predetermined boundaries imposed by teachers, geography, or legal schools. Two jurists from the same legal school, in the same geographic area, in the same time period, and with the same teachers might come to very different conclusions about why the principles and injunctions of their legal school are to be applied.

[9] It is likely that Peirce would himself approve of reading medieval legal theory manuals in light of his theory of abduction. He was convinced that medieval religious scholarship was consciously engaged in the kind of semiotics that assumes a logic of abduction which was abandoned by modern thinkers (William Pencak, 'Charles Peirce's Understanding of the Four Ages and of His Own Place in the History of Human Thought' (1991) 179 *Semiotica* 23, 29; Susan Petrilli and Augusto Ponzio, 'Peirce and Medieval Semiotics' in Vincent Colapietro and Thomas Olshewsky (eds), *Peirce's Doctrine of Signs* (Mouton de Gruyter 1996) 351ff. This should not be surprising if Peirce is correct that the origin of abduction was Aristotle; Peirce, *Pragmatism as a Principle and Method of Right Thinking* (n 2) 217—though in Peirce's conception this was actually retroduction; Peirce, *Reasoning and the Logic of Things* (Kenneth Ketner ed, Harvard University Press 1992) 141, a kind of prototype for abduction—since Aristotelean logic pervades medieval Latin and Muslim religious scholarship.

When jurists justify the inherited principles and injunctions, they are explaining the functional logic of their school's legal doctrines, and ultimately making a case for the proper function and purpose of Islamic law as an enterprise.

On first read of a classical legal theory manual, however, the 'why's are not forthcoming. They are buried deep within discussions on the nature of language, the applicability of prophetic reports, the limits of human reason, and the like. In almost all of these discourses, the principles and corresponding injunctions are already determined by preceding seminal jurists of legal schools. Reproducing these principles and injunctions gives the legal theory manual a veneer of continuity and, for the receiving community, authority within the legal school. There is no doubt that the jurists writing these manuals intended to keep their bolder assertions covert, so as to give novel ideas an air of historical legitimacy and avoid stigmatization within one's own legal school. But that makes it all the more difficult to determine the 'why' of Islamic law for which jurists are arguing. It is therefore understandable that most scholars, upon encountering the unchanging façade of legal theory, would assume that legal theory manuals are reified, uninteresting, uncreative tracts serving the twin causes of propaganda and polemics.

The present book, in fact, began out of an argument about the supposed homogeneity of legal theory manuals. In traditional Islamic religious schools, or, *madrasas*, legal theory is accorded a deep, yet distant veneration by those who teach and study the genre. The philosophical discourses and abstruse disquisitions on issues of linguistics and logic found therein are treated with a respect that borders on reverence. In a *madrasa* modeled on the Dār al-ʿUlūm Deoband in India, I studied legal theory with a teacher who described the subject as 'the most hallowed of all sciences' (*ashraf al-ʿulūm*). To him, this meant that legal theory could not be studied at all until all other Islamic sciences had been mastered, and even then the student must only study legal theory to memorize the principles laid out therein, not to engage or even understand them. This seems contradictory; legal theory, by definition, is supposed to provide a methodology upon which inherited Islamic law is predicated and novel Islamic law is derived. If one is not taught how principles are to be used, then one cannot derive injunctions that address novel circumstances. However, since the intricate details of Islamic jurisprudence have been extensively—and by my teacher's account exhaustively—elucidated by Muslim jurists, legal theory was assumed to be a scholastic rather than practical enterprise. I found this attitude in many seminaries across the Muslim world, and that legal theory was among the least studied of the Islamic sciences.

While conducting research on Zaydī legal theorists in Sana'a, Yemen, I fell in with local scholars of Shāfiʿī jurisprudence. Together we studied several Shāfiʿī legal theorists, and especially the legal theories of the eminent jurists Abū Ḥāmid al-Ghazālī (d. 505/1111) and Abū Isḥāq al-Shirāzī (d. 476/1083). I was struck by the Yemeni scholars' incredulous response to any suggestion that these two giants of Shāfiʿī jurisprudence held any significantly different opinions on legal theory. They took great pains to explain that any differences were in appearance only, and that the two were actually in harmony on every matter, as were all Shāfiʿīs. Their insistence on this point kept the study at a superficial level, and I figured that they were reluctant to take sides when jurists whom they held in such high esteem disagreed. So I went to a local bookshop to find legal theory works of Ḥanafī jurists whose differing theories we could discuss without the need to homogenize. I settled upon the works of two renowned Ḥanafī jurists: the *Taqwīm al-Adilla* of Abū Zayd ʿUbayd Allāh b. ʿUmar al-Dabūsī (d. 430/1039) and the *Muḥarrar fī Uṣūl al-Fiqh* of Muḥammad b. Aḥmad b. Abī Sahl al-Sarakhsī (d. 483/1090). A cursory glance at the two texts suggested that they were in consonance on most key issues, but if there were significant differences then perhaps they could be teased out through careful study and discussion. I returned to the scholars with renewed hope.

Within the first few days of discussing Dabūsī's *Taqwīm al-Adilla*, one scholar in particular had many objections. He asked if I was sure that Dabūsī was an actual Ḥanafī jurist, since his explanations for the positions he held, though couched in familiar language and promoting accepted positions, were unfamiliar and, according to the Yemeni scholar, unbecoming a Ḥanafī. I assured him that Dabūsī was one of the leading Ḥanafī jurists of his time and among the most celebrated in the medieval period, and so we agreed to continue discussing his theory. The next day, after having read more of Dabūsī's approach to legal theory, the scholar asked if I had not mistaken this Dabūsī with some other Dabūsī, who was perhaps a real Ḥanafī scholar. He explained that this was an understandable mistake; people regularly mistook the great Mālikī jurist Abū Bakr b. al-ʿArabī (d. 543/1148) with the mystic Muḥyī al-Dīn Ibn ʿArabī (d. 638/1240), the latter whom the scholar insisted was a disbelieving apostate (*kāfir murtadd*). I eventually persuaded him that this was indeed the correct Dabūsī, leaving aside for the moment Ibn ʿArabī's membership in the believing community.

The following day, in the middle of the discussion, the scholar closed his books, stood up, and refused to continue discussing Dabūsī. He protested that this Dabūsī character was clearly trying to undermine Islam with deviant opinions and that he was obviously out of line with the Ḥanafī tradition, which the scholar claimed to know well. In a bid to blacklist Dabūsī from being discussed in the mosques of Sana'a, he conferred with other scholars from his mosque and neighboring mosques, describing the ideas that Dabūsī had put forth in *Taqwīm al-Adilla.* He reported back that all of them agreed that Dabūsī was a dangerous threat to Islam in general and of true Ḥanafism in particular, no doubt an agent provocateur working for the enemies of Islam. He was more than happy, however, to move the discussion to the works of Sarakhsī, whom he praised as a true scholar and Ḥanafī.

The most noteworthy aspect of this whole interchange is that the works of Dabūsī and Sarakhsī are, at first glance, practically indistinguishable. Several of their chapters appear copied one from the other. They certainly owed much credit to their predecessor Abū Bakr al-Jaṣṣāṣ (d. 370/981), upon whose legal theory manual the two later jurists based much of their work. In fact, they often used the same terms and similar arguments as al-Jaṣṣāṣ to describe their own legal positions and principles. Yet, their justifications for *why* the principles and legal positions were to be applied reflect a deep divergence between their works. These justifications are located in their nuanced definitions of terms used to describe the principles and injunctions. By justifying a shared term in a slightly—or sometimes not so slightly—different way, the shape and application of Islamic law can change without disturbing the injunctions or principles.

In the above example of grape wine, the principle and the injunction are given and set; any attempt to change them would be immediately branded a departure from the boundaries of the legal school. However, there is a third element in the syllogism, the case, which is normally overlooked, but is completely up for grabs. Depending on how one justifies the terms within the principle or injunction, the case may be abduced to be more or less restrictive.

Justification is the main task of legal theory manuals; and here the difference between apology and justification is important. If one were trying to apologize for the injunction forbidding grape wine, one might point to Q. 5:90–91, or several prophetic reports that include the prohibition to explain why the latter exists in the juridical tradition. The concern of legal theory, however, is to justify how and why the prohibition—already enshrined in the tradition—should be applied. Whereas apology looks back to rationalize the tradition, justification looks forward to argue for the tradition's proper application.

Arguing for the way in which the received tradition should be applied requires a bit of guesswork on the part of the legal theorist when he engages in abduction. The legal theorist must justify inherited principles and injunctions by defining key terms such that they lead to particular conclusions. Using the example of the prohibition of grape wine, let us assume that we are moving from the injunction to the principle, the way the Ḥanafī model is 'supposed' to work. When justifying the prohibition in this model, a jurist might surmise that grape wine should be prohibited because it is a fermented drink. The jurist might then understand the principle that prohibits intoxicants as referring to other types of fermented drinks. The premises of the abductive syllogism would then look like this:

> Grape wine is forbidden because it is a fermented drink (Injunction)
> Fermented intoxicants in general are forbidden (Principle)

This leaves the jurist free to hypothesize about the application of jurisprudence regarding fermented intoxicants. The jurist might conclude that the prohibition of intoxicants applies narrowly to fermented drinks, and perhaps does not apply to other mind-altering substances like heroin or coffee. The jurist might then define what constitutes fermentation; whether the drink needs to be only a little fermented or if it needs to have progressed significantly in the fermentation process.

Alternatively, a jurist might justify the terms in the injunction and the principle differently to produce a different result. A jurist might surmise, for instance, that grape wine should be forbidden because it causes drunkenness (*sukārā*). The jurist might then understand the principle that prohibits intoxicants as referring to any drug that induces a state of, or like, drunkenness, making the premises of the abductive syllogism:

> Grape wine is forbidden to prevent drunkenness (Injunction)
> Intoxicants that cause a state of drunkenness are forbidden (Principle)

A jurist might then hypothesize that the application of the principle and injunction should be understood as forbidding all types of drugs, depending on how he defined 'drunkenness.' If drunkenness were defined as inebriation, then the prohibition would include all forms of fermented drinks, opiates, hard stimulants, hallucinogens, and the like. If, however, drunkenness were defined more generally as an altered state of mind, the prohibition might apply expansively to include caffeine and tobacco.

In both of the above examples, the injunctions and principles are maintained: grape wine is forbidden, as are intoxicants. However, the way in which jurists justified the key terms in the premises affected the abductions they might make about how the law is to be applied. In a sense, jurists were free to justify these terms as they saw fit; so long as they did not change the literal wordings of the premises, they could interpret at will. And indeed they did. When analyzing medieval works of *uṣūl al-fiqh*, one finds that jurists had very different justifications for why inherited jurisprudence—both its principles and injunctions—was to be applied. What is more, one finds that these justifications have a sort of coherence. When examining the justifications provided by a legal theorist in the aggregate, one finds that they were effectively arguing for a larger worldview, or narrative, within which one should situate the role and function of Islamic law as a whole.

In order to understand that larger narrative, it is necessary to get a feel for the justifications and abductions that jurists made in their legal theory manuals. The primary task of this book is to provide a glimpse into the methods that legal theorists employed for expressing disparate abductions about the application of Islamic law while simultaneously giving the appearance of uniformity. For this purpose, I have enlisted the works of the aforementioned Dabūsī and Sarakhsī to illustrate how two scholars from the same legal school, from the same geographic area, with the same intellectual heritage, and living in the same era might produce two legal theory manuals that look similar, but are poles apart in their arguments about the function of Islamic law.

Three chapters are devoted to uncovering their particular conceptions of three major sources of Ḥanafī law: the Qur'ān, the *sunna*, and opinion (*ra'y*). A chapter is dedicated to each source, and in each chapter we will closely examine three central concepts that shed light on how the source should be used in law. I have purposely avoided some of the vaguer topics, which were nonetheless extensively surveyed in legal theory manuals, like differentiating general (*'āmm*) and specific (*khāṣṣ*) terms or commanding (*amr*) and forbidding (*nahy*). Instead, I focus on subjects that directly relate to the nature of the legal source under study. The aim is to give the reader a taste for legal theory without getting so involved in theoretical debate that we lose sight of the practical ramifications of the theory itself.

This book by no means captures the full extent and argument of legal theory works. One will not become an expert in legal theory by having read it. But it will give one the *feel* of a legal theory work. The idea is to immerse the reader into a mode of argumentation and thereby enter the world of legal theorists by understanding the way they used complex technical terms. Each chapter also includes a *Brief Review* section and *Conclusion* that covers how the terms affect the understanding and application of the source under study.

By the third chapter, we start to see how Dabūsī and Sarakhsī structured their arguments to argue for larger, coherent worldviews. We will find that by justifying terms in the received principles and injunctions differently, they were able to argue for different cases. These cases, when taken together, present an argument for the relative authority and application of each source to the contemporary community. One begins to perceive that the two jurists understood the project of Islamic law in divergent ways. Their individual conceptions of the way in which God intended humans to apply divine law are clearly distinct, and their arguments, as a whole, suggest that Islamic law should be either a paradigmatic model for emulation or a set of ordinances designed for universal imitation. By examining their approaches to the sources of Islamic law, we can grasp their argument about the purpose of Islamic law as a whole. This underlying argument is the most exciting aspect of medieval legal theory manuals, both in the varied conceptions of Islamic law that it uncovers and in its diversity within contexts of assumed uniformity.

Before jumping into a close study of Dabūsī and Sarakhsī's works, a quick note about the context of the legal theories studied in this book. Although the development of Islamic law until the 11th century when Dabūsī and Sarakhsī wrote their tracts is important and interesting, it is not the subject of this book. One does not even need to know the biographies of the two legal scholars to enter their arguments, though brief biographies are provided in the appendix. It is enough to know two major facts for the purpose of this study. First, these contemporaneous and collocated scholars traced their legal pedigree to the Baghdad school of Ḥanafism, particularly in the persons of Abū al-Ḥasan al-Karkhī (d. 340/951) and Abū Bakr al-Jaṣṣāṣ (d. 370/981). Secondly, later Ḥanafī scholars considered Dabūsī and Sarakhsī to be the systematizers of Ḥanafī thought. They and their contemporary Abū al-Ḥasan al-Pazdawī (d. 482/1089) were regularly referred to as 'the three shaykhs' of the Ḥanafī school.[10] They are credited with providing the foundations upon which later Ḥanafī thought was based. All the more striking, then, that the thrust of their legal thought was so different.

My hope is that close attention to Dabūsī and Sarakhsī's arguments will disclose to the reader the narratives of law that these jurists were weaving, and that the reader will begin to enter those narratives and

[10] This is not to be confused with 'the three Imāms' regularly quoted in Ḥanafī texts. 'The three Imāms' refers to Abū Ḥanīfa, Muḥammad al-Shaybānī, and Abū Yūsuf.

interact with them. The study of legal theory is difficult—at times tedious—and requires one to juggle several complicated ideas at once. But it is deeply rewarding when read with an eye toward the narrative being presented. Patient study of the way jurists manipulated complex technical language will uncover unique and creative conceptions of Islamic law that stretch our assumptions about the boundaries of Islamic legal thought.

1

From God's Speech to Islamic Law: Defining the Qur'ān

The Qur'ān is considered the supreme source of Islamic law by all major legal schools of both the Sunnī and Shī'ī traditions. Early debates notwithstanding, there has been unanimous agreement since at least the 4th/10th-century that the Qur'ān captured the speech of God as revealed to the Prophet Muḥammad, which the latter authorized during his lifetime. These revelations were compiled into an authoritative codex by the third caliph, 'Uthmān b. 'Affān, and Muslims almost unanimously agree that this codex has been authentically preserved throughout the ages.[1] Being a pristine collection of divine revelation, the Qur'ān is considered an exceptional source of law that sits atop the hierarchy of legal sources.[2] Technically, then, legal proof derived from the Qur'ān should trump proof derived from any other source.

The Ḥanafīs in particular took pains to emphasize the radical superiority of the Qur'ān over all other sources of law. This was a point of pride for Ḥanafīs, especially in their debates with the rival Shāfi'ī legal school, whom the former criticized for making the Qur'ān and the *sunna* appear, at times, equal in terms of legal authority.[3] In response to what they perceived as an adulteration of the pristine status of the Qur'ān by al-Shāfi'ī and others, the Ḥanafīs argued that the Qur'ān was a miracle unlike any other and thus could not be expanded or constrained by

[1] Hossein Modarressi, 'Early Debates on the Integrity of the Qur'ān' (1993) 77 *Studia Islamica* 33.

[2] Fazlur Rahman, *Islam* (University of Chicago Press 1979) 69.

[3] Christopher Melchert, 'Qur'ānic Abrogation Across the Ninth Century' in Bernard Weiss (ed), *Studies in Islamic Legal Theory* (Brill 2002) 84.

any external source. Moreover, Ḥanafīs were united in their stances on major principles of Qurʾān interpretation and minimally differed on the injunctions that resulted from their method of interpretation.

Despite this apparent unanimity, Ḥanafīs disagreed as to how the Qurʾān was to be read and applied. These disagreements surface in the way Ḥanafīs justified inherited technical terms connected to the Qurʾān. For example, Ḥanafīs all agreed that the Qurʾān is 'the speech of God.' but debated whether the Arabic words used therein were literally God's speech. If they were literally God's speech, how could humans understand speech uttered by a being whose logic transcends human intelligence? If not, to what extent is God's speech mediated through the Arabic language and human interpretation? Ḥanafīs agreed that the Qurʾān is inimitable, but are the Arabic words themselves inimitable or is inimitability found in the messages contained therein? Ḥanafīs agreed that most verses of the Qurʾān were open to interpretation, but is there a method for knowing which interpretation is correct, or more correct than others?

The way a jurist answered these questions in his legal theory manual had a direct bearing on how he conceived of the Qurʾān's relationship to Islamic law. If, for example, the meaning of the Qurʾān and Qurʾanic passages could be known with certainty, then the Islamic law derived therefrom would be authoritative in perpetuity. If, conversely, the Qurʾān were assumed to be irremediably vague, then the law derived therefrom would only have conjectural force and relative authority. Ultimately, then, the answers that legal theory manuals provided in response to the above questions directly affected the role of the Qurʾān as a guide for the Muslim community. Taken broadly, they concern whether the Qurʾān was meant to dictate absolute laws for all time or to be interpreted differently based on time, place, and interpreter. Most legal theorists fell somewhere between these two extremes, and they argued for positions along the spectrum.

In their legal theory manuals, Dabūsī and Sarakhsī proposed distinct interpretations of the Qurʾān and its relationship to Islamic law. Since they did not disclose their thoughts overtly, we will have to get a picture of their conception of the Qurʾān through their treatment of key issues, acknowledging that they worked within the received Ḥanafī legal principles and injunctions. To do this we will look at three major issues: the inimitability of the Qur'ān, clear and ambiguous verses, and abrogation theory. In their justifications of technical terms associated with these central issues, Dabūsī and Sarakhsī revealed their discrete, underlying preconceptions about the nature of revelation, its purpose in the world, and the ideal relationship between the jurist and the Qur'anic text when deriving jurisprudence.

THE MIRACULOUSNESS AND INIMITABILITY OF THE QUR'ĀN

The issue of the inimitability of the Qur'ān (*i'jāz al-Qur'ān*) was often discussed in relation to Muḥammad's status as the last in a line of prophets delivering messages from God. The more prominent Qur'anic prophets—especially Noah, Moses, and Jesus—took part in miraculous events that could not be explained in naturalistic terms. Noah foretold a torrential rain that would flood the Earth, Moses had a staff that could turn into a serpent, and Jesus could heal the blind, lepers, and the otherwise infirm, among other miracles. These miracles served a dual purpose: they testified to the authority of the prophet himself and obliged the viewing audience to believe in the message being presented. The receiving community, for its part, expected prophets to prove their legitimacy through the performance of miracles.

Muḥammad, however, performed no such miracles. The Qur'ān itself testifies that Muḥammad would not perform miracles and, despite some extra-Qur'anic reports that Muḥammad performed supernatural phenomena, miracles of nature were not the foundation of his prophethood.[4] Instead, Muslim scholars posited that the Qur'ān itself was the miracle that proved the prophethood of Muḥammad. Scholars argued that the Qur'ān manifested its miracle in many ways, including prophesying the future and making scientific claims that transcended its 7th-century Arabian context. Positing these miracles required a certain

[4] See for instance, Qur'ān 11:12, 17:90–93, 28:48 and 29:48–51.

amount of reading-in by Muslim scholars and the miracles that they identified understandably reflected their socio-historical contexts.

In any case, prophesying the future or making scientific claims that could only be verified in posterity hardly seems a miracle for the receiving community. Such miracles may attest to the divinity of the Qur'ān for future generations living in the prophesied future, but they would not serve as proofs for the community receiving the Qur'ān. To accomplish that end, the Qur'ān would have to possess some type of self-evident, internal miracle. Thus, Muslim scholars, and indeed the Qur'ān itself, argued that the ultimate miracle of the Qur'ān is found in its inimitability (*i'jāz*). Scholars said that the challenge in Q. 2:23—'If you are in doubt concerning what We have revealed unto our servant, then bring one chapter like it'—was unmet in the time of Muḥammad, and remains unmet today. Hence, the Qur'ān, in its inimitability, is considered an abiding miracle.

Like all Ḥanafī jurists, Dabūsī and Sarakhsī believed that the Qur'ān was both miraculous and inimitable. They disagreed, however, on exactly how it was miraculous and about the precise location of its inimitability. This disagreement hinges on the way in which one defines 'inimitable.' For example, one might argue that the Qur'ān is inimitable in its ordering (*naẓm*). If this were the case, then the Qur'ān as redacted in the authoritative codex in its exact wording would be inimitable. As a result, each word and chapter would be inimitable and if the words were rearranged, then the inimitability—and hence, miraculousness—would no longer obtain. Therefore, a rational, well-intentioned reader of the codex would be convinced that the Qur'ān is miraculous by dint of the inimitability of its ordering, in that no other text could compare in terms of composition.

One might argue differently that the inimitability is found not in the ordering, but in the inner meaning (*ma'nā*) imparted by the text. If that were the case, then the words and chapters would not themselves be inimitable; rather, inimitability would be found in the meaning that those words and chapters impart. A rational, well-intentioned reader would recognize the inimitability of the meaning and message of the Qur'ān and would be obliged to believe in its miraculous, supernatural origin.

Of course, one could argue—and many scholars did—that the Qurʾān is inimitable in both its ordering and its inner meaning. Even amongst those who favored this combined vision of inimitability, there were debates about which takes precedence and in what ways the ordering and the meaning are inimitable.

The legal issue surrounding this subject is one of authority. If the Qurʾān is inimitable in its ordering alone, then the multivalent meanings that might lay within the text are not necessarily inimitable and are therefore not miraculous. Alternatively, if inimitability is found in the meaning of the Qurʾān, then qualified interpreters would be required to elucidate that discrete meaning and present it as inimitable. If the inimitability is found in both the ordering and the meaning, then that would suggest that the ordering of the text discloses a particular meaning to qualified interpreters, but they would then be practically unable to relate that meaning to others. That is because they would have to utilize words and phrases other than those found in the Qurʾān to explain the meaning found therein. If that explanation were claimed to be an exact reflection of the meaning within the Qurʾān, then the words and phrases of the explanation would compete with wording of the Qurʾanic text in disclosing the inner Qurʾanic meaning. Since the wording of the Qurʾān is inimitable, it would be impossible for a different wording to convey the same meaning.

The stakes for Islamic law, then, are quite high when justifying the role of 'inimitability' as the 'miracle' of the Qurʾān. The choice that a jurist makes in this regard determines whether Qurʾanic verses intend a particular meaning, if a jurist class is required to interpret that meaning, and if the Qurʾanic message can be conveyed universally. Put in legal terms, it is a choice between the Qurʾān providing a single law that can be understood only by jurists, many laws that can have relative authority, or law(s) that can never truly be known or implemented by mankind with certitude.

Dabūsī on Inimitability as the Qurʾanic Miracle

Dabūsī prefaced his discussion by defining the Qurʾān as that which 'has been passed down to us through multiple, uninterrupted chains of transmission (*mutawātir*)[5] and bound in redacted copies (*maṣāḥif*) in the seven known readings (*aḥrāf*).'[6] That the Qur'ān could be recited in seven variants was unproblematic for most jurists of the classical period. More troublesome was the reliance on *mutawātir* transmission. For Dabūsī, the transmission of the Qur'ān through multiple, uninterrupted chains ensures that the codified Qur'ān passed down through the generations is the same as that revealed to Muḥammad by God. Some of Dabūsī's critics questioned whether relying on any transmission, *mutawātir* or not, compromised the authenticity of the received text. They argued that if the Qur'ān was indeed the eternal Word of God and therefore miraculous, then it would not need human transmission to ensure its integrity. If that were indeed the case, then making the Qur'ān dependent on *mutawātir* transmission would be superfluous and serve only to undermine its miraculous nature.

Dabūsī responded to his critics by asserting that the very notion of revelation is phenomenologically predicated on a theory of transmission.[7] That is to say, Gabriel spoke to Muḥammad, who then repeated what he heard to his Companions. It was only after a verse was transmitted from Muḥammad to his Companions that it was established as revelation to the community. Hence, the idea of transmission was an essential element of revelation from the outset without which the Qur'an could never be disseminated. Dabūsī added that after Muḥammad's death, his Companions demanded verification from multiple transmitters before redacting the Qur'ān into an official volume.[8] During that process,

[5] Juynboll rightly translates *mutawātir* as it is used as a technical term in *ḥadīth* as 'broadly authenticated'; G H A Juynboll '(Re)appraisal of Some Technical Terms in Ḥadīth Science' (2001) 8:3 *Islamic Law and Society* 303, 326. I have chosen to use instead the somewhat clunky 'multiple, uninterrupted chains of transmission' because it reflects the perception of *mutawātir* that authors project in their discussions of both the Qur'ān and the *sunna*, but especially with the Qur'ān. Concerning the Qur'ān, the *mutawātir* are more than broadly authenticated reports; they are *mutawātir lafẓī*, in that every word was transmitted widely through uninterrupted transmissions. To reduce confusion, I used the same translation in the *sunna* chapter; though authors regularly treat the *ḥadīth* that reach their definition of *mutawātir* as *mutawātir lafẓī*, even if it is clearly *mutawātir ma'nawī*, they do not explicitly use either term (see Chapter 2, note 15).

[6] Abū Zayd al-Dabūsī. *Taqwīm al-Adilla* (Khalīl al-Mays ed, Dār al-Kutub al-ʿIlmiyya 2001) 20. On early controversies surrounding the *muṣḥaf* and the evolving understanding of the Qur'ān as written, see Travis Zadeh, 'Touching and Injesting: Early Debates over the Material Qur'an' (2009) 129:3 *Journal of the American Oriental Society* 443, 452ff.

[7] Dabūsī (n 6) 20. [8] Ibid 20.

if a Companion of the Prophet claimed that a verse was recited by Muḥammad and should be included in the official redaction, but could not find other Companions to support that claim, then the proposed verse was not accepted into the official codex.[9] Once the codex was completed, it was memorized and disseminated across the Muslim Empire. Dabūsī concluded that the fact that the Qur'ān was preserved throughout the ages despite relying on a process of transmission was a miracle in and of itself. *Mutawātir* transmissions, therefore, were the conduit for the miraculous preservation of the exact words revealed to Muḥammad.[10] As a miracle, the Qur'anic codex generated indubitable knowledge (*yūjib ʿilm al-yaqīn*) of the authenticity of the verses contained therein as the Word of God revealed to Muḥammad.

Having established the authenticity of the Qur'ān, Dabūsī turned his attention to its contents. According to Dabūsī, the verses of the Qur'ān were all inimitable in their exact ordering (*naẓm*) found in the official codex. No human could produce a work like the Qur'ān nor could any of its verses be reworded. This meant that words within a verse could not be substituted for others, even if the general meaning of the verse were retained. Of course, this did not mean that the Qur'ān resisted any attempt at explanation, but that any explanation would be necessarily limited. To clarify, Dabūsī made a critical distinction between *tafsīr* and *ta'wīl* as methods of interpretation. He defined *tafsīr* as 'an explanation that claims to leave no doubt as to its verity' (*bayān lā yabqá fīhi shakk*).[11] Dabūsī argued that this type of interpretation was impermissible, since it would suggest that two wordings—one found in the redacted text and one articulated through *tafsīr*—were equally veracious. Since the Qur'anic codex generated indubitable knowledge (*ʿilm al-yaqīn*) of its veracity, a *tafsīr* that claimed to similarly vitiate all doubt in its veracity would be imitating the Qur'ān. Thus, Dabūsī concluded that

[9] The obvious exception being Khuzayma b. Thābit, whose single testimony was considered by the principal compiler of the official Qur'anic codex, Zayd b. Thābit (no relation), equal to two witnesses; Jalāl al-Dīn al-Ṣuyūṭī, *al-Itqān fī ʿUlūm al-Qur'ān* (Muṣṭafā Dīb ed, Dār Ibn Kathīr 2000) 1:185; Ella Landau-Tesseron (trs), *The History of al-Ṭabarī Vol. XXXIX* (SUNY Press 1998) 131. For full accounts of the Qur'ān's redaction, see Daniel Madigan, *The Qur'ān's Self-Image: Writing and Authority in Islam's Scripture* (Princeton University Press 2001) 13–52.

[10] Dabūsī (n 6) 20. [11] Ibid 169.

the inimitability of the text precluded any *tafsīr* of the Qur'ān from being an authoritative expression of its meaning (*ma'nā*). He did allow, however, for an interpretation known as *ta'wīl*. This is a more tentative, non-authoritative attempt to explain the intention of verses and will be examined further in the next section.

Despite insisting that Qur'anic verses were inimitable and generated indubitable knowledge in their veracity, Dabūsī did not conflate the inimitability (*i'jāz*) of the wording of the Qur'ān with its miraculousness. For him, the fact that the Qur'ān could not be replicated did not in itself constitute a miracle. Dabūsī argued that a miracle (*mu'jiza*) was some sort of sign that indubitably verifies a claim to prophethood. Miracles are unmistakable manifestations of God's power, like Jesus raising the dead or Moses transmogrifying his staff; and so whatever the Qur'ān's true miracle, it should accomplish the same end.[12] Specifically, the miracle should result in the witness to the miracle conceding the performer's claim of prophethood. Dabūsī noted that individual verses of the Qur'ān, especially short verses, do not lead a reader to believe that Muḥammad was a prophet. Therefore, he concluded that not all verses of the Qur'ān were miracles (*kullu āya minhu laysat bi-mu'jiza*).[13]

Nevertheless, Dabūsī stated that there were verses in the Qur'ān that fit his definition of a miracle. Such verses, he said, were 'clear' (*muḥkam*) and concern the nature and attributes of God. Dabūsī said that these clear verses, which assert the unity of God and laud His many attributes, would lead any well-intentioned reader to recognize that Muḥammad spoke the truth; though the verses themselves, like any miracle, do not compel this recognition. Rather, a reader must engage in minimal reflection (*ta'ammul*) to realize that only a prophet of God could have conveyed these clear verses.[14] Dabūsī cautioned that if clear verses compelled this realization without any reflection on their meaning, then there would be no rationale for rewarding believers and punishing disbelievers in the afterlife.[15] Reward and punishment, he said, only make sense in a system

[12] Ibid 13.
[13] Ibid 20. See also 'Abd al-'Azīz al-Bukhārī, *Kashf al-Asrār 'an Fakhr al-Islam al-Bazdawī* (Muḥammad Baghdādī ed, Dār al-Kitāb al-'Arabī 1997) 1:69–70.
[14] Ibid 14. [15] Ibid 14.

wherein individuals are free to choose and free to err, a capacity that is removed when compulsion is introduced.

Dabūsī acknowledged that some individuals do not recognize the prophethood of Muḥammad despite being exposed to the clear verses of the Qurʾān and having thought about them; but he dismissed such people as ignorant.[16] Their ignorance may be due to either an honest misreading of the text or mendacity, but either way the ignoramus would have some impairment keeping him from accepting the miracle. In Dabūsī's system, the result of proper reflection on clear verses is always recognition that Muḥammad is the messenger of God.[17] By extension, the reflecting reader accepts that the message itself has a supernatural origin. Once the message is acknowledged as supernatural, it must be considered, by definition, inimitable. Inimitability of the whole text, then, is a byproduct of the clear, miraculous verses of the Qurʾān.

This last position has ramifications for the authority of juridical interpretation of Qurʾanic passages. Dabūsī presented a kind of stratification of verses, such that some are miraculous while others are not. Miraculous verses are only those that deal with theology, meaning that legal verses are not miraculous. The law contained in the Qurʾān, therefore, is not a miraculous law, and enacting that law would not necessarily lead one to recognize the Qurʾān's divine origin. Legal verses are, nonetheless, inimitable in their ordering (*naẓm*) and one can be certain that they were revealed by God. However, the result of this inimitability is that these legal verses cannot be interpreted beyond their literal wordings or else they lose divine authority. So although the Qurʾān could be used as a legal document, any legal interpretation derived from the Qurʾān is tentative at best and can never claim divine sanction.[18]

[16] Ibid 14. [17] Ibid 443.

[18] This became a point of contention amongst later Ḥanafīs who sought to reconcile Dabūsī with the likes of Sarakhsī and Pazdawī. ʿAlāʾ al-Dīn al-Bukhārī, for example, wrote, 'because Dabūsī was firm [in his belief] that the injunctions found in the Qurʾān constituted authoritative evidence [for deriving law], he did not need to call [legal verses] miraculous.' Bukhārī (n 13) 1:70. This re-reading admits Dabūsī's position, but apologizes for it as well.

Sarakhsī on Inimitability as the Qur'anic Miracle

Despite appearing to agree with Dabūsī, Sarakhsī had a different understanding of the miraculous nature of the Qur'ān. Like Dabūsī, he defined the Qur'ān as the redacted codex that has been passed down through *mutawātir* transmission and said that any religious teachings transmitted through such a methodology would generate indubitable knowledge.[19] Sarakhsī held that, among completely transmitted texts, only the Qur'ān could claim to have been passed down so rigorously, from the individual collections of the Companions of Muḥammad to all contemporary copies. For him, the fact that the Qur'ān was copiously transmitted was the miracle of the Qur'ān for contemporary readers.[20] He argued that no other teaching would have been preserved so carefully and this care is itself proof of the veracity of Muḥammad's prophetic claim. In this regard, Sarakhsī was in lock step with Dabūsī and his Ḥanafī compatriots. He further agreed with them by stating that the miracle of transmission does not impute miraculousness onto the meaning of the Qur'ān. Rather, the *mutawātir* transmission of the Qur'ān is a miracle that is exterior to the text; one that merely requires the reader to have indubitable knowledge that the text is preserved. Thus, the miracle of *mutawātir* transmission is an assurance to contemporary readers that the Qur'ān that they are reading is the same as that revealed to Muḥammad. Sarakhsī concluded that since the Qur'anic codex reflects revelation from God, there must be some inimitability inherent in the text itself.

Sarakhsī offered two possible loci for the inimitability of the Qur'ān. The Qur'ān, he said, might be inimitable in either its ordering (*naẓm*) or its inner meaning (*ma'nā*).[21] If the inimitability were located in the ordering, then the text as a whole, as compiled by the Companions of the Prophet and passed down through *mutawātir* transmissions, would be inimitable. In that case, only the exact redacted copy, with its particular chapter and verse sequence with the exact Arabic wording would be admissible in legal proceedings or in ritual obligations requiring recitation of the

[19] Muḥammad b. Aḥmad al-Sarakhsī, *al-Muḥarrar fī Uṣūl al-Fiqh* (Ṣalāḥ b. Muḥammad ed, Dār al-Kutub al-'Ilmiyya 1996) 1:210.
[20] Ibid 1:210. [21] Ibid 1:211.

Qur'ān. If the verses were re-ordered or translated into some other language then the inimitability would no longer obtain and the new text would not be considered the Qur'ān. Sarakhsī said that this could not be the case, since individual verses are not all, in and of themselves, inimitable. It would be a stretch to consider short verses in particular, some of them containing only a few words like 'and ten nights' or 'the Calamity!' to be impossible to imitate. However, these verses become inimitable when they are read within the context of the chapter (*ṣūra*) to which they belong, often alongside verses that rhyme and build on the short verses.[22] Sarakhsī said that it is the chapter that is inimitable, not its constituent parts. The individual verses are still considered revelation and the reader must have indubitable knowledge of their status as such, but they are not inimitable.

There is a subtle difference between Dabūsī and Sarakhsī here that has broad implications. Recall that all Ḥanafīs agree that the Qur'ān is miraculous and that its miracle is found in its inimitability. There is a disagreement, however, about whether the inimitability is found in the ordering (*naẓm*) or the meaning (*maʿnā*), or both. Unless these terms are kept firmly in mind, it might appear that Dabūsī and Sarakhsī are arguing the same point. Dabūsī held that not all verses were miraculous, but they were nonetheless inimitable in their wordings because they were revealed by God. Sarakhsī, also argued that not all verses are miraculous, but added that the meaning of the verses when read in context is inimitable. Put another way, Dabūsī affirmed that all verses of the Qur'ān in their *naẓm* were inimitable, but they do not function as miracles because they do not all attest to the divinity of the message. So, despite failing to serve as a miracle, the ordering of the Qur'ān is nevertheless inimitable because it has a supernatural origin and cannot be altered. For Sarakhsī, by contrast, individual verses are not inimitable in and of themselves, but when gathered and contextualized in a chapter their meaning is inimitable and therefore miraculous.

Sarakhsī admitted that considering the context of verses to be inimitable suggests that only the meaning (*maʿnā*) that the chapter imparts is

[22] Ibid 1:211.

inimitable, and not the ordering of the constituent verses of the chapter.[23] That is, it may be that the ordering of the verses in the chapter is merely a particular method utilized to produce a certain meaning—a meaning that is independent from the words used to convey that meaning—that is inimitable. This meaning, once understood, might then be reworded or retranslated in a way that preserves the meaning but changes the ordering. If, in fact, the meaning imparted by the ordering is the miracle intended by God, then the wording of the Qur'ān is incidental to the fact that it was revealed in 7th-century Arabia. The Qur'ān could, at least in theory, be reworded while maintaining the inimitability of the meaning. In essence, then, Sarakhsī's argument that the inimitability of the Qur'ān is to be found only in the chapter as a whole meant that the chapter was not inimitable in the exact ordering and wording of its constituent verses in Arabic as received through *mutawātir* transmissions, but that inimitability is found in the meaning that the chapter and its constituent verses impart.

Sarakhsī conceded that both positions on the issue—one holding the Qur'ān to be inimitable in its *naẓm* and the other in its *maʿnā*—were meritorious and not necessarily mutually exclusive. Certainly, he wrote, the ordering of the Qur'ān was done by design and was intended by God to impart a specific meaning.[24] It is therefore not surprising that many people erroneously thought that the Qur'ān was inimitable in its exact redacted order in Arabic. He pointed out, however, that Arabic is a language: languages being systems of signs that humans create in certain times and spaces. Sarakhsī warned that to equate the Word of God to something created, like a language, would be to engage in anthropomorphism, a crime that was to be avoided at all costs.[25] Equating

[23] Ibid 1:211.

[24] Sarakhsī, *Kitāb al-Mabsūṭ* (Kamāl ʿInānī ed, Dār al-Kutub al-ʿIlmiyya 2001) 1:138.

[25] Sarakhsī (n 19) 1:211. It is significant that Sarakhsī did not use al-Sighnāqī's more textually-based, straightforward argument. Sighnāqī used the saying of Muḥammad 'The Qur'ān was revealed in seven recitations' to argue that the *naẓm* of the Qur'ān is important, but not essential to its miracle and recitation in prayer. To say otherwise would be to contradict the above *ḥadīth*. al-Ḥusayn b. ʿAlī al-Saghnāqī [*sic*] *Kitāb al-Wāfī fī Uṣūl al-Fiqh* (Muḥammad Akhsīkathī ed, Dār al-Qāhira 2003) 1:204. This method of argumentation was surely available to Sarakhsī, but his non-use emphasized his doctrinal bent and concern. It was more important for him to insist on the primacy of his doctrine than to make a simpler, more legally-efficacious argument.

any creation or created thing to God or any of His attributes would be to engage in the greatest sin possible.

Interestingly, Sarakhsī took pains to construct a rational argument to defend his claim. He reasoned that since God Himself spoke the words of the Qur'ān, the Qur'ān comprised God's Speech. This Speech, being divine, must be beyond time and space, and certainly beyond anything created. If the Word of God must be radically other than all creation, then one must accept that the Word of God cannot be contingent upon any language for its ultimate expression. Due to the theological constraints that Sarakhsī said were of paramount importance, he decreed that 'the inimitable meaning is [located] in the aggregate meaning' (*maʿnā al-iʿjāz fī-al-maʿnā tāmm*) imparted by the text.[26] Sarakhsī acknowledged that it logically follows from this position that the Qur'ān could be translated into other languages or reworded in a way that preserves its meaning and still retain its inimitability.[27]

Some of Sarakhsī's detractors argued that a translation would adulterate the word of God such that it would no longer be inimitable. Sarakhsī was undaunted by this critique and provided a detailed rebuttal to those who would deny that a translation of the Qur'ān could retain inimitability.[28] The major criticism to which he responded calls attention to the 'undisputed fact' that no non-Arab (*ʿajamī*) could produce any work in Arabic comparable to the Arabic Qur'ān.[29] The critics contend that the inability (*ʿajz*) of the non-Arab to produce the Qur'ān precludes the possibility of his producing an exact translation in his own language. Sarakhsī dismissed this argument by questioning the applicability of the premise. He conceded that no non-Arab could produce something like the Qur'ān in Arabic, but argued that it is also true that no non-Arab could produce poetry in Arabic comparable to great Arab poets like Imru' al-Qays. That does not mean that non-Arabs cannot understand Imru'

[26] Sarakhsī (n 19) 1:211.
[27] Sarakhsī appears to have been the last major Ḥanafī scholar to hold this position, see Bukhārī (n 13) 1:77–8.
[28] For a discussion of the polemics surrounding the translatability of the Qur'ān and the perniciousness of foreign words, see Travis Zadeh, *Translation, Geography and the Divine Word* (PhD Diss, Harvard University 2007) 2:369ff.
[29] Sarakhsī (n 19) 1:211.

al-Qays in translation, nor does it mean that the poetry of Imru' al-Qays is somehow miraculous in its inimitability.[30] Besides, the Prophet was sent to all of humankind, both individuals who speak Arabic and those who do not. The existence of non-Arabic speaking peoples is therefore further proof that the inimitability of the Qur'ān must reside in its aggregate meaning; else the mission of the Prophet would be restricted to Arabs and Arabic speakers.[31]

Sarakhsī said that it was for those very reasons that Abū Ḥanīfa allowed Persians who could not speak Arabic to recite the Qur'ān in Persian during obligatory prayers.[32] Although this position was disputed even within the Ḥanafī school, Sarakhsī described it as normative, using Abū Ḥanīfa as a champion for his own stance. Still, he cautioned that if a translation of the Qur'ān were to be used in prayer, that translation must be precise. Exegesis of the Qur'ān was not permitted in prayer and so the translator must be certain that the words utilized in Persian refer to their exact equivalents in Arabic.[33] Noting that Abū Ḥanīfa's most prominent students, Muḥammad al-Shaybānī and Abū Yūsuf, held that the Qur'ān was inimitable in both its *naẓm* and *maʿnā*, Sarakhsī provided ways in which their position could be reconciled with Abu Ḥanīfa's such that, for all practical purposes, the inimitability of the Qur'ān was confined to its *maʿnā*.[34] He stressed that however unpalatable the consequence, the Qur'ān must transcend any anthropomorphic qualities, lest one be guilty of heresy, and so the inimitability must be confined to the *maʿnā*.

It is important to note that Sarakhsī referred to the inner meaning of the Qur'ān and not the inner *meanings*. In stark contrast to Dabūsī, Sarakhsī was confident that if a scholar utilized the proper hermeneutic, he would arrive at the true, inimitable inner meaning of any given Qur'anic passage. Sarakhsī argued that legal scholars (*ʿulamā'*) were able to ascertain this inner meaning with regard to legal verses and, once having understood it, could apply that inner meaning authoritatively in legal matters. He embraced the idea that *tafsīr* and *ta'wīl*, when practiced by jurists, could produce an interpretation of legal verses that could

[30] Ibid 1:211.
[31] Ibid 1:211. [32] Sarakhsī, *al-Mabsūṭ* (n 24) 1:137. [33] Ibid 1:139.
[34] Sarakhsī, *al-Muḥarrar fī Uṣūl al-Fiqh* (n 22) 1:211.

claim to be a manifestation of the inimitable meaning inherent in legal verses of the Qur'ān.

When compared to Dabūsī, Sarakhsī's conception of inimitability gives the scholarly community a great deal of power when approaching the Qur'ān as a legal document. For Dabūsī, miraculousness was equated with the pragmatic effect that some verses had in causing a reader to assent to the divinity of the message. Inimitability, however, was only the logical consequent of a divine text, in that no human could produce a work authored by God. When inimitability is confined to the *naẓm* of the Qur'ān, it is difficult to derive an authoritative inner meaning, since the articulation of that inner meaning would no longer be Qur'ān, and thus no longer inimitable. Sarakhsī's association of inimitability with the inner meaning of the Qur'ān, by contrast, required that qualified interpreters, whom Sarakhsī only identified as 'the *'ulamā','* derive the authoritative inner meaning for the benefit of the believing community. The inner meaning so derived would serve to guide the believers in matters theological, legal, spiritual, and otherwise. Without the interpretations of these *'ulamā'*, the inner meaning would be lost and the Qur'ān would be unable to guide the community.

The discussions recounted above concerning the inimitability of the Qur'ān appear highly theoretical. This is especially true because the two divergent positions did not affect Ḥanafī Qur'ān interpretation, especially regarding the injunctions that Ḥanafīs derived from the Qur'ān, in any significant way. Nevertheless, they do affect how one might regard Qur'anic interpretations and injunctions. If the interpretations are authoritative, then one has no choice but to accept them and act upon them. If they are merely conjectural, then one might appreciate the interpretations and accept them as possible, but deviate from them in one's personal life. Of course, we cannot get a clear picture of the Qur'ān's relation to practice and Islamic law through a study of its inimitability alone.

There are other theoretical debates that, in conversation with the inimitability debates, help provide a more robust view of the Qur'ān as a source of law. One such debate concerns the ability to understand figurative language. For Dabūsī, legal verses that utilize figurative language may remain forever vague or tentative given his belief that the inimitability of the Qur'ān precludes definitive interpretations of legal verses. Sarakhsī, on the other hand, was forced to develop a hermeneutic that delineated the precise meaning of figurative language if he was to salvage the inimitable inner meaning. As can be expected, the highly personal and subjective discussions of figurative language were not prominent and overt. Rather, they were couched in far more familiar—and mundane—recapitulations of established Ḥanafī positions concerning 'clear' and 'ambiguous' verses.

THE CLEAR AND THE AMBIGUOUS IN THE QUR'ĀN (*MUḤKAMĀT WA MUTASHĀBIHĀT*)

Muslim scholars frequently disagreed about how to identify clear and ambiguous verses. The most notable disagreement arose from differing reports attributed to the Companion Ibn ʿAbbās and the Successor Mujāhid concerning the following verse:

> He it is Who has sent down to you the Book—in it are verses that are clear (*muḥkamāt*), they are the foundation of the book (*umm al-kitāb*), and others that are ambiguous (*mutashābihāt*). But those in whose hearts is perversity follow the part thereof that is ambiguous, seeking discord and seeking its interpretation (*ta'wīlihi*). And none know its interpretation except for Allāh. And those endowed with knowledge say, 'We believe in it, the whole of it is from our Lord.' And none pay heed except the people of understanding. (Q. 3:7)

There is a history of lively debate amongst religious scholars regarding the meaning of this verse as well as its proper reading. The most famous debate captured in the reports of Ibn ʿAbbās and Mujāhid concerns the portion of the above verse that reads 'and none know of its interpretation except for Allah. And those endowed with knowledge say, "We believe in it, the whole of it is from our Lord." '[35] In this reading, endorsed by

[35] Ṣuyūṭī (n 9) 1:642.

a report from Ibn ʿAbbās,[36] no one knows the interpretation of the ambiguous verses of the Qur'ān except God; anyone who would even attempt to interpret them is perverse. However, a report from Mujāhid states that the relevant part of the verse should, in fact, read, 'and none know of its interpretation except for Allah *and* those endowed with knowledge. Say, "We believe in it, the whole of it is from our Lord."' In this latter reading, God and those endowed with knowledge know the interpretation of ambiguous verses. This reading assumes a class of individuals 'endowed with knowledge' who can interpret ambiguous verses for the rest of the community. This reading would appear to sanction interpretations derived by these knowledgeable individuals. Since there is no punctuation in the original Arabic, both sides can claim that their reading accurately reflects the intent of the text. The two larger issues that drive the debate between these two readings are interpretive possibility and interpretive authority. Specifically, can ambiguous verses remain forever ambiguous or does a scholarly community provide their interpretation?

Based on what we know of Dabūsī and Sarakhsī thus far, one might assume that Dabūsī would endorse Mujāhid's reading, such that only God knows the true interpretation of ambiguous verses and humans should leave off trying. One might assume that Sarakhsī favored Ibn ʿAbbās' view, such that God and the jurists alone know the true interpretation. In fact, Dabūsī and Sarakhsī both agreed with the report of Ibn ʿAbbas, which by the 5th/11th century was the dominant Sunnī position. To do otherwise would bring suspicion upon themselves from their Sunnī compatriots. Yet, by providing discrete justifications for the terms 'clear' (*muḥkam*), 'ambiguous' (*mutashābih*), and verses that fall in between the two, they were able to forge a hermeneutic wholly reconciled with their individual justifications of Qur'anic inimitability.

[36] Note that the report from Mujāhid has Ibn ʿAbbās in its *isnād*. Sunnī scholars on the whole, however, held that the more reliable Ibn ʿAbbās reports were those that uphold the traditional Sunnī interpretation of the verse and are found in the *Tafsīr* of ʿAbd al-Razzāq and the *Mustadrak* of al-Ḥākim. A succinct summary of the debate can be found in Ṣuyūṭī (n 9) 1:643–4.

Dabūsī on the Clear and the Ambiguous

Dabūsī held that the clear verses (*muḥkamāt*) mentioned in Q. 3:7 are so clear that they require no elaboration at all. Their plain-sense meaning is sufficient for every reader and they are applicable in all times and all places. Therefore, he reasoned, these verses must refer to something that was always true and will always be true; so they must refer to a truth beyond time and space. The only truth that transcends time and place is God Himself, in His essence and attributes. Clear verses, then, are necessarily those that discuss the nature of God's essence or attributes. The converse of the above statement is also true according to Dabūsī; that is, if a verse refers to God's essence or attributes, then it is necessarily clear.

By way of example, Dabūsī considered the phrase, 'And God is knowledgeable of all things (29:62).' The truth of the statement contained in this verse will always be true because God will always be knowledgeable of all things and there can never be anything that escapes God's knowledge. Hence, the verse is clear because the content will never change in response to the context of the interpreter. More importantly, the verse must be clear because it refers to God's attribute of knowledge. Thus, the interpreter need not interrogate whether the content will always be true or not; the fact that the verse refers to God's attribute of being all-knowledgeable precludes any need for interpretation or explanation.[37] This proscription from interpretation results in part from the limitations of the human intellect. Since Dabūsī held that the human intellect is incapable of cognizing God, any attempt to explain these verses would presuppose an intimate understanding of God's nature beyond that explicitly mentioned in the Qur'ān. To claim such an understanding would be tantamount to heresy, and so Dabūsī forbade any interpretation of clear verses. In any case, since both the individual words and the meaning of these verses were clear, interpretation of either the entire clear verse or its constituent words was unnecessary. The verse could never be abrogated, nor could its meaning fail to obtain,

[37] Dabūsī (n 6) 117.

regardless of time and place. It is for this reason that God designated these verses to be 'the foundation (*umm*) of the Book.'[38]

Ambiguous verses were similarly beyond the pale of hermeneutics for Dabūsī. Being the 'opposite of clear,'[39] these verses are merely to be believed in exactly as they are worded without any consideration for meaning or legal applicability. On the Day of Judgment, God will test the believer concerning his belief in the literal wording of ambiguous verses and the believer will only pass this test if he believes in their literal wording apart from any exegesis.[40] Specifically, believers must say, 'We believe in it, the whole of it is from our Lord' and nothing further in order to pass their test. Dabūsī did not provide a rubric for identifying ambiguous verses, nor did he cite examples of them.[41]

For Dabūsī, only a few verses of the Qur'ān were classified as either 'clear' or 'ambiguous'; in fact, the majority of verses did not belong to either category.[42] Indeed, since Dabūsī exempted clear and ambiguous verses from hermeneutical and juridical inquiry, he could not classify all verses as either clear or ambiguous without exempting the entire Qur'ān from interpretation. In Dabūsī's system, the 'clear' and the 'ambiguous' were a subclass of Qur'anic verses to be believed in, but not expounded upon. By providing such a defintion, Dabūsī effectively relegated clear and ambiguous verses to the margins of Qur'anic interpretation theory.

For the verses that could be subject to interpretation, including all legal verses, Dabūsī introduced a middle term, *mu'awwalāt*,[43] which describes

[38] Ibid 117. [39] Ibid 117. [40] Ibid 118.

[41] This is particularly curious given Dabūsī's frequent references to Abū Bakr al-Jaṣṣāṣ, who wrote extensively on this topic. Citing Ibn ʿAbbās, Jaṣṣāṣ asserted that all verses of the Qur'ān could be formally divided into verses that are ambiguous and clear. He discussed competing definitions and classifications of clear and ambiguous verses, and though giving them various levels of credence, ultimately concluded that the terms refer primarily to abrogation. For him, 'ambiguous' verses were those that were abrogated (*mansūkh*), despite their presence in the Qur'ān, and the abrogating verses (*nāsikh*) were those that were 'clear'; Aḥmad b. ʿAlī al-Jaṣṣāṣ, *Aḥkām al-Qur'ān* (ʿAbd al-Salām Shāhīn ed, Dār al-Kutub al-ʿIlmiyya 1994) 2:3–4. Dabūsī's approach differed from Jassās' most significantly in that, according to Dabūsī, verses of the Qur'ān could not all be formally classified as either clear or ambiguous.

[42] Dabūsī (n 6) 173.

[43] The term '*mu'awwal*' was a contested one in Ḥanafī circles, and so the definition provided here is particular to Dabūsī. For other Ḥanafī understandings, see Bukhārī (n 13) 1:118. I have deliberately focused on the *mu'awwal* and not the *mushtarak* because Ḥanafīs unanimously considered the *mu'awwal* to require use of the intellect, meaning

verses that can be interpreted with more or less clarity.[44] These verses comprise the majority of the Qur'ān and do not disclose their meanings and juridical applications without a reader who engages in some level of interpretation. Verses that are subject to interpretation can be found on a spectrum of relative clarity—some are clearer and therefore require less interpretation while others are vaguer and require more interpretation. One could tell whether more or less interpretation was required based on the use of literal (*ḥaqīqī*) or figurative (*majāzī*) language within that verse.[45] If a verse were largely composed of literal terms then less interpretation would be required, whereas figurative language required more interpretation.

Dabūsī briefly defined the literal word as that which presents an obvious meaning to the reader.[46] The meaning is obvious when the sense (*irāda*) of a word unambiguously points the reader to its literal referent (*waḍʿ*).[47] For example, if a reader were to come across the phrase 'a star is born,' and the phrase was intended to make the reader think of the nascence of a celestial ball of luminous plasma, then the phrase is *ḥaqīqī*. If, however, the intention of the phrase 'a star is born' is to inform the reader that someone will be a great entertainer, then the phrase is *majāzī*. The reader can determine whether a term is intended literally if the sentence still makes sense in its context after a literal reading. If a passage does not

that the resulting interpretation could be wrong, whereas that was not necessarily the case with the *mushtarak*; al-Qāsim b. ʿAbd Allāh b. Quṭlubughā, *Khulāṣat al-Afkār* (Thanāʾ Allāh Zāhidī ed, Dār Ibn Ḥazm 2003) 80–3; Muḥammad b. Walī al-Dīn al-Farfūr, *Mukhtaṣar al-Afkār* (Walī al-Dīn al-Farfūr ed, Dār al-Farfūr 2001) 60–1; Muḥammad b. ʿAlī al-Ḥaṣkafī, *Ifāḍat al-Anwār* (Muḥammad Saʿīd Burhānī ed, n.p. 1992) 105; Muḥammad b. Zayd al-Lāmishī, *Kitāb fī Uṣūl al-Fiqh* (ʿAbd al-Majīd Turkī ed, Dār al-Gharb al-Islamī 1995) 79. For Dabūsī and Sarakhsī in particular, see Saghnāqī (n 25) 1:259.

[44] Dabūsī (n 6) 169.

[45] The *ḥaqīqī-majāzī* dichotomy was well-established in *uṣūl al-fiqh* texts by the 5th/11th century, and was closely linked by legal theorists to discussions on the miraculous nature of the Qur'ān; Wolfhart Heinrichs, 'On the Genesis of the *Haqīqa-Majāz* Dichotomy' (1984) 59 *Studia Islamica* 111, 129.

[46] Dabūsī (n 6) 95.

[47] Ibid 119. The term '*irāda*' literally means 'will' or 'desire', depending on the context. I have intentionally used Fregean terms here to differentiate the use of *irāda* in the text under study with its use in theology (divine will/intentionality) and Sufism (desire); for the use of *irāda* in theology, see Frank Griffel *al-Ghazālī's Dialectical Theology* (Oxford University Press 2009) 160ff; for the use of *irāda* in relation to Sūfism, see Alexander Knysh (trs) *al-Qushayri's Epistle on Sufism* (Garnet Publishing 2007) 214–17.

make immediate and unambiguous sense to the reader, the reader must conclude that the author's intention was to use figurative language.[48] Interpretation, therefore, is only required when the intention of a word used in the Qur'ān points to other than its literal referent. Understanding requires a link between a word and its referent (*ittiṣāl baynahumā*), a link that is obvious when the word is literal. In the case of figurative language, the link is established through some internal logic (*bi-wajhin mā*)[49] that needs to be determined by the reader.

Dabūsī used the example of metaphor (*istiʿāra*) to demonstrate how figurative language should be interpreted.[50] If one were to describe a person who is brave as a 'lion,' the speaker would be using metaphor because the literal referent of 'lion'—a mammal of the species *panthera leo*—is not what was intended by the speaker. Nevertheless, the interpreter understands the speaker because they both participate in a shared vernacular (*samāʿ*).[51] Thus, the interpretation required is minimal and it is obvious to the interpreter that the intended referent of 'lion' is 'brave.' Dabūsī said that the process involved here is more of word substitution in ordinary language than engaged interpretation.[52] When the speaker creates metaphors and allusions (*ibdāʾ istiʿārāt wa-taʿrīḍāt*) that are not part of the vernacular, a deeper level of interpretation is required. This deeper interpretation requires the reader to use reason (*raʾy*) and analogy (*qiyās*) in order to determine a meaning.

Dabūsī recognized that when an interpreter uses reason and analogy there is room for error in determining a referent. It may well be that the referent determined by the reader is different than the one intended by the speaker. This, for Dabūsī, is an insurmountable problem. In the absence of the speaker himself, the interpreter is forever denied the actual authorial intention. The intention is therefore hidden (*bāṭin*) and will remain so unless it somehow becomes clear on its own

[48] Ibid 120.
[49] Ibid 119. Although '*bi-wajhin mā*' literally means 'in some way', I have translated it here as 'by some internal logic' as it more accurately reflects the context in which it is found.
[50] For a succinct discussion of the difference between *majāz* and *istiʿāra* in the Ḥanafī and Shāfiʿī legal schools, see Bukhārī (n 13) 2:110–11.
[51] Dabūsī (n 6) 119.
[52] Ibid 95.

(*taẓhiru bi-ṭarīquhā*).[53] By admitting the irremediably inexact nature of figurative interpretation, Dabūsī absolved interpreters from finding an exact referent for non-conventional metaphors. Interpreters might make educated guesses about the referents, but are not charged with determining the referent with certainty. To justify the futility in trying to determine non-conventional metaphoric referents, Dabūsī paraphrased Q. 2:286, 'God does not burden us beyond our capacities.'[54]

The inability to determine exact referents for verses needing interpretation presented Dabūsī with a problem regarding the derivation of law from the Qur'ān, particularly because he held that most verses require interpretation. He could solve this problem by stating either that law cannot be derived from any verses that are not entirely composed of literal words, or that using reason or analogy to derive the law would preclude the resulting interpretation from being authoritative. Though he argued for the latter, both options seem to render most of the Qur'ān juridically impotent. Dabūsī conceded that using reason when interpreting could only result in a possible explanation of an unclear verse.[55] This would most likely result in multiple interpretations from disparate interpreters. When several possible interpretations for a single verse have been proffered, knowledgeable individuals would need to determine which possibility is preponderant (*rājiḥ*) over all others. Dabūsī elsewhere went into some detail as to how the process of determining preponderance occurs, but ultimately concluded that preponderance (*tarjīḥ*) was an inexact science. What is most important is not finding the 'right' interpretation, but that interpreters interpret with the express aim of genuinely understanding the *sharī'a*, not simply justifying whims (*hawā*).[56] Dabūsī did not restrict interpretation of figurative language in the Qur'ān to the purview of juridical scholarship, though he did say that only jurists could accurately determine preponderant interpretations of legal verses.

53 Ibid 100.
54 Ibid 101. 55 Ibid 169.
56 Ibid 169. Ḥaṣkafī was particularly interested in the issue of preponderance, his discussions on the Qur'ān are peppered with rules of *tarjīḥ*, and he outlined the rules for *tarjīḥ* with regard to the *sunna*—Ḥaṣkafī (n 43) 214–18—and for *qiyās*—Ḥaṣkafī (n 43) 286–8.

Dabūsī anticipated that his detractors would balk at the imprecise nature of the law derived by his proposed practice. It is conceivable that, based on Dabūsī's theory, two jurists could come up with completely different readings of a passage using figurative language and both claim authenticity. Dabūsī embraced this criticism and agreed with its implication. Since the authorial intentions behind figurative language are hidden, he argued that no one could ever definitively know if an interpretation was correct. Therefore, verses that utilize figurative language, even those with legal implications, do not require all readers, or more specifically all believers, to act on them with uniformity.[57] Rather, one is permitted to act in accordance with an interpretation for which preponderance could be plausibly argued.

At the very least, arguing for preponderance provides the interpreter a tentative rationale for acting upon a legal command found in a verse, even if he were not certain that his actions were definitely in line with the verse's intention. Dabūsī called this rationale 'surface knowledge' (*ʿilm ẓāhir*) that does not reach the level of certainty (*yaqīn*) or even complete comprehension (*iḥāṭa*), but nevertheless compels the interpreter to act.[58] Dabūsī did not seem concerned that this might result in differing opinions and actions. He was content so long as the process of preponderance was followed and the interpreter was aware that his interpretation might not correspond to the exact authorial intention. To those who would say that such an approach to Qur'anic law destabilizes a unified exposition of Islam and that interpretation should be highly restricted, Dabūsī gave a curious reply. He said that free interpretation must be allowed or else scholars would be unable to adapt to evolving criticisms of the Qur'ān. 'If [interpretation] were not permitted,' he argued, 'we would not be able to respond to the attacks of those who espouse heretical beliefs about the Qur'ān.'[59] It is interesting that Dabūsī was less concerned with defending the interpretations of his legal school than with arguing against heretics. Differing interpretations that do not involve heresy appear to have been perfectly acceptable to Dabūsī. For him, interpreting the Qur'ānic message couched in figurative language was less about generating a

[57] Dabūsī (n 6) 100. [58] Ibid 169. [59] Ibid 169.

linear interpretation of law than about ensuring good-natured, well-reasoned interpretation itself.

Sarakhsī on the Clear and the Ambiguous

Sarakhsī's definition of clear (*muḥkam*) and ambiguous (*mutashābih*) verses was similar to Dabūsī's. Sarakhsī said that 'clear' verses could not be abrogated and do not admit interpretation,[60] and used the same verse as Dabūsī to illustrate his point, 'And God is knowledgeable of all things.' Sarakhsī said that such verses pertaining to the nature of God could not be reworded or interpreted; they are simply to be accepted, maintained, and believed in based on their literal wording and meaning.[61] Sarakhsī gave scant attention to ambiguous verses, but provided slightly more detail concerning them than did Dabūsī. Like Dabūsī, he said that ambiguous verses are those that humans cannot hope to understand. He provided an example with Q. 75:22–23, 'On that day faces will be bright, looking toward their Lord.' Sarakhsī remarked that the literal meaning of this verse could not have been intended here, because God has no direction and thus humans cannot look toward Him.[62] Quite the contrary, humans are limited in their understanding and cannot think beyond directionality (*jiha*). Since no amount of interpretation can make sense of non-direction, Sarakhsī concluded that the verse must therefore be ambiguous. As such, the verse must be believed in but cannot be

[60] Sarakhsī, *al-Muḥarrar fī Uṣūl al-Fiqh* (n 19) 1:124

[61] Ibid 1:124. It should be noted here that some later Ḥanafīs tweaked this position so that the *muḥkamāt* might include aspects of the *sharīʿa*. In an example that simultaneously highlights the way in which the historical legal theory works of a school were replicated and subverted at the same time, Ibn Quṭlubughā in his gloss of Nasafī's *uṣūl* work recounted Nasafī's definition of the *muḥkam* as relating to the attributes of God and that which cannot be abrogated or changed (strangely enough, this was the same definition he provided for the *mutashābihāt*); Ibn Quṭlubughā (n 43) 97. He added, however, that when a legal dictate was repeated, as in the case with prayer, that dictate also takes on the level of *muḥkam*; Ibn Quṭlubughā (n 43) 91. Thus he was able to include some legal punishments, such as those for adultery and imbibing intoxicants, among the rights of God (*ḥuqūq Allāh*), thereby making these aspects of the *sharīʿa* unchanging and unchangeable; Ibn Quṭlubughā (n 43) 173. It was a subtle change to the definition of the *muḥkamāt*, but it was a move that opened the door for later Ḥanafīs to include legal verses in the *muḥkam* category and make certain aspects of the *sharīʿa* immutable; see Farfūr (n 43) 67 and 221–4.

[62] Sarakhsī, *al-Muḥarrar fī Uṣūl al-Fiqh* (n 19) 1:127.

understood, nor should anyone attempt to explain it in the hopes of making it intelligible. Similar verses dealing with unintelligibles—like the hand of God, or God's rising above his throne—are to be believed in as ambiguous and that belief should be sufficient for the believer. To anyone who might ask how (*kayf*) God rises above his throne or how humans might look to their Lord if not literally, Sarakhsī glibly responded, 'it's ambiguous, that's how!' (*huwa mutashābih wa-huwa kayfiyya*).[63] By thus defining ambiguous verses, Sarakhsī effectively cut off all discussion about God's essence and attributes.

Sarakhsī introduced several middle terms describing verses that fall in between the categories of clear and ambiguous. These verses have various levels of clarity and ambiguity, a spectrum similar to that proffered by Dabūsī. Also similar to Dabūsī, clarity and ambiguity hinged on words being understood as literal (*ḥaqīqī*) or figurative (*majāzī*). Sarakhsī defined literal words as those with a primary referent (*mawḍūʿ fī-al-aṣl*) that is known (*maʿlūm*) to the author and reader. A figurative word, in contrast, was defined as one that is used metaphorically (*mustaʿār*) to connote something other than its primary referent.[64]

The figurative word, for Sarakhsī, is that which a speaker uses to metaphorically allude to an intended referent. He often equated figurative language (*majāz*) with metaphor (*istiʿāra*), and in fact used them interchangeably throughout his work, though the former was often utilized as a technical descriptor that related more to the structure of language than its performance. Sarakhsī remarked that figurative language is found throughout literature, including the Qur'ān and the *hadīth*, and that figurative language is often more prevalent than literal language.[65] This did not pose a problem for Sarakhsī, because he provided a methodology by which the primary referents of all metaphors may be precisely determined.

According to Sarakhsī, the Arabs used two exhaustive processes that would successfully connect a figurative word with its proper referent. He called the first process a formal connection (*ittiṣāl al-ṣūra*), wherein a figurative word and its referent shared an essential, often physical

[63] Ibid 1:127. [64] Ibid 1:127. [65] Ibid 1:128.

feature.[66] For example, Sarakhsī said that Arabs would use the word 'sky' when referring to 'rain.' This is understandable, he said, partly because Arabs called everything above them 'sky', but also because rain comes from the clouds that are in the sky. Thus, the literal referent of the word 'sky' is connected to 'rain' through a formal, physical relationship. In this scheme, the literal meaning of a figurative word is not erased through metaphor, but is used to determine the intended referent.

The second type of connection that figurative words have with their intended referents is a connection in meaning (*ittiṣāl al-maʿnā*).[67] This type of connection is found not in some physical link between the figurative word and its primary referent, but in the figurative word sharing or describing a characteristic of its intended referent. Sarakhsī employed the same example as Dabūsī by using the word 'lion' to connote 'brave.' The literal referent of 'lion' is an animal that displays both strength (*quwwa*) and bravery (*shujāʿ*). Therefore, the word 'lion' can be used as a substitute or metaphor for those two qualities. By utilizing either of these two methods, those of formal connection and connection in meaning, a person can come to be certain of the primary referent intended by the author.[68] Reflection (*taʾammul*) is required on the part of the reader in his search (*ṭalab*) for the intended referent, in contrast to the intuitive process by which literal words are understood, but the reader can nonetheless hope to know the referent with certainty.[69] Once the reader has obtained this certainty, the figurative word becomes, for all intents and purposes, literal for the reader.[70]

Theoretically, then, a reader who is skilled in making formal connections and connections in meaning might be able to determine the referents of figurative terms in the Qurʾān with a level of certainty. This certainty, though, could only apply to verses that discuss mundane

[66] Ibid 1:133.
[67] Ibid 1:133.
[68] This similarity between Sarakhsī's 'connections' and Aristotle's primary and secondary qualities is striking. However, it is difficult to explore Aristotle's influence on Sarakhsī primarily because historical literature on the topic sometimes confuses our Muḥammad b. Aḥmad al-Sarakhsī with Aḥmad ibn Ṭayyab al-Sarakhsī (d. 285/899), the disciple of al-Kindī (d. ca. 259/873) and champion of Aristotelian thought. Aristotelian thought is palpable in Sarakhsī's works and merits further study.
[69] Sarakhsī, *al-Muḥarrar fī Uṣūl al-Fiqh* (n 19) 1:134
[70] Ibid 1:146.

matters like law and history, since interpreting verses that discuss God and His attributes is off-limits. Hence, the Qur'ān as a legal document might be interpreted by qualified scholars to lay bare the exact meaning intended by the author, regardless of whether the legal dictates are couched in literal or figurative language.

Sarakhsī built on his theory of metaphor to describe not only how Qur'anic legal dictates could be known with certainty, but how the bulk of Islamic law could be known with certainty. Sarakhsī argued that the rules of ordinary language could be extended to demonstrate the way in which Islamic law is derived and applied. In ordinary language, he contended, the reader can know the intended referent by thinking about the characteristics, whether formal or in meaning, it shares with a figurative term.[71] In this process, the figurative word is the limiting term. That is, though the intended referent may be known through the specific qualities it shares with the figurative word, the opposite is not true. A figurative term cannot be derived by enumerating the qualities of its intended referent. In practical terms, while a reader can deduce 'bravery' or 'strength' from 'lion,' one cannot deduce 'lion' from 'bravery' and 'strength.'[72] The connection, it would seem, only moves one way. Sarakhsī pointed out that a figurative word may have many characteristics—in the case of our 'lion' example, characteristics like 'carnivorous,' 'large,' 'menacing'—which may or may not be appropriate for denoting 'brave' or 'strong.' Hence, there is something special about the word 'lion' that it signifies bravery and strength, and only bravery and strength, to the reader. Sarakhsī did not detail how these connections are established, but took it for granted that language works in the way that he suggested. These points are foundational to the parallel that Sarakhsī then made between ordinary language and the derivation of law.[73]

[71] Ibid 1:135. [72] Ibid 1:136.

[73] Interestingly, Sarakhsī did not liken his hermeneutic method to analogical reasoning (*qiyās*) in Islamic law. At first glance, this would appear to have been the most logical and straightforward means of explication, and indeed several of his contemporaries and later Ḥanafīs made that link; see Bukhārī (n 13) 1:164. The fact that Sarakhsī did not make this link says a great deal about his view of *qiyās* as a strong foundational source for Islamic law. For *qiyās* to retain certainty, it would have to use as little personal reasoning as possible and resemble mathematics more than art. Someone like Pazdawī, for instance, could afford to liken determining a referent to *qiyās* precisely because he

For Sarakhsī, the example of metaphor maps the process of inducing a paradigmatic case (*aṣl*) that provides a rationale for inherited injunctions.[74] He compared the intended referent of a figurative word to the paradigmatic case, and the figurative word itself to the injunctions. Sarakhsī argued that by reflecting on the applications of law—meaning the specific injunctions of Ḥanafī jurisprudence—one could induce the paradigmatic cases that underlie those injunctions. He posited a special connection between the injunction and its paradigmatic case, wherein the injunction can point to the paradigmatic case if one reflects on the injunction properly. The paradigmatic case, however, can never directly point to the injunction, nor can it be used to establish novel injunctions.[75] The connection from injunction to paradigm only moves one way, just like the connection between the figurative word and its intended referent. In that case, knowing the paradigmatic case of an injunction is merely an academic exercise, a helpful bit of information that can aid someone in understanding an injunction completely, but is not necessary knowledge for acting upon the injunction. Sarakhsī assumed that paradigmatic cases lie behind each injunction, but argued that these paradigmatic cases need not be induced. Thus, a person can, in theory, act upon an injunction without understanding its rationale, yet trusting that there is a paradigmatic case behind it that would be unearthed through sufficient reflection.

To illustrate the logic that informs this unquestioning adherence to received injunctions, Sarakhsī said that prior to knowing the paradigmatic case of an injunction, that injunction acts like a figurative word with the intended referent unknown.[76] Similar to the way metaphor works, once the paradigmatic case is known, the injunction no longer functions like a

was more dubious of *qiyās* than was Sarakhsī. Nevertheless, Pazdawī and Sarakhsī both presented overall conceptions of Islamic law as mostly predetermined and replicable because Pazdawī offset his doubt in *qiyās* with faith in Consensus (*ijmāʿ*). Such a seemingly minor point as likening determining a referent to *qiyās* (or not, as in the case of Sarakhsī) demonstrates the internal coherence of legal theory works and reflects a consciousness on the part of legal theorists that their arguments pertaining to the minutiae of legal hermeneutics have a larger bearing on the place and applicability of Islamic law and its sources.

[74] Sarakhsī, *al-Muḥarrar fī Uṣūl al-Fiqh* (n 19) 1:135.
[75] Ibid 1:135; Saghnāqī (n 28) 1:355.
[76] Sarakhsī, *al-Muḥarrar fī Uṣūl al-Fiqh* (n 19) 1:136.

figurative word and becomes more like a literal word. This knowledge, though, is unnecessary for accepting and acting upon the injunctions laid down in Ḥanafī jurisprudence,[77] just as one does not need to interrogate the way in which figurative words operate in ordinary language in order to understand and act upon their intentions.

Through his discourse on figurative language, Sarakhsī developed a key concept that pervades much of his work. That is the notion that something might necessitate action, even if it is not understood. He developed this idea later in his discussion of the single-narrator *ḥadīth* (*khabar al-wāḥid*), but his discussion of metaphor provides a backdrop for his theory regarding that which necessitates action but not knowledge (*yūjib al-ʿamal lā al-ʿilm*). Action, in this framework, is not predicated on understanding, but on belief. Once an individual believes that an injunction has a divine origin, that belief is enough to act upon the injunction, trusting that there is wisdom behind it. Metaphorical passages function similarly, necessitating action on the applications of law as described by, presumably Ḥanafī, scholars of jurisprudence. The lay believer need not understand the meaning of a passage except in its manifestation as an injunction in the legal tradition. Jurists, however, are able to determine the intended referents of metaphorical terms in Qur'anic passages by utilizing the hermeneutic outlined above. What this means for the interpretation of the Qur'ān is that all verses—other than verses that are 'clear' and 'ambiguous,' meaning those that deal with God's essence and attributes—are potentially literal in that their intended meaning can be known. The wording of a verse may be figurative, but juridical reflection will always remedy (*tuṣliḥ*) any ambiguity created by metaphor and provide the intended meaning.[78]

Sarakhsī argued that Ḥanafī juridical scholars have already determined most of the meanings intended by figurative language in the Qur'ān. These intended meanings were then elaborated by seminal scholars and captured in the Ḥanafī juridical tradition. Reflection upon the injunctions that these scholars enumerated would lead one to understand the paradigmatic cases behind them, though such reflection

[77] Ibid 1:136. [78] Ibid 1:137.

is unnecessary. Acting upon these injunctions would assuredly put one in fidelity with the Qur'anic message, regardless of whether or not the actor understands the underlying rationale. Essentially, then, the meaning of every verse of the Qur'ān, other than theological verses, can be known through recourse to the Ḥanafī legal tradition and acted upon with certainty.

By analogizing jurisprudence with his conception of ordinary language, Sarakhsī argued for a system wherein jurists are the arbiters of the Qur'ān who, through their juridical injunctions, make the Qur'ān clear to the rest of mankind.

BRIEF REVIEW

At this point, it will be helpful to recap the views of Dabūsī and Sarakhsī in order to gain some insight into their views on the nature of the Qur'ān. For Dabūsī thus far, the Qur'ān is a book that, for the most part, requires interpretation. He did not suggest that the Qur'ān had only one authentic interpretation nor did he argue for any particular interpretation over another. Reason and analogy played a large part in his framework, and the inherent fallibility of the interpretive enterprise as he described it results in a vagueness that Dabūsī accepted as a necessary reality. Though he treated the physical text of the Qur'ān as inimitable, static, and redacted, Dabūsī admitted that interpretation of the text in varying times and places would produce different meanings. These meanings should be judged and compared to determine which one is preponderant, but none are absolutely authoritative. Thus, the text is performative in the life of the legal community, and jurists were not limited by the jurisprudence of their forbears when extracting meaning from the text.

Dabūsī limited the scope of interpretation, however, in his discussion of clear and ambiguous verses. Clear and ambiguous verses can never be subject to interpretation, and must retain the same meaning to all people. Likewise, Dabūsī said that miraculous verses of the Qur'ān cannot be interpreted and were meant to generate the same response in all readers: affirmation of the prophethood of Muḥammad. Taking his discussion on *iʿjāz al-Qurʾān* into account, 'clear' verses seem to have a similar structure and function to those that are 'miraculous.' Though Dabūsī did not make this connection overtly, the similarity in definition is unmistakable. Miraculous verses lead a person to recognize God, result in indubitable knowledge, and cannot be interpreted. Dabūsī characterized clear verses as dealing with God, resulting in indubitable knowledge, and serving as the foundation—though a hermeneutically impotent one—of the Qurʾān. The definitions are not identical, but there are obvious correlations. What this intimates is a commitment to a particular message in the Qurʾān that Dabūsī held to be central to revelation. Thus far, this commitment manifested itself in knowing the Godhead and recognizing His intervention in history in the form of a divine text. The legal verses do not appear to be similarly foundational to the message of the Qurʾān, which perhaps accounts for the multivalent readings that Dabūsī allowed for interpretable verses.

Sarakhsī's conception of the meanings of the Qurʾān is far more reified than Dabūsī's. The Qurʾān intends to convey particular meanings, and those meanings were ascertained and delineated by jurists in the past.[79] Therefore, the legal interpretive process has, for the most part, ceased with the coalescence of Ḥanafī juridical thought. The jurisprudence proffered by Ḥanafī scholars reflects the true meaning, or, at least, the range of possible meanings available from the text. Sarakhsī resolved the issue of conflicting opinions in his discussion on Consensus (*ijmāʿ*), but for now it suffices to say that revelation, apart from the ambiguous verses, was fully coherent and cognizable for Sarakhsī, especially in the form of jurisprudence.

[79] This attitude toward the text is also found is Sarakhsī's discussion of the *mujmal* and *ishārat al-naṣṣ*, especially in contrast to Dabūsī. Whereas Dabūsī held that the true meaning of *mujmal* verses could never be known with certainty, Sarakhsī held that their meaning could be known through recourse to *tafsīr* works; Bukhārī (n 13) 1:146. Whereas Dabūsī argued that by going beyond the texts itself, indications extracted from the text (*ishārat al-naṣṣ*) could not be subject to specification (*takhṣīṣ*), Sarakhsī argued that the indications were obvious to the learned and could thus be specified; Bukhārī (n 13) 2:463 and Saghnāqī (n 25) 1:533. Sarakhsī allowed for *qiyās* to be used when determining the *dalālat al-naṣṣ* whereas Dabūsī said that the *dalālāt* can only be extratextual connections made intuitively when one hears a word or phrase; Lāmishī (n 43) 52.

Sarakhsī also repeatedly exhibited a dedication to doctrinal integrity in his legal theory. He demonstrated this in his discussion of inimitable verses when he refused to consider the possibility of inimitability being located in the ordering of the Qur'ān, since that might result in anthropomorphism. It is with similar justification that Sarakhsī argued against ambiguous verses being interpreted in certain ways.[80] In the example of Q. 75:22–23, Sarakhsī denied the possibility of a literal interpretation when he argued that the meaning of this verse could not be that humans will actually look toward God. He aligned himself with strict literalists who affirmed the literal reading of the passage 'without [asking] how' (*bi-lā kayf*). The doctrinal justifications that Sarakhsī provided for his views are especially striking when contrasted with Dabūsī, who rarely engaged interlocutors on a doctrinal level. It is important to recognize that while Sarakhsī claimed that the possible meanings of the Qur'ān were clearly laid out in Ḥanafī jurisprudence, he held certain doctrinal concerns to be paramount and that jurisprudence must, at least nominally, conform to these doctrinal concerns. Sarakhsī further argued that the interpretation of legal verses in the Qur'ān was restricted to the Ḥanafī injunctions that were in harmony with his doctrinal positions.[81]

[80] Margaret Larkin observes a similar connection in the case of ʿAbd al-Qāhir al-Jurjānī, who shares Sarakhsī's views on figurative language stemming from a concern for the inimitability of the Qur'ān; *The Theology of Meaning* (The American Oriental Society 1995) 164. Larkin further observes that equating the process of determining a metaphorical referent with straightforward analogy is itself rife with theological undertones and overtones, ibid 91ff. I am grateful to an anonymous reviewer for pointing me to this text.

[81] It is interesting to note that in the discussion of clear and ambiguous, Dabūsī and Sarakhsī departed from the associations they explicitly embraced. As mentioned in footnote 41 above, Dabūsī not only disagreed with Abū Bakr al-Jaṣṣāṣ' conception of clear and ambiguous verses, he did not even mention it as a possibility. Similarly, Sarakhsī's contention that the verses of the Qur'ān are mostly clear and that meaning is laid down in the injunctions in Ḥanafī jurisprudence goes against the dominant Ḥanafī view. Al-Māturīdī, for instance, embraced the ambiguities in the text, and most Ḥanafīs held some mix of Māturīdī's opinion and that of the Mālikī jurist al-Baqillānī (d. 403/1013) that most Qur'anic verses are irremediably vague and that they are partial expressions from which the Divine Will is inferred; David Vishanoff, *Early Islamic Hermeneutics: Language, speech and meaning in preclassical legal theory* (PhD Diss, Emory University 2004) 117ff. It is therefore certain that the doctrinal concerns that Sarakhsī held paramount were at least in part concerns that did not conform to the major doctrinal school of the Ḥanafīs, to which Sarakhsī himself claimed allegiance. The same can be said for Dabūsī, whose discussion cannot be classified as wholly belonging to any doctrinal or juridical tradition.

One might be tempted to view Dabūsī and Sarakhsī as proxies for larger debates about the merits of pragmatism versus empiricism, or between truth as experience and truth as observed reality. Indeed, Dabūsī appears to have been interested in the truth of the Qur'ān insofar as it produces an effect in the reader, whereas Sarakhsī identified a tangible truth that can be extracted from the text itself. Comparisons to contemporary philosophical discourses are helpful, but limited. We must remember that both jurists were working within strict frameworks wherein the principles and injunctions were fixed. It is only within these frameworks that the arguments put forth by these legal theorists have any weight, and in some cases the strictures placed on them by their received history precluded anything so sweeping as a Gestalt shift. This is most evident in their discussions of Qur'anic abrogation, a subject fraught with theological difficulties and a received tradition that rigidly defined the boundaries of the topic. Nevertheless, we find that amidst these tight restraints, Dabūsī and Sarakhsī were able to argue for unique ways of conceiving the subject.

THE ABROGATING AND THE ABROGATED (*AL-NĀSIKH WA-AL-MANSŪKH*)

For a text that claims divine authority, the Qur'ān projects a surprisingly self-conscious sense of its own abrogation (*naskh*). It states that some verses abrogate others and that God intended for some verses to be either forgotten or barred from the codex. The most referenced verse that deals with the topic of abrogation is Q. 2:106,[82] 'We do not abrogate a verse or cause it to be forgotten except that We replace it with something that is better or similar to it.' The meaning of abrogation, however, is and has been a contested issue. The eminent jurist and exegete Abū al-Qāsim al-Khū'ī (d. 1317/1899) provided a concise definition of abrogation as a technical term,

[82] See John Burton, 'The Exegesis of Q. 2:106 and the Islamic Theories of naskh' (1985) 48:3 *Bulletin of the School of Oriental and African Studies* 452.

> Technically, the term *naskh* signifies the abolition of an ordained matter in the Sharīʿa because of the passage of its period [of applicability], regardless of whether this abolished matter is related to the divinely ordained injunctions or to noncanonical laws; or whether it is related to the divinely ordained positions or other matters that revert to God, because of His being the Lawgiver.[83]

It is noteworthy that in this definition, abrogation is applicable to the Qur'ān only in matters related to the *sharīʿa*. For jurists in particular, abrogation essentially occurs when one injunction in the Qur'ān abrogates another injunction. Exactly which verses abrogate and which are abrogated is hotly debated. Muslim scholars throughout history have attempted to enumerate the verses that abrogate, and the number has historically fluctuated from 5 to over 500,[84] depending on the abrogation theory employed. The number of verses that a jurist considers abrogated directly affects the law that he would then derive. The abrogated verses would be invalid sources for legislation, and thus a jurist who considered more verses to be abrogated would have fewer valid sources available to him when deriving law, but would also have less conflicting verses with which to contend.

In modern times, abrogation theory has taken a leading role in revivalist and reformist movements. For example, Medinan-based abrogation is championed by those who hold that Islam is primarily a socio-politico-economic system that demands establishment in the form of a nation-state.[85] In the Medinan-based framework, the more legal and antagonistic verses revealed in Medina abrogate the Meccan verses, the latter which, on a political level, called for something more like passive civil disobedience. Counter to this theory, many reformists suggest that the more universal Meccan verses are the core of the religion and the Medinan verses were but a limited juridical instantiation of the general

[83] Abū al-Qāsim al-Khū'ī, *Prolegomena to the Qur'ān* (Abdulaziz Sachedina tr, Oxford University Press 1998) 187.
[84] Shāh Walīullāh, *al-Fawz al-Kabīr fī Uṣūl al-Tafsīr* (Salman al-Ḥusaynī ed, Dār al-Bashā'ir n.d.) 53–60.
[85] See Olivier Carré, *Mysticism and Politics: A Critical Reading of Fī Ẓilāl al-Qur'ān by Sayyid Qutb* (Carol Artigues tr, Brill 2003) 31.

principles revealed in Mecca.[86] When the time and place changes, those instantiated verses are abrogated and new instantiations have to be derived from the Meccan verses apropos the novel circumstances. Other figures have argued that abrogation should be understood as 'specification' (*takhṣīṣ*),[87] meaning that God altered the conditions or stipulations of previous juridical commands without actually abrogating them, or that abrogation only applied to previous scriptures.[88] While abrogation theory did not enjoy as central a role in 5th/11th-century models of Islamic law, the various theories sketched above were nevertheless present and were the subject of much debate. Though Dabūsī and Sarakhsī addressed and acknowledged the many and varied theories circulating in their time, they worked within the particular Ḥanafī abrogation theory that their contemporaries upheld.

Jurists who identified themselves with one of the four Sunnī schools of law had diverse conceptions of the nature and scope of abrogation theory, and each school caricatured the others' positions on abrogation to defend their own stances. Ḥanafī scholars were particularly incensed by Shāfiʿī scholars, whom the former claimed to only allow Qur'anic verses to abrogate other parts of the Qur'ān and only a *sunna* to abrogate another *sunna*.[89] In the Ḥanafī protrayal, Shāfiʿīs held that the Qur'ān could not abrogate a *sunna* nor vice versa, though the reality of the Shāfiʿī position is far more nuanced. Ḥanafī scholars defined their own position in contrast to their description of the Shāfiʿīs, holding that the Qur'ān could abrogate a *sunna* and further that a *sunna* could abrogate the Qur'ān.[90] Ḥanafīs argued that personal opinion (*ra'y*) and analogy

[86] Abdullahi an-Na'im, *Toward an Islamic Reformation: Civil liberties, human rights and international law* (Syracuse University Press 1990) 18.

[87] Muhammad Ghazali, *A Thematic Commentary on the Qur'ān* (International Institute of Islamic Thought 2000) 40.

[88] David Powers, 'On the Abrogation of the Bequest Verses' (1982) 29:3 *Arabica* 246, 247.

[89] Melchert, 'Qur'ānic Abrogation Across the Ninth Century' in Bernard Weiss (ed), *Studies in Islamic Legal Theory* (Brill 2002) 86.

[90] Murteza Bedir, 'An Early Response to Shāfiʿī: ʿĪsā b. Abān on the Prophetic Report' (2002) 9:3 *Islamic Law and Society* 285, 304. For an example of the Shāfiʿī approach to Qur'anic abrogation by the *sunna* and vice versa as it was conceived by Shāfiʿīs themselves, see Bernard Weiss, *In Search of God's Law: Islamic Jurisprudence in the Writings of Sayf al-Dīn al-Āmidī* (University of Utah Press 1992) 534ff.

(*qiyās*) should have no role in abrogation, a position that Shāfiʿīs shared in principle, though, as some Ḥanafīs argued, not always in practice.[91] Although Ḥanafīs defined themselves in part by their adherence to a particular method of abrogation, scholars within the school were able to work within the confines of the Ḥanafī framework to promote divergent conceptions of abrogation that had significant juridical impact.

Dabūsī on Abrogation

Along with his Ḥanafī contemporaries, Dabūsī claimed that there were four ways for a revealed text to be abrogated, all of which dealt with the text (*naṣṣ*) itself and the injunction (*ḥukm*) that the text—whether abrogated or not—imparted on its readership. The first possibility is that both the injunction and the wording (*tilāwa*)[92] of the text that stipulates the injunction were abrogated. Dabūsī said that this was the case with previous scriptures, particularly those of Abraham and David.[93] These scriptures, referenced in the Qur'ān as the 'scrolls (*suḥuf*) of Abraham'[94] and the '*zabūr* of David,'[95] are lost forever, as are their injunctions. These 'lost scriptures' could also include the Torah, the original text of which was believed by most Muslims to have been corrupted and, for all intents and purposes, lost. In any case, Dabūsī argued that all of these texts—their injunctions and their wordings—were abrogated by the arrival of Muḥammad and the Qur'ān.[96]

This presents two immediate theological problems relating to the temporality (*muddat al-baqā'*) of God's commandments. First, temporality suggests that God's speech might not address all peoples in all times, or that a command that might be beneficial for one community might be injurious to another. If that were the case, then it could be argued that the same Qur'anic injunctions that were beneficial for 7th-century Arabia might be injurious to other societies. The second

[91] Sarakhsī, *al-Muḥarrar fī Uṣūl al-Fiqh* (n 22) 2:51.
[92] I translate *tilāwa* as 'wording', following the practice of John Burton (n 82) 452 as opposed to the more literal translation of 'recitation.' I find that 'recitation' becomes unwieldy in English, and 'wording' allows for greater descriptional clarity.
[93] Dabūsī (n 6) 231. [94] Qur'ān, 87:19. [95] Qur'ān, 4:163.
[96] Dabūsī (n 6) 231.

major theological problem that the temporality of God's command raises, which is related to the first problem, is that God may command an action that is good (*ḥasan*) for one people yet may be evil (*qabīḥ*) for another. One might commit an evil act by following an abrogated command in the scripture of other nations; yet, it was God who originally issued the command. In that case, it would seem that following God's command might lead to evil. Dabūsī said that it was not possible for God to command evil and dedicated the majority of his work on the topic of abrogation to responding to these two problems.

To those who would claim that the *sharīʿa* of Muḥammad was applicable only temporally, Dabūsī was unambiguous. He began one of his chapters on abrogation by stating:

> The *sharīʿa* of Muḥammad permanently endures (*thābita*) after [his death] because it cannot be abrogated except by a direct report (*khabar*) from God Most High. And it is established by the text that [Muḥammad] is the last of the Prophets. Therefore, we can be sure of the perpetuity (*dawām*) of [the *sharīʿa*] because there is no Prophet after him.[97]

He ended the same chapter in a similarly unambiguous manner, maintaining that the injunctions (*aḥkām*, sing. *ḥukm*) of the Qurʾān abide until the Day of Judgment.[98] Yet, Dabūsī significantly qualified his rhetorical overtures to the eternal applicability of Qurʾanic injunctions by introducing the idea of 'precipitating causes' (*asbāb*, sing. *sabab*). Every injunction, he argued, is built (*bināʾ*) upon a precipitating cause, and the text always explicitly or implicitly delineates that cause.[99] For example, the declination of the sun from its zenith is the precipitating cause for the necessity of praying the noon prayer. Also, the month of Ramaḍān is the precipitating cause for the necessity of fasting. Similarly, four individuals testifying to having witnessed fornication (*zinā*) is the precipitating cause for punishing the accused fornicators. In each of these cases, the text presents a cause that gives rise to an instance wherein the injunction (*ḥukm*) must be enacted. If, for whatever reason, the cause does not obtain in a particular circumstance, then the injunction cannot be applied.[100]

[97] Ibid 235. [98] Ibid 238. [99] Ibid 236. [100] Ibid 236.

Dabūsī took pains to clarify that the cause must obtain in its entirety, as meticulously defined by its exact description and relationship to its injunction given in the Qur'ān and according to the manner in which it was understood in the time of Muḥammad. If only a part of the cause obtains in a scenario, then the injunction cannot be applied. For example, the punishment for fornication can only be applied if the cause—the witnessing of fornication—obtains in totality. Based on the Qur'anic stipulations, this means that four individuals must witness sexual penetration between a man and woman who do not have a licit sexual relationship. If the cause does not obtain in its entirety, like the four witnesses not observing the actual penetration, or there being fewer than four witnesses, then the injunction cannot be applied. Furthermore, since the precipitating cause for the injunction is the illicit intercourse of a man and woman, homosexuality does not fall under the jurisdiction of the cause and, by extension, the injunction.[101] By linking the injunction to its stated cause, Dabūsī responded to the first theological criticism by saying that God's injunctions in the Qur'ān are indeed established forever, but that those injunctions can only be applied in specific circumstances. Thus, one should not think that God's commands are temporal, but that precipitating causes are temporal and change when societies evolve, requiring new injunctions that speak to the new circumstances.

As to the second major problem that Dabūsī faced, that of God prescribing evil, Dabūsī centered his discussion on God's purpose (*ḥikma*). Behind every command that God enjoins upon mankind is a higher purpose that leads people closer to God.[102] Dabūsī believed that the most instructive example of this purpose is found in the case of Abraham, who was commanded to sacrifice his son. Sacrificing one's son is an evil action under any circumstance, and if indeed Abraham had killed his son then he would have committed an evil act. At the point at which he was going to

[101] Ibid 134. This is an extension of Abū Ḥanīfa's own reasoning on the subject, see Saghnāqī (n 28) 1:494–5. Muḥammad al-Shaybānī and Abū Yūsuf disagreed with Abū Ḥanīfa on this issue, arguing that the punishment for fornication should apply to homosexuals; Sarakhsī, *al-Mabsūṭ* (n 24) 9:119. Sarakhsī himself went one step further and argued that homosexuality was in fact a mark of apostasy, basing his opinion on a prophetic report, and thus warranted the death penalty; Sarakhsī, *al-Mabsūṭ* (n 24) 9:88–9.

[102] Dabūsī (n 6) 229.

kill his son, though, God sent down a lamb to be sacrificed in place of the son. This story might give one the impression that God recognized that His original command was evil and thereafter changed the command to one that was good. Dabūsī, while acknowledging the apparent (*ẓāhir*) reading of the story, asserted that God does not change His mind and knows all things. What is hidden (*bāṭin*) in the story is the purpose of God in that He wished to bring Abraham closer to Him. God knew that He would replace the child with the lamb, but wanted to use the pretext of Abraham sacrificing his son to test Abraham. This testing, in the form of willingness to sacrifice, succeeded in bringing Abraham closer to God (*mutaqarrib bi-hi bi-dhibḥihi*).[103] Once Abraham was close to God, the test was concluded and the sacrifice could change, at which point sacrificing the lamb would bring Abraham closer to God. After the conclusion of the test, the command to kill the son became evil and the command to sacrifice a lamb was good. Throughout the story, the purpose behind both commands remained the same: bringing Abraham closer to God.

Dabūsī argued that each and every injunction was informed by a particular purpose (*ḥikma*). Again using the case of fornication, Dabūsī said that the purpose of punishment by one hundred lashes—as prescribed by Q. 24:2—was deterrance (*zajr*), not injury (*talaf*). The guilty parties are to be deterred from returning to their sin, not injured by the punishment. If the result of the punishment were not deterrence but mere injury, then the punishment would not achieve its intended purpose. Dabūsī said that if, for example, the guilty parties were extremely sick and lashing might cause death, then the punishment could not be exacted because it would not accomplish the intended purpose.[104] If the purpose was no longer being fulfilled despite trying to enact an injunction (*ishtaghal al-ʿabd bi-al-iqāma*), then God might choose to abrogate that injunction entirely.[105] Dabūsī was adamant, however, that every injunction from God could be, at one time or other, enacted by humans. If an injunction was impossible to enact or was never meant to be enacted, then it would seem that God had prescribed a useless (*ʿabath*) injunction. Since God does not engage in useless acts,

[103] Ibid 237. [104] Ibid 237. [105] Ibid 237.

Dabūsī said that an injunction would never be abrogated unless it was at some time possible for humans to enact it.[106] Once the injunction was carried out at some time, it might fulfill the purpose that God intended and could then be abrogated if conditions changed. Dabūsī said that this was the case with revelations to previous nations that God abrogated in both their injunctions and their wordings through new revelations.

Having defended the complete abrogation of entire scriptures, Dabūsī described partial abrogation of the Qur'ān, starting with the injunction (*ḥukm*) being abrogated, but not the wording (*tilāwa*) that establishes that injunction. Dabūsī provided precious little elaboration on this form of abrogation. He cited the example of punishment for fornication in the Qur'ān, and pointed out that the Qur'ān first commanded confinement and rebuke of the guilty parties (Q. 4:15) and then later commanded lashing (Q. 24:2). Dabūsī said that the verse commanding lashing abrogated the verse calling for confinement and rebuke. He based his view on the maxim that an injunction is established for all times unless there is compelling proof for its cessation (*ḥattā yaqūmu dalīl al-ziwāl*).[107] The verse of lashing in this case is compelling proof for the cessation of confinement and rebuke, despite the fact that the verse regarding confinement and rebuke remained in the codex. This is an example of the injunction—in this case confinement—being abrogated, but not the wording. Dabūsī did not attempt to explain why the verse remained in the codex, but he did argue that the mere existence of a verse does not guarantee the applicability of its injunction. For him, the official wording of the Qur'ān simply established what can be recited in the prescribed prayers and what constitutes the Qur'ān as inimitable.[108] Rather than explaining why abrogated texts remained in the codex, he simply suggested that the abrogated injunctions serve as starting points for the law and are important to know, despite their having been abrogated by

[106] Ibid 237. The description of a useless act is somewhat similar to the Muʿtazilite position; Margaretha Heemskerk, *Suffering in the Muʿtazilite Theology* (Brill 2000) 125ff, but it differs in that Dabūsī does not focus on whether the action is beneficial or not—or whether or not it is a good idea either—but on the potential for enactment.

[107] Dabūsī (n 6) 232.

[108] Ibid 232.

other verses.[109] Dabūsī emphasized that the abrogated injunctions and verses could only be abrogated by the Qur'anic text itself and that nothing outside of the Qur'anic text should be allowed to have a role in this type of abrogation.

The form of abrogation described above wherein the injunction is abrogated but not the wording is the most commonly referenced and has the most significant impact in jurisprudential works. Dabūsī endorsed the popular notion that certain injunctions found within the Qur'ān were not to be enacted nor were they to be used when deriving law. Though this was an accepted practice, the legal effect of claiming such an abrogation was quite severe. It meant that the abrogated verse could never become operative again, since God Himself abrogated it. It is unsurprising, therefore, that identifying verses that are abrogated in their injunction but not their reading has been the most contested form of abrogation. Dabūsī, though acknowledging that such abrogation regularly occurred, did not attempt to enumerate all the verses that abrogate nor those that were abrogated in this way.

Dabūsī next covered the form of abrogation wherein the wording was abrogated, but the injunction still operated in jurisprudence. To describe how this form of abrogation works, he described two types of revelation. The redacted Qur'ān contains a type of revelation called 'recited revelation' (*waḥy al-matlū*). The other type of revelation was revealed to Muḥammad, yet for some reason was not considered part of the Qur'ān, and is known as 'unrecited revelation' (*waḥy ghayr matlū*).[110] This latter type of revelation may not have been included in the Qur'ān due to a dictate from the Prophet, or because the paper upon which the original revelation was written went missing, or because multiple witnesses could not be found to verify that Muḥammad had authorized it as revelation. In all of these cases, Muslim scholars assumed that it was God who, for whatever reason, intended that the revelation not be included in the codex. To accomplish this task, He might have commanded Muḥammad to strike it from the codex or may have caused the original writings to be lost.

[109] Ibid 232. [110] Ibid 232.

Dabūsī explored abrogation of a wording but not its injunction through his analysis of unrecited revelation. He pointed out that some Companions of the Prophet had personal copies (*maṣāḥif*) of the Qurʾān that had slightly different wordings than did the redacted Qurʾān. Sometimes these were minor differences that expressed a similar meaning as the redacted Qurʾān, perhaps with some added flourish or emphasis. Sometimes, however, the wordings in those disparate copies commanded different injunctions.

Dabūsī cited in this regard the Companion ʿAbd Allāh Ibn Masʿūd and his personal Qurʾān, which contained a slightly different injunction regarding the expiation of an unfulfilled oath. Whereas the redacted Qurʾān requires an individual seeking expiation to 'fast for three days' (Q. 5:89), Ibn Masʿūd's rendition ordered the same person to 'fast for three days in succession (*mutatābiʿīn*).'[111] The accepted Ḥanafī practice for expiating an unfulfilled oath is to fast for three days consecutively, despite the fact that the redacted Qurʾān does not mention the need to fast consecutively. Dabūsī said that this is an example of the wording being abrogated but the injunction remaining. Despite its absence from the codex, he maintained that it is proper for a person to fast for three days in succession to expiate an unfulfilled oath. That is because when the 'recited revelation' is abrogated, what remains is 'unrecited revelation,' which is still revelation.[112]

However, based on Dabūsī's own theory of revelation, only that which was passed down through multiple (*mutawātir*) transmissions could be accepted as the Qurʾān. He could not, therefore, equate Ibn Masʿūd's version of the Qurʾān with the redacted Qurʾān since Ibn Masʿūd's version was not narrated though multiple transmissions. But Dabūsī also could not simply ignore Ibn Masʿūd's version of the Qurʾān since the latter

[111] Though both Dabūsī and Sarakhsī accorded this wording to the *muṣḥaf* of Ibn Masʿūd, Jaṣṣāṣ presented it as the opinion of Ibn Masʿūd as relayed by Mujāhid. He ascribed the wording to Ibrāhim al-Nakhaʿī, who was Abū Ḥanīfa's teacher, but not a Companion. Jaṣṣāṣ defended the Ḥanafī position by recourse to several *aḥādīth* relayed by prominent Companions affirming the necessity to fast three days consecutively. He then professed that this was a case wherein the wording was abrogated, but not the injunction, thus maintaining the dominant Ḥanafī discourse through different means; Jaṣṣāṣ (n 41) 2:577.

[112] Dabusi (n 6) 232.

was a reliable transmitter, a respected Companion of the Prophet, and a source of legislation for early Ḥanafī scholars. So Dabūsī argued that the unrecited revelation in Ibn Masʿūd's Qurʾān was the 'intended injunction' (*ḥukm maqṣūd*) and that it was the preferred course of action, though it was permissible to act only upon the injunction mentioned in the redacted copy of the Qurʾān.[113] In this way, Dabūsī was able to preserve both the integrity of Ḥanafī reliance on Ibn Masʿūd and the integrity of the redacted copy of the Qurʾān.

The final method of abrogation that Dabūsī considered was addition to the text (*ziyāda ʿalā al-naṣṣ*).[114] Addition to the text occurs when an injunction found in the Qurʾān is made more general or specific in its application than a literal reading of the text allows. Dabūsī warned that tampering with the text in this manner is impermissible, and stated that though most scholars similarly claim that it is prohibited, they nonetheless promote such a practice under the guise of specification (*takhṣīṣ*).[115] He claimed that scholars regularly added to the text while maintaining that they were simply elucidating the restrictions or additions inherent in the text. For example, Q. 5:89 states that one may free a slave to expiate an unfulfilled oath. Dabūsī chided juridical scholars who insisted that the slave being freed must be a Muslim, a condition that is not specified in the text.[116] Along the same lines, Dabūsī cited some scholars who claimed that the punishment of lashing for fornication must be accompanied by banishment (*nafy*), another stipulation not found in the text. Some of these specifications were applied to the text due to corresponding reports from the *sunna* of the Prophet or from the practice of the Companions. Despite this, Dabūsī was adamant that if the specifications are found anywhere

113 Ibid 232.

114 Abū al-Barakāt al-Nasafī called this type of abrogation 'abrogating the characteristic of the injunctions' (*naskh al-waṣf al-ḥukm*), which succinctly captures the way *ziyāda ʿalā al-naṣṣ* actually functions; Ḥaṣkafi (n 43) 231. Ibn Quṭlubughā defended Nasafī's nomenclature since the foundation of the injunction remains though the application may differ, so that *ziyāda ʿalā al-naṣṣ* is merely bringing out the different facets of the foundation that underlies the injunction; Ibn Quṭlubughā (n 43) 156.

115 Dabūsī (n 6) 233.

116 Ibid 233.

other than in the text of the Qur'ān itself, then the scholars promoting the specification are in fact adding to the text.[117]

He reasoned that the danger in adding to the text goes back to the issue of the precipitating causes (*asbāb*) of the law. Dabūsī stated earlier that every injunction has a precipitating cause that necessitates the injunction. If the cause is not found in its entirety, then the injunction cannot be enacted. Similarly, if enacting the injunction does not fulfill the purpose (*ḥikma*), then the injunction should not be enacted. Adding to the text, Dabūsī argued, can easily change the cause or divert the injunction from its purpose, both of which invalidate the injunction.[118] He believed that it was for this reason that Abu Ḥanīfa and Abu Yūsuf were so careful when they dealt with the injunction on consuming alcohol. The text, they noted, forbids both drinking grape-wine (*khamr*) in particular and intoxication (*sakr*) in general. Therefore, if someone were to consume a drink that was fermented, but not fermented in the manner of grape-wine—either through the use of different ingredients or a different fermenting process—and were not to drink it in sufficient quantity to cause intoxication, then neither the injunction concerning intoxication nor the injunction concerning the consumer of grape-wine could obtain.[119] Dabūsī clearly agreed with the approach of Abū Ḥanīfa and Abū Yūsuf, which was rejected by many of his Ḥanafī contemporaries, if only to preserve his theory of the cause and purpose connected with injunctions.

Dabūsī's reliance on the cause and the purpose when discussing abrogation theory reflects his appreciation for the role of circumstance in discussions of legal injunctions. The jurist must take circumstance into account before determining whether the cause of the injunction obtained or if the injunction will fulfill its purpose. Failure to consider circumstance might result in a jurist erroneously applying an injunction found in the Qur'ān. Hence, Qur'anic injunctions cannot be applied

[117] Ibid 234. Al-Tamartāshī provided examples such as requiring the recitation of al-Fātiḥa as a *rukn* of prayer and being in a state of ritual ablution prior to circumambulating the Ka'ba as unacceptable abrogations of the text masquerading as *ziyāda ʿalā al-naṣṣ*; Muḥammad b. ʿAbd Allāh al-Tamartāshī, *al-Wuṣūl ilā Qawāʿid al-Uṣūl* (Muḥammad Sharīf ed, Dār al-Kutub al-ʿIlmiyya 2000) 270.

[118] Dabūsī (n 6) 233.

[119] Ibid 234.

without careful consideration of both their status as either abrogated or abrogating and their applicability given the circumstances surrounding their application.

Sarakhsī on Abrogation

Sarakhsī defined abrogation narrowly, such that it dealt only with licitness or illicitness (*ḥalāl wa-ḥarām*). 'Abrogation,' he said, 'is nothing except [God] forbidding what was permitted or permitting what was forbidden.'[120] He nevertheless followed the same approach as Dabūsī when outlining the possible methods of abrogation. He began by considering the scenario of both the wording (*tilāwa*) of a text as well as its injunctions (*aḥkām*) being abrogated, as was the case with the texts of the prophets Abraham and David. Like Dabūsī, Sarakhsī was forced to confront the difficulties raised by the prospect of such abrogation. The two major issues that Sarakhsī dealt with in this vein are similar to those attended to by Dabūsī—namely, why God reveals injunctions only to rescind them later, and how God's command can be good (*ḥasan*) in one context and evil (*qabīḥ*) in another.

As to the first issue concerning the divine wisdom behind injunctions, rather than discuss the temporality of God's command, Sarakhsī asked the reader to consider the objectives (*maqāṣid*) of divine injunctions. He rejected the likes of Dabūsī, who said that an injunction's purpose is to incite a believer to engage in particular action that will bring him closer to God. Instead, he posited that the objective of God's command is to test His subjects to determine which of them will have firm conviction (*ʿaqd al-qalb*)[121] that the injunction is the truth from God.[122] Passing the test is not contingent upon successful implementation of the injunction, but is contingent upon believing it to be a divine injunction that *should* be implemented. Sarakhsī cited the example of ambiguous verses to prove his point. Ambiguous verses cannot be comprehended or acted upon but are merely to be believed. If the slave of God believes, then he passes

[120] Sarakhsī, *al-Muḥarrar fī Uṣūl al-Fiqh* (n 22) 2:44.
[121] Ibid 2:49.
[122] Ibid 2:51.

the test posed by the ambiguous verse.[123] In the same way, the primary objective of all other verses, including legal injunctions, is not to act upon the command, but to have firm conviction in the injunction's origin and applicability. Sarakhsī concluded that having this firm conviction is, in fact, the fundamental injunction (*ʿaqd al-qalb huwa al-ḥukm al-aṣlī*) underlying all of God's commands. As a result, Sarakhsī claimed that abrogation could only occur after the reader was afforded the ability to have firm conviction in the divine injunction, not, as Dabūsī claimed, after the reader has the opportunity to act upon that injunction.

Firm conviction in God's injunctions is the bedrock of Sarakhsī's abrogation theory. He repudiated anyone who argued that the objective of an injunction was anything other than producing firm conviction. He cited as 'misguided' those who, like Dabūsī, claimed that there is some intended purpose that is fulfilled by acting upon a particular injunction. Sarakhsī further charged with heresy those who, like Dabūsī again, claimed that abrogation could only take place after the commanded party had the ability to enact the injunction, equating them with his doctrinal rivals, the Muʿtazila.[124] Sarakhsī tried to divorce God and His injunctions from any contingency upon human action (*ʿamal*) in an effort to sanctify the Godhead from any anthropomorphic qualities. 'Action [on the part of another],' he wrote, 'is only desired by someone who seeks to profit from [that action], and God is above that.'[125] For Sarakhsī, then, God is a commanding being whose command requires no rationalization, fulfillment, or understanding. God can command something and negate that same command without any need for humans to understand the logic of the change. Nor does God have any need for humans to act in a certain way. Given Sarakhsī's position regarding the absolute transcendence of God and His logic, it is a simple move for him to thereafter claim that all of God's actions are good (*ḥasan*) regardless of time, place, or circumstance and can never be classified as evil (*qabīḥ*).[126] God is privy to algorithms that transcend human logic, and so cannot be measured by human modes of judgment. Hence, abrogation of an injunction does not suggest

[123] Ibid 2:51.
[124] Ibid 2:49.
[125] Ibid 2:51.
[126] Ibid 2:48.

vileness of either the command or the Commander, since the objective of the injunction in the first place was only belief. After abrogation, so long as people believe that the abrogated injunction was from God, the injunction achieves its objective and is, therefore, good.

By asserting the primacy of firm conviction, Sarakhsī created a platform for himself from which he could explain the idea of abrogated readings and injunctions in a rather straightforward manner. He said that humans are charged with believing that certain wordings and injunctions existed in the past, but that God, for whatever reason, willed them to be forgotten or destroyed.[127] He briefly mentioned that God sent down different injunctions for different times and places, but did not elaborate on the reasoning behind God's decision to do so.[128] Sarakhsī instead devoted the majority of his discussion on this topic to establishing the enduring quality of the Qur'anic injunctions. He maintained, on pain of heresy, that no abrogation could take place after the death of the Prophet. Citing Q. 15:9, 'Certainly we have sent down the Reminder, and indeed We are surely its Guardian,' Sarakhsī argued that the codex is under Divine protection and will never be compromised.[129] He then moved on to consider the abrogation of a verse's injunction while its wording remains extant.

Sarakhsī argued that the agreed-upon wording of the Qur'ān that comprises the codex serves two purposes. Like Dabūsī before him, Sarakhsī posited that, first, the official codex determines what can be read during the prescribed prayers, and second, it is integral for knowing the correct ordering of the text.[130] The mere fact that injunctions are present in their wordings does not testify to their enduring applicability. To the contrary, injunctions may be abrogated even though the wording remains, if only so that they can be read during prayers and maintain the ordering of the Qur'ān. Once again, Sarakhsī cited 'ambiguous' verses as an example of how a verse may serve only the purpose of recitation in prayer as well as maintaining the order of the Qur'ān and nothing more,[131] since ambiguous verses were not to be understood or acted upon.

[127] Ibid 2:61. [128] Ibid 2:47. [129] Ibid 2:61.
[130] Ibid 2:63. [131] Ibid 2:63.

Sarakhsī had to reconcile his emphasis on the codex as necessary for maintaining the ordering of the Qur'ān with his aforementioned stance that the ordering of the Qur'ān is not inimitable. He did so by explaining that when the Companions of the Prophet thought it 'good to begin committing the wording [of the Qur'ān] to written form upon these two stipulations [of codifying both what can be read in prayer and maintaining the ordering of the Qur'ān], only the first [stipulation, that of denoting what can be read in prayer,] survived.'[132] Thus, the Qur'ān in the time of the Prophet had an inimitable ordering that did not retain its inimitability when compiled into the codex by the Companions. Having dispensed with this technicality, Sarakhsī reiterated that the wording of a Qur'anic verse might remain in the codex though the injunction is abrogated. In contrast to Dabūsī's lack of explanation for this phenomenon, Sarakhsī argued that this abrogation took place for the expressed purpose of properly executing religious rituals.

The third method of abrogation that Sarakhsī considered involves the abrogation of the wording such that it is not included in the redacted Qur'ān while the injunction contained in that abrogated wording remains operational in jurisprudence. Just as Dabūsī had done, Sarakhsī used the example of fasting as expiation for an unfulfilled oath to demonstrate this type of abrogation. To quickly review this issue, whereas the redacted Qur'ān mentions that one must fast for three days to expiate an unfulfilled oath, Ibn Masʿūd's wording of the same verse added that the fasting must be for three consecutive days. Sarakhsī was faced with the same challenge as Dabūsī: to simultaneously preserve the integrity of the Qur'anic codex, the integrity of Ibn Masʿūd, and the intergrity of Ḥanafī injunctions that are based on Ibn Masʿud's Qur'ān. 'There is no doubt,' said Sarakhsī, 'of the moral probity (ʿ*adala*) of Ibn Masʿūd… [therefore] we believe in [his reading's] status as recitation (*matlū*), that it is Qur'ān, and that it is the Word of God.'[133] Sarakhsī explained that if a wording was considered part of the Qur'ān at any time during Muḥammad's life, then it maintains the status of revelation forever and must be believed in. For some reason, however, God decided to cause this particular reading to be

[132] Ibid 2:63. [133] Ibid 2:63.

lifted from all hearts other than that of Ibn Masʿūd.[134] Sarakhsī provided no explanation for God's action and, given his conception of God's transcendent wisdom, he did not need to. What mattered to Sarakhsī was that revelation—whether recited (*matlū*) or not (*ghayr matlū*) and whether in the codex or not—is applicable to all persons.

What is curious is that Sarakhsī accepted Ibn Masʿūd's reading at face value. He admitted that the wording attributed to Ibn Masʿūd could not be authenticated through multiple transmissions (*mutawātir*),[135] which Sarakhsī earlier posited as a necessary prerequisite for a verse to be considered part of the Qurʾān. To overcome this dilemma he brought together two of his foundational positions: deference to the juristic tradition and the absolute transcendence of God. He defended a juridical opinion that was ensconced in the Ḥanafī tradition by appealing to God's inscrutable will. He acknowledged that it is the position of 'our scholars'—meaning the Ḥanafīs—that the fast of expiation must span three consecutive days.[136] The prescriptive nature of this juridical opinion, as opposed to the more suggestive nature of Dabūsī's position, required Sarakhsī to classify a non-*mutawātir* account of Ibn Masʿūd's reading as equivalent to the Qurʾān. Sarakhsī attributed this to the will of God, citing Q. 17:86 in his defense: 'And if We willed, We could take back that which We revealed unto you.' God chose to abrogate the wording of Ibn Masʿūd while retaining the injunction because He willed it to be so. Sarakhsī was not trying to make sense of Divine abrogation, but sought to explain its workings through the received tradition. That is, the existence of the injunction in the legal tradition was evidence that the wording did indeed exist as unrecited revelation, whether or not it was narrated through multiple transmissions or included in the official codex.

Sarakhsī's discussion of the fourth type of abrogation, addition to the text (*ziyāda ʿalā al-naṣṣ*), is remarkable in its similarity to Dabūsī's. The examples he used are identical, as are the conclusions he reached. Sarakhsī repudiated any addition to the text after the death of the Prophet, which

[134] Ibid 2:63.
[135] Ibid 2:63.
[136] Ibid 2:63. Sarakhsī accepted the injunction as fact, and in his work of jurisprudence did not question the need to fast consecutively; Sarakhsī, *al-Mabsūṭ* (n 24) 8:166–8.

included adding stipulations to injunctions that are not found in the text. To do so, he warned, would result in failure to enact the injunctions of God as they were intended to be enacted.[137] While Sarakhsī's discussion is more verbose than Dabūsī's, the content is almost exactly the same.

The most striking difference between these two juridical scholars in their approaches to abrogation is found in their conceptions of the purpose (*ḥikma)* and objective (*maqṣad*) of Qur'anic injunctions. For Dabūsī, laws were intended to bring believers closer to God through acting upon injunctions. It is therefore understandable that Dabūsī would hold action and practice central to his theory. Abrogation, he said, cannot take place before humans are able to act upon the injunction, lest the injunction become meaningless. Further, if the precipitating cause of an injunction does not obtain in its entirety, or if enacting the injunction does not fulfill the purpose for which it was intended, then it cannot be enacted. Believers, while bound by the text, are forced to interact with it in relation to their circumstance. Thus, every new circumstance requires a fresh look at the injunction. Jurisprudence, therefore, is not a static science, despite the presence of clear textual injunctions.

Sarakhsī, in contrast, held firm conviction to be the centerpiece of his theory. The believer is expected first and foremost to believe in injunctions as divinely ordained and to believe that they should be enacted regardless of circumstance. In Sarakhsī's framework, the circumstances surrounding the enacting of an injunction is, quite simply, circumstantial; meaning that circumstance is peripheral to the need to believe that all non-abrogated injunctions should be enacted. Only minimal reflection is required to enact God's injunctions and the reality of abrogation is only to be acknowledged, not necessarily understood. God may, or may not, abrogate at will; and anyway, God's abrogation follows no standard or methodology that humans can comprehend. As Sarakhsī claimed in his discussion of clear and ambiguous verses, believers need not understand God's commands to act upon them.[138]

[137] Sarakhsī, *al-Muḥarrar fī Uṣūl al-Fiqh* (n 19) 2:64.

[138] Despite their stated deference to the Ḥanafī tradition, particularly to the jurisprudence that they inherited, Dabūsī and Sarakhsī's justifications of abrogation do not fully conform to any of the *uṣūl al-fiqh* models of their Ḥanafī predecessors. Jaṣṣās, for example, said that abrogation occurs when God eases a command that was previously

CONCLUSION

It is now becoming clear that Dabūsī and Sarakhsī had very different functional conceptions of Islamic law as a project. Based on his approach to the Qurʾān—which only betrays part of his view of Islamic law—Dabūsī appears to promote a relationship between the Qurʾān and context. In this scheme, the jurist needs to interpret the legal verses of the Qurʾān to derive an injunction that fulfills a particular purpose based on the context of its application. This interpretation will never be completely authoritative, but the jurist can argue for the preponderance of his interpretation. With regard to legal application of juridical interpretations, purpose and circumstance play an important and intertwined role. Jurists must always examine the circumstances surrounding an injunction's enactment to ensure that the precipitating causes obtained in their entirety and that the injunction fulfills its purpose.

Sarakhsī, on the other hand, appears to have regarded revelation as a definitive set of injunctions and regulations that are passively received by believers and jurists alike.[139] One need only believe in the revelation and its commanding nature to fulfill the true objective of any injunction. And

difficult; Jaṣṣāṣ (n 41) 1:71–2, a position that both Dabūsī and Sarakhsī disavowed (Dabūsī does not mention it and Sarakhsī rejects it; Sarakhsī, *al-Muḥarrar fī Uṣūl al-Fiqh* (n 19), 2:49). The theory of precipitating causes (*asbāb*), which Dabūsī discussed in the 'clear and the ambiguous' section and which Sarakhsī discussed in the present one, appears to be a novel idea in that it did not exist in Ḥanafī thought prior to the 5th/11th century and was repudiated even by their contemporaries. Al-Samʿānī (d. 489/1095) said of Dabūsī's theory of *asbāb*, '[it] is an error and invention (*khaṭāʾ wa ikhtirāʿ*), which, I think, no one before him has espoused.' Aron Zysow, 'Muʿtazilism and Māturīdism in Ḥanafī Legal Theory' in Bernard Weiss (ed), *Studies in Islamic Legal Theory* (Brill 2002) 260. Abū al-Ḥasan al-Pazdawī (d. 482/1089), normally an ally of Sarakhsī yet indebted to the work of Dabūsī, rejected his theory of *asbāb* outright as unnecessary and misleading; ibid 261. Dabūsī and Sarakhsī's frameworks and deference to received jurisprudence paid homage to the Ḥanafī juridical tradition, but departed on the theoretical level in ways that make possible new and novel methods of interpretation and, at least theoretically, novel jurisprudence.

[139] The more legalistic bent of Sarakhsī compared to Dabūsī in the interpretation of the Qurʾān was not missed by later Ḥanafī scholars; see for example, Bukhārī (n 13) 1:192. Bukhārī also noted that Dabūsī was hesitant to utilize anything other than definitive (*qaṭʿī*) sources when deriving jurisprudence, preferring to use reason and admit to its tenuousness rather than posit divine law based on dubious sources; Bukhārī (n 13) 3:468.

it is not only revelation to which Sarakhsī accorded such a relationship. The jurisprudential tradition also demands such a passive reception: the jurist can try to understand the tradition if he so desires and will find in it sound principles, but that understanding is not necessary and is, ultimately, superfluous. Similarly, it is not necessary to understand the intended referents of legal verses that utilize figurative language, since the legal tradition provides all the clarity required to understand their literal intent. Sarakhsī's distaste for a dialogical relationship with the Qur'ān was palpable, as has been noted by other scholars,[140] and it is clear that he considered a believer to be primarily one who submits uncritically and entirely to the message, not one who interacts with it creatively. With respect to the Qur'ān as a source of jurisprudence, Sarakhsī espoused a vision of Islamic law as transcendent and universally applicable.

Nevertheless, neither Dabūsī nor Sarakhsī changed inherited principles and injunctions in any significant manner. They covered the same topics under the same topic headings, and for the most part employed the same technical terms. Yet, by justifying those inherited principles and injunctions and associated technical terms differently, they were able to hypothesize about different cases. Seemingly synonymous terms like purpose (*ḥikma*) and objective (*maqṣad*) were utilized so as to promote competing views of the law. By linking injunctions to their purpose, Dabūsī was able to argue that God's injunctions do not always need to apply, so long as they could have been enacted at some time in history. By defining the objective of God's law as producing belief, Sarakhsī was able to promote a conception of Islamic law that requires believers to have conviction that injunctions should be enacted in all times and places, barring some extreme situation that precludes their enactment.

These differing definitions yielded concrete results in the application of Islamic law by encouraging different abductions that justify the inherited principles and injunctions. If we take the example of lashing

[140] Ya'akov Meron, 'Marghīnānī, His Method and His Legacy' (2002) 9:3 *Islamic Law and Society* 410, 413.

fornicators in accordance with Qur'anic dictate, we have the following Ḥanafī principle and injunction stemming from Q. 24:2:

> Fornication is a punishable offence (Principle)
> Fornicators must be lashed 100 times (Injunction)

The Qur'ān specifically prescribes 100 lashes as punishment for fornication and the Ḥanafī school holds that fornicators must be punished. These premises do not change and will not change unless a jurist wishes to work outside of the Ḥanafī school. However, the way in which these premises are justified significantly influences a jurist's abductions about how they are to be applied. Dabūsī, for instance, justified the principle in light of God's purpose and the injunction in light of precipitating causes. The premises of his abductive syllogism from which he would hypothesize about how to apply the law would look like this:

> Fornication is a punishable offence for the purpose of deterrance (Principle)
> Fornicators must be lashed 100 times when all the precipitating causes obtain (Injunction)

By calling attention to precipitating causes and God's purpose, Dabūsī challenges jurists to assess the circumstances around which the law is applied. The jurist then needs to make an informed decision about whether to enact the injunction at all. Yet apart from the particular justifications, the principle and injunction are undisturbed. If one were not looking for the author's personal definitions for the terms 'purpose' and 'precipitating causes,' Dabūsī would be seen as merely perpetuating traditional Ḥanafī positions in his work of legal theory.

In contrast to Dabūsī, Sarakhsī's employment of the term 'objective' to justify the received Ḥanafī tradition encourages a different abduction about how the law is to be applied. For Sarakhsī, the premises that lead to the abduction look like this:

> Fornication is a punishable offence with the objective of testing belief (Principle)
> Fornicators must be sentenced to 100 lashes if the jurist truly believes (Injunction)

Since belief is the centerpiece of Sarakhsī's framework, it colors the justification of both the principle and injunction. A jurist working within Sarakhsī's framework might abduce that he should apply the punishment to convicted fornicators despite his own personal feelings or the circumstances surrounding the case. Failure to do so would reflect poorly on the jurist's religious convictions, and in fact Sarakhsī intimated that those who question the universal applicability of God's injunctions—applying the punishment for fornication in particular—are weak in faith.[141]

The subtle differences in definition of key terms create unique justifications of inherited law that not only speak to the way a jurist is to apply Islamic law in his context, but also to the larger project of Islamic

[141] That is not to say that Sarakhsī did not require strict stipulations before meting out punishment; including examining the moral probity of witnesses, determining the virginity of the accused, defining fornication and its witnessing, and the like. But Sarakhsī was adamant that when the requirements were met and fornication was proved in court, that punishment should not be withheld for any reason. In contrast to Dabūsī, who said that the punishment would fail to achieve its purpose if it injured the accused instead of preventing sin, Sarakhsī said that the punishment for fornication was not meant to purify, but to injure. The point of the punishment for fornication—which Sarakhsī said was stoning, more on this in the next chapter—was death, and so it does not matter if the accused is sick or elderly; Sarakhsī, *al-Mabsūṭ* (n 24) 9:117. He seemingly responds to those who, like Dabūsī, suggest that context has a defining role in enacting punishment. In his discussion on the theoretical individual who is coerced into fornication, Sarakhsī insists that the coerced must be stoned, because 'injunctions are premised upon precipitating causes, not upon context.' Sarakhsī, *al-Mabsūṭ* (n 24) 24:105. This principle appears to inform Sarakhsī's unequivocal refutation of any male who claims to have been coerced into fornication, both because of the difficulty in proving that one was coerced and because, unless the Caliph is doing the coercing, one can always appeal to a higher authority for a reprieve. If one is threatened with something less than death, like imprisonment, unless he engages in fornication, then he should accept imprisonment over fornicating, because there is always a chance for eventual release. And if, in fact, the coerced is threatened with death and is convinced that he will be killed, it is better that he be killed than commit fornication, for which he will be stoned anyway. This can be compared to Jaṣṣāṣ' discussion on the same subject, wherein he claims that the traditional Ḥanafī opinion is that if someone were coerced into fornication by a person in authority then he should not be punished. The reason given by Jaṣṣāṣ was that '[punishable] fornication does not occur without desire (*shahwa*),' and so if the person is coerced, then desire is not a motivating factor, thus the punishment cannot be enacted. Jaṣṣāṣ quoted Ṭaḥāwī as presenting this as the normative Ḥanafī opinion, as agreed upon by Abū Ḥanīfa, Muḥammad, and Abū Yūsuf; Aḥmad b. ʿAlī al-Jaṣṣāṣ, *Sharḥ Mukhtaṣar al-Ṭaḥāwī* (Dār al-Bashāʾir al-Islamiyya 2010) 8:454–6. Sarakhsī took the opposite tack, saying, 'fornication cannot take place unless the man has an erection, and an erection cannot be achieved without sensual pleasure, and that is evidence of willingness [on the part of the fornicator]. And herein lies the difference between men and women [in this regard]: when fornication occurs, women are [merely] the site of intercourse, and they may still serve in that capacity despite fear.' Sarakhsī, *al-Mabsūṭ* (n 24) 24:103.

law. In one conception, applying law requires a dialogical relationship with the source-texts and in another it demands universal application of inherited jurisprudence. Telling the difference between the two requires our close attention to terms that, on the face of it, seem identical, like 'purpose' and 'objective,' or 'inimitable' and 'miraculous.'

Though we now have an insight into their approach to the Qur'ān's legal applicability, it is too soon to make sweeping judgments about Dabūsī and Sarakhsī's conceptions of Islamic law. For that, we will have to analyze other sources of law, namely *sunna* and opinion (*ra'y*). For example, the two jurists have to reconcile the inherited jurisprudence about fornication mentioned above with prophetic reports that prescribe stoning adulterers. Their treatment of the *sunna* will clarify the way the sources of law interact to produce legal judgments that can then be called 'Islamic law.' Still, understanding the myriad and complex arguments of Dabūsī and Sarakhsī in their treatment of the Qur'ān helps us understand the way in which they argued. It calls our attention to the fact that minor disagreements about the interpretation of, say, figurative language or the expiation of unfulfilled oaths, reflect larger preconceptions about the proper function of Islamic law. A Ḥanafī jurist reading these arguments would then be presented with divergent possibilities for how to apply the received injunctions from the Ḥanafī tradition. While Dabūsī and Sarakhsī's treatment of the Qur'ān does not completely capture their nuanced conceptions of Islamic law, it does give us insight into the trajectory of their larger arguments.

2

Re-creating the Prophetic Model: *Ḥadīth* as the Gateway to the *Sunna*

The *sunna* is considered the second most authoritative source in classical Islamic legal theory, even if the term itself is highly contested. At its most basic level, the *sunna* is the normative practice of the Muslim community and is predicated on an historical precedent that defines model behavior. The concept of normative practice is common to every organized society, and individual groups within societies often claim that their particular practice defines the boundaries of normative behavior. Pre-Islamic Arabia, for example, held manliness (*muruwwa*) and tribalism (*'aṣabiyya*) to be integral values and practices of their *sunna*, but these values may have been understood in different ways and invoked for separate purposes.[1] What, then, makes a practice normative, what constitutes the bounds of its normativity, and how does one deviate from it if necessary? Such questions came to the fore with the advent of Muḥammad's prophetic call, because Muḥammad affirmed, changed, or supplanted many pre-Islamic patterns of behavior. In the process, Muḥammad was transforming the *sunna* of the pagan Arabs into a new, Islamic *sunna*. This new *sunna* emanated not only from Qur'anic injunctions, but from the practice of Muḥammad himself. Muḥammad is reported to have said, 'The book was given to me, as well as something that is [in extent or importance] similar to it.'[2] The 'something that is similar to it' was unanimously understood by Muslim scholars to refer to the speech and actions of Muḥammad. Thus, the speech and actions of the Prophet abrogated the *sunna* of the

[1] Stefan Sperl and Christopher Shackle (eds), *Qasida Poetry in Islamic Asia and Africa: Eulogy's Bounty, Meaning's Abundance* (Brill 1996) 8.

[2] G H A Juynboll, *Muslim Traditions* (Cambridge University Press 1983) 58.

pagan Arabs and defined normative practice for the life of the Muslim community.[3] Thereafter, the actions and statements of the Prophet were known as 'the *sunna.*'

Ḥanafī scholars of the 5th/11th century argued that the *sunna* of the Prophet was normative for the Muslim community because Muḥammad was 'protected' (*maʿṣūm*) by God from persistent error. As a result, Muslims could be certain that by following the Prophet, they were themselves free from error. The Ḥanafī doctrine of protection held that, first and foremost, the Prophet could not err (*zāla*) in transmitting the exact text of the Qurʾān as revealed by God.[4] By this token, the integrity of the Qurʾān was ensured and beyond reproach. Nonetheless, many Ḥanafī jurists admitted that the Prophet could be incorrect (*khaṭaʾ*) concerning judgments involving his personal opinion (*raʾy*) in matters both religious and secular. However, since the Prophet was the conduit of revelation (*ṣāḥib al-waḥy*), God would correct any mistake he made through means of revelation. Hence, though the Prophet could potentially err, he could not persist (*qarra*) in that error because God would rectify his actions.[5] The Muslim community could therefore be certain that any action in which the Prophet persisted had implicit divine sanction. The Ḥanafīs thereby argued that the Muslim community should consider the *sunna*, defined as the actions and statements of Muḥammad, to be divinely sanctioned and thus normative for believers.

In theory, the *sunna* could be accessed through the observed words and the deeds of Muḥammad. However, the scholars of the 5th/11th century were hamstrung by the temporal disconnect between themselves and their Prophet. The disconnect required narrators from the generation of Muḥammad to report to the succeeding generation what they

[3] Yasin Dutton, '*ʿAmal* v. *Hadith* in Islamic Law: The Case of *Sadl al-Yadayn* (Holding One's Hands by One's Sides) When Doing the Prayer' (1996) 3:1 *Islamic Law and Society* 13, 14.

[4] See Shahab Ahmed's excellent discussion of the development of this doctrine in light of *ḥadīth* studies and polemics in his 'Ibn Taymiyyah and The Satanic Verses' (1998) 2 *Studia Islamica* 67–124.

[5] For a full treatment of changing medieval Ḥanafī conceptions on the doctrine of *ʿiṣma* and prophetic error, see Rumee Ahmed 'The Ethics of Prophetic Disobedience: Qurʾān 8:67 at the Crossroads of the Islamic Sciences' (2011) 39:3 *Journal of Religious Ethics* 440ff. For the origins of the principle of *ʿiṣma*, see M M Bravmann, *Studies in Semetic Philology* (Brill 1977) 455ff.

heard the Prophet say or what they saw him doing. That succeeding generation would then convey those reports to the next, and so on for four centuries. The *sunna* of the Prophet as available to later generations was encapsulated in these reports, known as *ḥadīth* (pl. *aḥādīth*).[6] As a matter of juridical necessity, *aḥādīth* were viewed by later generations as the embodiment of the *sunna* and enacting the *sunna* was seen as commensurate with acting upon the *aḥādīth*.[7]

Jurists, therefore, looked to the *ḥadīth* literature in order to define normative practice. As one can imagine, by the fifth century A.H. there were copious *ḥadīth* reports in circulation that purported to reflect the *sunna*. These reports contained many and varied aspects of ritual and social life, and so they helped expand the purview of Islamic jurisprudence by giving expressed prophetic sanction to specific injunctions not found in the Qur'ān. Despite a reliance on *aḥādīth* for conveying the *sunna*, jurists recognized that some *aḥādīth* might not be authentic accounts of the Prophetic example.[8] To gauge the reliability of these reports, two sciences of *ḥadīth* criticism emerged, known as *ʿilm al-riwāya* and *ʿilm al-dirāya*. The first examined the chain of transmission (*sanad*) through which each *ḥadīth* was narrated.[9] A sub-science known as *ʿilm al-jarḥ wa al-taʿdīl* developed wherein every narrator in the chain was scrutinized in an attempt to establish their moral probity (*ʿadāla*), their memory (*ḍabṭ*), and the probability of their interaction with the narrators from which they claimed to have heard the *ḥadīth*. If all of these factors suggested that the transmission contained reliable information about the Prophet, then the *ḥadīth* would be considered sound (*ṣaḥīḥ*). If not, then the *ḥadīth* was accorded a more dubious status; though, as will be seen, *ḥadīth* of dubious status were often used to derive jurisprudence. The second science of *ḥadīth*, *ʿilm al-dirāya*, was far less prevalent and concerned the text (*matn*) of the narration. In this mode of criticism, the text of the *ḥadīth*

[6] Fazlur Rahman, *Islam* (University of Chicago Press 1979) 54.

[7] It was an accepted tenet of the Ḥanafī school in particular that the *sunna* could not be known except when there is some evidence (*dalīl*) that the report is veracious; 'Abd al-ʿAzīz al-Bukhārī, *Kashf al-Asrār ʿan Fakhr al-Islām al-Bazdawī* (Muḥammad Baghdādī ed, Dār al-Kitāb al-ʿArabī 1997) 2:565.

[8] Aḥmad b. ʿAlī al-Jaṣṣāṣ, *Uṣūl al-Jaṣṣāṣ* (Muḥammad Tāmir ed, Dār al-Kutub al-ʿIlmiyya 2003) 1:273.

[9] Rahman (n 6) 54.

would be examined based on its internal composition and its consistency with other Islamic sciences. Different scholars had different standards for assessing the accuracy of the text of *aḥādīth*, but more often than not, if the chain of transmission were deemed sound, then the *ḥadīth* would be accepted at face value.[10] A common refrain amongst *ḥadīth* scholars and jurists alike reflected this: 'accepting *ḥadīth* means knowing the persons [in the chain of transmission] (*ʿilm al-rijāl*).'[11]

Jurists had diverse standards by which they would judge the soundness and subsequent applicability of *aḥādīth* based on their chains of transmission,[12] which directly affected the nature of their jurisprudence. If they judged the majority of *aḥādīth* to be sound, then the corpus of *ḥadīth* literature would be seen as an accurate and exhaustive reflection of the *sunna*. Consequently, juridical application of the *sunna* would be synonymous with applying the dictates found in the *aḥādīth*. If, conversely, jurists judged only a small number of *aḥādīth* to be sound, then the *aḥādīth* would be an incomplete and tenuous expression of the prophetic *sunna*. In that case, the articulation of jurisprudence would require greater reliance on the Qurʾān, Consensus, and human reasoning. Basically, the place that jurists accorded the *sunna* as a source for deriving authoritative jurisprudence depended on the extent to which they viewed the *aḥādīth* as a reliable source for determining the *sunna*.

Three major issues determined the ability for *aḥādīth* to serve as arbiters of the *sunna* in Islamic legal theory manuals. The first two deal with levels of transmission and the third deals with the *sunna*'s ability to abrogate the Qurʾān. We will analyze these subjects and find that despite the Ḥanafī school having historically established positions on these matters, Dabūsī and Sarakhsī managed to promote unique and competing ideas about the accessibility of the *sunna* through *aḥādīth*. They were once again able to work within inherited boundaries to argue for divergent conceptions of the applicability of Islamic law.

[10] Jonathan Brown, *Hadith: Muhammad's Legacy in the Medieval and Modern World* (Oneworld 2009) 31.

[11] Juynboll (n 2) 161.

[12] See Christopher Melchert, 'Traditionist-Jurisprudents and the Framing of Islamic Law' (2001) 8:3 *Islamic Law and Society* 383.

MULTIPLE-CHAINED TRANSMISSIONS (*MUTAWĀTIR*) AND WELL-ESTABLISHED (*MASHHŪR*) TRANSMISSIONS

The Ḥanafī school divided *ḥadīth* transmissions into three categories: *mutawātir*, well-established (*mashhūr*), and single-transmission (*āḥād*). These categories reflected levels of reliability that *ḥadīth* were accorded based on the number of their independent chains of transmission (*ṭuruq*). Of the three, single transmissions were given the most scholarly attention and generated the most controversy.[13] By contrast, there was a general consensus amongst Ḥanafī scholars regarding *mutawātir aḥādīth*. This was reflected in the writings of Dabūsī and Sarakhsī, whose chapters on the subject read almost identically. The same authorities were invoked, the same criticisms were considered and rejected, and the same examples were provided as proofs. Though Sarakhsī's treatment of *mutawātir* transmission was more verbose, the ideas presented in their works were indistinguishable. Their only point of difference concerned the well-established (*mashhūr*) *aḥādīth*, which were discussed alongside the *mutawātir*. The difference in their understanding of the *mashhūr* appeared slight, but had a significant impact on their resulting articulation of Islamic law.

The *Mutawātir* in the Thought of Dabūsī and Sarakhsī

The two juridical scholars defined *mutawātir* transmissions as conforming to three criteria.[14] First, the narration must have been heard directly by the narrator in such a way that the narrator's audition (*samāʿ*) was in no way compromised. Secondly, there must be a continuous chain of narrators, all of whom heard the narration directly, understood it, and transmitted exactly what they heard. Finally, the narration must

[13] Murteza Bedir, 'An Early Response to Shāfiʿī: ʿĪsā b. Abān on the Prophetic Report' (2002) 9:3 *Islamic Law and Society* 285, 295.

[14] For a brief summary of Dabūsī's treatment of the *mutawātir* see Abū Zayd al-Dabūsī. *Taqwīm al-Adilla* (Khalīl al-Mays ed, Dār al-Kutub al-ʿIlmiyya 2001) 22 and for the *mashhūr* 170–3; for Sarakhsī see Muḥammad b. Aḥmad al-Sarakhsī, *al-Muḥarrar fī Uṣūl al-Fiqh* (Ṣalāḥ b. Muḥammad ed, Dār al-Kutub al-ʿIlmiyya 1996) 1:212–21 and Sarakhsī, *Uṣūl al-Sarakhsī* (Abū al-Wafā' ed, Dār al-Kutub al-ʿIlmiyya 2005) 1:282–95.

have been simultaneously reported by different individuals in so many different places that the multiple chains of transmission (*ṭuruq*) vitiate any claims of fabrication. If a report met these conditions, it attained the status of *mutawātir*. Once so classified, the content of the narration ought to generate indubitable knowledge (*ʿilm al-yaqīn*) of its veracity. This effectively put *mutawātir aḥādīth* on par with the Qurʾān as a miraculous source of knowledge, since the Qurʾān was miraculous and generated indubitable knowledge because it was preserved through *mutawātir* transmission. Indeed, Dabūsī and Sarakhsī explicitly accorded *mutawātir* transmissions a legal status equivalent to the Qurʾān.

Conspicuously missing from Dabūsī and Sarakhsī's discussion was any mention of text (*matn*) criticism of *mutawātir* transmissions. Neither scholar delved into issues surrounding the meaning (*maʿnā*) of a *mutawātir* transmission or its phrasing (*lafẓ*), despite the likelihood that a widespread transmission would have been transmitted using different phrasings, and perhaps conveying slightly different meanings. Many legal scholars attempted to delineate the minimum level of divergence between the phrasings that would lead two comparable *aḥādīth* to be classified as either synonymous or disparate. Dabūsī and Sarakhsī, however, only briefly alluded to the fact that multiple narrations with slightly different phrasings could still be considered *mutawātir* because it would be unrealistic to expect that all the transmissions would have utilized the exact same words.[15] Though they clearly believed that the text of the transmissions needed only conform to a uniform meaning and not to a uniform phrasing, they did not explore the issue further or deal with criticisms of their position. The reason for this will not be speculated upon, but what is important is that the thrust of Dabūsī and Sarakhsī's discussion was on the status of the *mutawātir* transmissions as legally authoritative evidence (*ḥujaj*, sing. *ḥujja*) for extrapolating a

[15] Wael Hallaq, 'On the Authoritativeness of Sunnī Consensus' (1986) 18 *International Journal of Middle East Studies* 427, 444. Hallaq suggests that Sarakhsī meant *tawātur bi-al-maʿnā* when the latter discussed *tawātur* and I agree, but it is important that the technical term is neither used nor alluded to in his discussion. Regarding the split between *tawātur lafẓī* and *tawātur maʿnawī*, Juynboll convincingly demonstrated that *tawātur lafẓī* was never a realized phenomenon; G H A Juynboll, '(Re)appraisal of Some Technical Terms in Ḥadīth Science' (2001) 8:3 *Islamic Law and Society* 303, 343–4.

judicial decision. Their primary concern was to defend the particular Ḥanafī utilization of *mutawātir* transmissions in legal theory, not to define its internal structure.

It is important that Dabūsī and Sarakhsī held that *mutawātir* transmissions did not require scrutiny of the narrators within their chains of transmission (*isnād*). Although both jurists gave the issue of *isnād*-criticism much import in other discussions, they presumed that the widespread nature of the *mutawātir* transmission precluded lying and conspiracy. It is not in the nature of humans, they argued, to perpetuate conspiracies and hide the truth. As Dabūsī explained, 'it is not possible for a person to perpetually hide his secrets. He eventually divulges it to a close friend, who then tries to keep the secret but then divulges it to his close friend. That friend then tells another, and [thereby] the secret becomes public.'[16] Further, they felt that in order for a narration to achieve the status of *mutawātir*, that narration would require a high level of plausibility since so many different people not only narrated it, but also believed it to be authentic. After all, argued Sarakhsī, someone might be able to convince a small colony of people that he divorced his wife in Mecca and freed a slave in Kufa on the same day, but that story would not be believed by people in neighboring towns due to its implausibility.[17] Therefore, in order for a transmission to reach the status of *mutawātir*, it would have to surmount the natural tendency for lies to be exposed and for the masses to accept only what is plausible. Thus, if a *ḥadīth* reaches the level of *mutawātir*, then it is, *ipso facto*, reliable and trustworthy. This absolved Dabūsī and Sarakhsī from demanding that all the narrators in all the chains of transmission of a *mutawātir ḥadīth* be reliable and trustworthy; a process that would preclude almost all reports from reaching *mutawātir* status and render the category purely theoretical.

While this trust in humanity's transmission-vetting capabilities allowed for a larger number of reports to reach *mutawātir* status, it also allowed for a broader range of narrators to have their transmissions accepted. Elsewhere, Dabūsī and Sarakhsī stated that legitimate

[16] Dabūsī (n 13) 208.
[17] Dabūsī (n 14) 209; Sarakhsī, *al-Muḥarrar fī Uṣūl al-Fiqh* (n 14) 1:214.

narrators must be, at minimum, Muslim, trustworthy, reliable, sane, and of a mature age (*bālighh*) if their transmissions were to be accepted.[18] All of these stipulations were dropped in the case of the *mutawātir* out of necessity. As stated earlier, criticizing the chains of transmission would render most all *mutawātir aḥādīth* invalid. However, there was a major unintended consequence to dropping all stipulations for narrators in *mutawātir* transmissions, particularly the stipulation of religious affiliation. If being Muslim was not a prerequisite for having one's transmissions accepted, then, theoretically, other widespread, competing non-Muslim narratives could similarly be considered *mutawātir* and therefore legally binding upon believers. The manner in which Dabūsī and Sarakhsī dealt with the problem of *mutawātir* transmissions from other religious groups tells us a great deal about their perception of other religious groups and of Islam as ascendant over all other religions.

The most obvious competing narrative that Dabūsī and Sarakhsī considered was the crucifixion of Jesus. While the Jewish and Christian *mutawātir* reports claimed that Jesus died on the cross, Q. 4:157 states, 'They did not kill [Jesus] and they did not crucify him, but it was made to appear to them [that they had done so].' The Qur'ān claims that at the time of the crucifixion, Jesus was lifted to God, which led most commentators to believe that another person was tortured and killed in Jesus' place whom God caused to look like Jesus. This presented a problem because, based on Dabūsī and Sarakhsī's methodology, the claims of Jews and Christians that Jesus was tortured and killed were encapsulated in reports so widespread that they reached the level of *mutawātir*. As *mutawātir* reports, they would have the same status as the Qur'ān and thus generate indubitable knowledge of their veracity. Some legal scholars objected that in Dabūsī and Sarakhsī's conception of *mutawātir*, the diametrically opposed claims of Christians and the Qur'ān regarding Jesus both generated indubitable knowledge.

Dabūsī and Sarakhsī responded to this criticism by reminding their detractors of the premise of their theory. In order to be considered *mutawātir*, the original narrators must have witnessed the event being

[18] Dabūsī (n 14) 175; Sarakhsī *al-Muḥarrar fī Uṣūl al-Fiqh* (n 14) 1:258.

narrated, understood it, and then transmitted what they observed. In the case of Jesus' torture, Dabūsī and Sarakhsī argued that the torturers did not know Jesus well enough to definitively identify whom they were torturing. In addition, Jesus' close associates were not present at the time of his torture to make a positive identification. Therefore, the people who narrated reports regarding his torture were not in a position to make a substantive claim about who was actually being tortured. However, regarding the crucifixion itself, Dabūsī and Sarakhsī admitted that the general populace would have been able to witness Jesus on the cross, including his close associates. So even if the torturers misidentified Jesus, his companions certainly would have recognized their master. To reconcile the Qur'anic account with their theory of *mutawātir*, Dabūsī and Sarakhsī said the body on the cross was so mutilated after its torture that even Jesus' close associates would not have been able to definitively identify the individual hanging from the cross. Since the original narrators of the crucifixion did not conclusively witness his torture and death, the Jewish and Christian claims of Jesus' death cannot be considered *mutawātir*.

Although Dabūsī and Sarakhsī preserved their theory of *mutawātir* against the above criticism, they simultaneously raised questions about God's machinations. That is not least because in the Qur'anic passage cited above, God made it appear to onlookers that Jesus was being crucified. In the absence of any evidence to the contrary, it is perfectly understandable that Jews and Christians would propagate reports that Jesus was, indeed, crucified, such that those reports would be known far and wide. In essence, then, in safeguarding their theory of *mutawātir*, Dabūsī and Sarakhsī argued that God knowingly misled two nations: namely, the Jews and the Christians. Even if Muḥammad eventually came with the truth to clear up the matter, the 600 years between the disputed crucifixion and the advent of Muḥammad's prophethood would be characterized not only by ignorance (*jahiliyya*) but by God's willful misguidance. Sarakhsī explained that sometimes God achieves His will by obfuscating the reality of a situation, like when He caused the Meccan pagans to underestimate the strength of the Medinese Muslim army. Dabūsī linked the issue with the purpose (*ḥikma*) that underlies all of God's rulings. He suggested that the greater purpose behind the crucifixion was for God to deliver Jesus from his enemies to Himself (*al-dafʿ ḥikma ʿaẓīma*). By creating a likeness of Jesus to be killed, God was able to subtly deliver Jesus (*al-tashbīh dafʿ laṭīf*), because God's deliverance is always subtle. The collateral result of this subtle deliverance, however, was the misguidance of the people witnessing the event. This might have been regrettable, but both he and Sarakhsī argued that God was only increasing in misguidance people who were already misguided because of their own actions. This position demonstrated Dabūsī and Sarakhsī's low regard for the early Christians as well as their regard for Islam as a pristine message that has no equal. Their understanding of the *mutawātir* also esteems the Muslim community above other communities since the *mutawātir* transmissions of other nations may actually be the result of divine misguidance. The Muslim community was protected from such misguidance, a theme further explored in their treatments of legal Consensus (*ijmāʿ*).

The juridical effect of Dabūsī and Sarakhsī's conception of *tawātur* was that *mutawātir* transmissions were to be accepted and applied juridically without considering either transmission (*riwāya*) or content (*dirāya*) criticism. The impossibility of conducting narrator-criticism of *mutawātir* transmissions precluded *riwāya* criticism and the inscrutability of God's will precluded *dirāya* criticism. Hence, *mutawātir* transmissions were to be applied in jurisprudence with impunity and the jurist can have indubitable knowledge in the veracity of that application.

The *Mashhūr* in the Thought of Dabūsī and Sarakhsī

After having agreed on a single definition of the *mutawātir*, Dabūsī and Sarakhsī proposed divergent definitions for the more imprecise category of well-established (*mashhūr*) *aḥādīth*. The difference appears small, but it has palpable ramifications in their discussions of the *sunna* abrogating the Qurʾān. Dabūsī defined *mashhūr aḥādīth* as reports that were transmitted through various chains. Whereas the *mutawātir* were of such common knowledge that neither uniform text nor sound chains of transmission were necessary to establish their veracity, the *mashhūr* were *aḥādīth* that were not quite so widespread and thus were to be subject to both text (*matn*) and chain of transmission (*isnād*) criticism. Dabūsī held that a few of these *mashhūr aḥādīth* were narrated with uniform wordings and in such numbers as to warrant them having the legal status of *tawātur* (*'alā ḥadd al-mutawātir*). That is to say, though they were not *mutawātir aḥādīth*, they were nevertheless treated as such juridically because of the high likelihood of their authenticity. As a result, believers were charged with having indubitable knowledge of the veracity of this subgroup of *mashhūr aḥādīth*. The majority of *mashhūr aḥādīth*, however, did not reach the level of *tawātur*, and so they were accorded the same juridical status as a single transmission (*khabar al-wāḥid*). Dabūsī said that these inferior transmissions did not impart indubitable knowledge, but believers could have peace of mind (*ṭum'anīnat al-qalb*)[19] in the veracity of their contents.[20] Since believers were only required to follow that which is known indubitably, they need follow only those *mashhūr aḥādīth* that reach the level of *tawātur*. Dabūsī did not explain the difference between the *mashhūr* that are at the level of the *mutawātir* and those that are not, though he intimated in another discussion that a *mashhūr ḥadīth* becomes *mutawātir* if there are over ten identical transmissions.[21] The difference between the *mashhūr* and the *mutawātir*, though, was left vague and Dabūsī did not delve into the subject in detail.[22]

Sarakhsī provided even less detail and clarity on the *mashhūr aḥādīth* than did Dabūsī. He offered no clear definition of the *mashhūr* and often used the term interchangeably with *mutawātir*. Like the *mutawātir*,

[19] A quick look at the transliteration will demonstrate that I have taken liberties with the translation here. Josef van Ess calls it *Geborgenheit des Herzens* (security of the heart) in *Die Erkenntnislehre des 'Adudaddin al-Içi* (Weisbaden 1966) 76; and George Makdisi calls it 'tranquility of the heart' in *Ibn Aqil: Religion and Culture in Classical Islam* (Edinburgh Press 1997) 246. Both are more technically accurate, but the idiom 'peace of mind' suggests the repose coupled with a kind of certainty that our authors intend.

[20] Not all Ḥanafīs made a distinction between *yaqīn* and *ṭum'anīnat al-qalb*. Al-Aḥsā'ī and his teachers, for instance, equated the two explicitly; Abū Bakr al-Aḥsā'ī, *Zawāhir al-Qalā'id 'alā Mahammāt al-Qawā'id* (Yaḥyā b. Abī Bakr ed, Dār al-Nu'mān lil-'Ulūm 2002) 45. For all intents and purposes, Sarakhsī equated the two functionally.

[21] Dabūsī (n 14) 171.

[22] It should be noted that *mashhūr* transmissions are normally associated with reports whose authenticity is established by the widespread dissemination of the content of the report in the generation following that of the Companions; al-Qāsim b. 'Abd Allāh b. Quṭlubughā, *Khulāṣat al-Afkār* (Thanā' Allāh Zāhidī ed, Dār Ibn Ḥazm 2003) 130. Although this was a common conception in classical Islamic law, I did not find evidence of it in either Dabūsī or Sarakhsī's works.

Sarakhsī said that the *mashhūr* generated indubitable knowledge and that believers were obliged to believe in them. This position is distinct from that of Dabūsī, who said that the majority of *mashhūr aḥādīth* did not attain the level of *mutawātir*. In contrast, Sarakhsī made almost no distinction between *mutawātir* and *mashhūr aḥādīth* and in fact regularly categorized *aḥādīth* as *mutawātir* in one discussion and the same *ḥadīth* as *mashhūr* in another.

The result of this undefined relationship between two juridically equivalent categories was that Sarakhsī had two types of *ḥadīth* that he could claim generated indubitable knowledge. If he felt that a *ḥadīth* did not attain the level of *tawātur*, or if others would not deem it so, then he could retain its function in generating indubitable knowledge by arguing that it was *mashhūr*. Indeed, Sarakhsī did so when defending traditional Ḥanafī opinions regarding the *sunna* abrogating the Qurʾān. When discussing the same issue, Dabūsī was hampered by a dearth of *aḥādīth* at his disposal that generated indubitable knowledge. That discussion will follow below, for which it is important to bear in mind the subtle difference in their definitions.

The *mutawātir* and *mashhūr aḥādīth* have great juridical impact because they can legislate at the level of the Qurʾān, and their practical ramifications are most apparent in discussions on the *sunna* abrogating the Qurʾān. Yet, the fact that these reports needed to be widespread through multiple chains of transmission keeps their numbers somewhat limited. The far more prevalent—and controversial—type of report is that of the single transmission. It is the single transmission that brings out the stark differences in Dabūsī and Sarakhsī's conception of the *sunna*'s relationship to Islamic law.

THE SINGLE TRANSMISSION (*AL-KHABAR AL-WĀḤID*)

The role of single transmissions in the articulation of Islamic law is an intensely debated subject amongst juridical scholars.[23] The single

[23] Josef van Ess, 'Ḍirār b. ʿAmr und die 'Cahmiye': Biographie einer vergessenen Schule' (1967) 43 *Der Islam* 241–7.

transmission refers to a *ḥadīth* ascribed to the Prophet that was narrated by only one or two of his Companions. The injunctions contained therein are therefore problematic because single transmissions potentially contain truth or falsehood (*yaḥtamil al-ṣidq wa-al-kidhb*) with equal probability, depending on the probity and memory of the narrator.[24] In general, Sunnī scholars were not concerned with the moral probity of the Companions, whom they believed would not lie about the Prophet. However, they were concerned about someone in a later generation capriciously inventing a prophetic saying and then reverse-attributing that saying to the Prophet by way of a Companion. Since single transmissions, by definition, do not have corroborating transmissions from other Companions, they cannot be externally validated through comparison with other reports. They are—again, by definition—unable to demonstrate the level of reliability that *mutawātir* and *mashhūr* transmissions afford through their wide circulation. The Shāfiʿīs often tried to mitigate this shortcoming of the single transmission by determining if all the narrators in the chain of transmission (*sanad*) of a *ḥadīth* were trustworthy characters.[25] If such a trustworthy chain were established, Shāfiʿīs believed that the *ḥadīth* would then be sound (*ṣaḥīḥ*), barring patently fabricated text in the wording of the *ḥadīth*. In the former case, the *ḥadīth* would be considered to accurately reflect the words of the Prophet, would command obedience from believers, and could be used as a trustworthy source of jurisprudence.

Ḥanafīs were largely unimpressed by the Shāfiʿī methodology. Their major objection was that if a transmission could be accepted with certainty as accurately reflecting the words of the Prophet then that transmission might be considered *waḥy ghayr matlū*. Ḥanafīs argued that in that case, for all intents and purposes, single transmissions would have the same legal status as the Qurʾān and the *mutawātir*.[26] This not only meant that the status of the Qurʾān and the *mutawātir* would

[24] Wael Hallaq, 'The Authenticity of Prophetic Ḥadīth: A Pseudo-Problem' (1999) 89 *Studia Islamica* 75, 82.
[25] Muhammad Hashim Kamali, *A Textbook of Hadīth Studies* (Islamic Foundation 2005) 57.
[26] Ibid 4.

be diminished, but that the single transmission would be sufficient to abrogate the Qur'ān if the two were in conflict. Further, rejecting a *ḥadīth* that was transmitted through a sound single transmission would be juridically equivalent to rejecting the Qur'ān. The Shāfiʿīs, of course, did not accept the Ḥanafī criticism, rejecting it as an extreme caricature of their intended position. Ḥanafīs, for their part, had their own issues to resolve regarding single transmissions. Despite their criticism of the Shāfiʿīs and the radical distinction they tried to maintain between the Qur'ān and single transmissions, there was tension between the Ḥanafī position on the single transmissions as an inferior source of jurisprudence—when compared to the Qur'ān and the *mutawātir*—and the dominant methodology they used to derive law.

When engaging in apologetics, Ḥanafī juridical scholars claimed to articulate legal theory by starting with jurisprudence and working backward.[27] That is, scholars supposedly induced the paradigmatic cases (*uṣūl*) behind laws from the legal applications (*furūʿ*) in the form of injunctions that were inherited from their predecessors. Oftentimes, it was impossible to link a legal application to a paradigmatic case without recourse to single transmissions.[28] Thus, single transmissions were used to apologize for most of the jurisprudence in the Ḥanafī school. This was not in and of itself problematic for Ḥanafīs, except when the inherited injunction was inconsistent with an imperative from a source with a higher status than the single transmission, such as the Qur'ān. A scholar's understanding of the status of single transmissions determined how they resolved the conflict between inherited injunctions that were supported by single transmissions and Qur'anic dictates that commanded the opposite.

Dabūsī on Single Transmissions

Dabūsī's major concern regarding single transmissions was in describing their ability to function as authoritative evidence (*ḥujaj*, sing. *ḥujja*)

[27] Kamali, *Principles of Islamic Jurisprudence* (Islamic Texts Society 1991) 9.
[28] Hallaq, 'The Authenticity of Prophetic Ḥadīth' (n 24) 88.

for extrapolating juridical injunctions. In doing so, he had to mediate what he described as two extremes. On the one hand, if it were possible to accept a single transmission as a *ḥujja*, then all single transmissions would necessitate action (*yūjib al-ʿamal*) upon the imperative contained therein. On the other hand, if single transmissions were not considered *ḥujaj*, then the bulk of Ḥanafī jurisprudence would be founded upon conjecture (*ẓann*). Dabūsī admitted that the conjectural nature of the single transmission itself was unmistakable and unavoidable. Regardless of the content of a *ḥadīth* or the reported soundness of its narrators, there remained the possibility that falsehood seeped into the report somewhere along the chain of narrators or that the report and its chain were entirely fabricated.[29] As mentioned earlier, single transmissions that trace their lineage back to a single Companion of Muḥammad cannot be verified by comparison to other, similar *aḥādīth*, nor can the overwhelming sentiment of the believing community attest to their veracity. Since they are not *mutawātir*, single transmissions do not have the overwhelming approval of the community behind them, nor do they enjoy the miraculous protection given by God to *mutawātir* transmissions. Because it was impossible to externally validate the authenticity of single transmissions, Dabūsī said that all avenues for ascertaining certainty (*yaqīn*) in the veracity of these reports are forever closed (*masdūd*).[30]

As if to ameliorate the consternation this might cause a jurist trying to derive sound law, Dabūsī warned that if single transmissions were to have a high level of certainty then believers would be required to act upon them.[31] In that scenario, single transmissions could obligate (*faraḍa*) believers to carry out certain acts, meaning that those who failed to enact them would flirt with disbelief. Given the immense number of single transmissions, this would lead to a situation wherein innumerable actions would be obligatory upon believers. Believers would then assuredly fail to fulfill the dictates of all single transmissions, whether due to ignorance or through incapacity.[32] Dabūsī explained that instead of focusing on the

[29] Dabūsī (n 14) 170.
[30] Ibid 173.
[31] Ibid 172.
[32] Ibid 173.

minutiae that are found in single transmissions, believers are first and foremost required to fulfill the claims that God has over His servants (*ḥuqūq Allāh*), like prayer and the prescribed almsgiving.[33] These claims, however, can only be ascertained from sources that generate indubitable knowledge—the Qur'ān and the *mutawātir* traditions—not from single transmissions. Dabūsī argued that whatever information the single transmissions might contain was not of primary importance, and so the content of those transmissions could not oblige believers to action.

Dabūsī added that believers are not only exempt from acting upon single transmissions in day-to-day matters, but that they should not use single transmissions as a basis for action in foundational matters. He cited Q. 17:36, 'And do not pursue that of which you have no knowledge' to argue that single transmissions could not be used as authoritative evidence (*ḥujaj*) for extrapolating juridical injunctions.[34] If one cannot be certain of the veracity of single transmissions, then any action based upon them would be founded on less than indubitable knowledge. Dabūsī claimed that in matters that are foundational to Islam, action without knowledge is invalid (*al-ʿamal bi-ghayr ʿilm bāṭil fī al-aṣl*).[35] Foundational matters for Dabūsī were those dealing with the claims of God, which include rituals due to Him and belief in Him.[36] As mentioned above, these rights were only enumerated in the sources that generate indubitable knowledge. Thus, single transmissions should have no role in defining the foundational issues of Islam, apart from which believers are not required to act.

Still, there are certain claims between humans (*ḥuqūq al-ʿibād*) that are guided by Islamic law. These include codes of action (*muʿāmalāt*) and social laws. The details of these laws as articulated by Ḥanafī scholars were almost entirely founded upon single transmissions. Nevertheless, Dabūsī said that if the veracity of a report is not known with indubitable knowledge, it could not be considered authoritative evidence in any arena, including the *ḥuqūq al-ʿibād*.[37] Dabūsī was left, then, to explain how social laws were to be established if not by the content of single

33 Ibid 172.
34 Ibid 170.
35 Ibid 168.
36 Ibid 170.
37 Ibid 178.

transmissions. He posited that if there were a lack of evidence from the Qur'ān and *mutawātir* transmissions regarding a particular social matter, one could then use a single transmission to validate a particular position. However, if another jurist were to choose a conflicting single transmission to validate a different position, he would be at liberty to do so. In either case, the positions for which jurists argue through single transmissions would have no binding authority upon other jurists.[38]

Moreover, there were two situations in which jurists were encouraged to reject the use of single transmissions altogether when arguing a position. The first is if there is evidence for a conflicting position that is expressed in the Qur'ān, the *mutawātir* transmissions, or a strong analogy (*qiyās*).[39] The second is if following the relevant single transmission causes some kind of constraint (*ḥaraj*) on the community. Dabūsī argued that Q. 22:78, 'God does not desire to place upon you any constraint (*ḥaraj*) in the religion (*al-dīn*),' meant that whatever is from God does not constrain believers, and thus what can be known with certainty to be divinely sanctioned cannot be constraining.[40] Therefore, if a single transmission resulted in constraint for the community, it must be rejected since it would violate God's desire. Dabūsī did not provide a rubric by which to judge injunctions as 'constraining' or not, but the indictment of a single transmission as causing constraint would be proof that it was not divinely sanctioned. 'Whatever does not generate certainty,' wrote Dabūsī, 'is rejected [if] it results in constraint.'[41]

Sarakhsī on Single Transmissions

Sarakhsī significantly disagreed with Dabūsī's approach to single transmissions. In particular, he questioned the underlying assumption that single transmissions are irremediably conjectural (*ẓannī*). Dabūsī argued that single transmissions could not be externally verified, allowing capricious individuals to ascribe their own thoughts to the Prophet through these reports. Sarakhsī, on the other hand, argued that it was improper to doubt the veracity of single transmissions—in

[38] Ibid 174. [39] Ibid 197. [40] Ibid 173. [41] Ibid 173.

the process impugning the narrators of the report—simply because of the mere potential for deceit. Instead, he said that believers should have a positive opinion (*ḥusn al-ẓann*) of one another and hence narrators should be accorded a positive opinion in the absence of evidence to the contrary.[42] Therefore, a narrator's transmission should be rejected only if he proves himself to be an unrepentant sinner (*fāsiq*).[43] Barring such proof, one should assume that narrators and their transmissions tend to be trustworthy (*bi-jānib al-ṣidq*).[44] In defense of this assertion, Sarakhsī invoked a *ḥadīth* that explained that God aids and endows with knowledge those who propagate His message.[45] Consequently, Sarakhsī reasoned, if an individual were conveying God's message by narrating a report from the Prophet, then he must be the beneficiary of divine blessing. The fact that narrators of *aḥādīth* were recipients of divine blessing should only increase their stature in the eyes of believers. Sarakhsī thereby concluded that the moral probity (*ʿadāla*) of *ḥadīth* narrators should be assumed as a fact.

Though Sarakhsī assumed that narrators were scrupulous moral beings, this character did not speak to the exactitude (*ḍabṭ*) of the narrators in transmitting precise narrations. The possibility remained that a narrator might have been righteous, yet forgetful (*ghāfil*), and as a result transmitted *aḥādīth* incorrectly. Sarakhsī defended *ḥadīth* narrators by describing two levels of exactitude. The first, he said, was perceptible exactitude (*ḍabṭ ẓāhir*), which referred to a narrator's ability to reliably memorize the exact phrasing (*lafẓ*) of a transmission and its context.[46] The second and more important exactitude was concealed exactitude (*ḍabṭ bāṭin*), which refers to a narrator's ability to retain the inner meaning (*maʿnā*) of a transmission, particularly in its relation to the injunctions of the *sharīʿa* as manifested in substantive jurisprudence (*fī mā yabtanī ʿalayhi aḥkām al-sharʿ wa-huwa al-fiqh*).[47] Sarakhsī explained

[42] Sarakhsī *al-Muḥarrar fī Uṣūl al-Fiqh* (n 14) 1:259.

[43] Although the term *fāsiq* connotes 'corrupt,' I have used the translation utilized by Wilferd Madelung— 'Early Muslim Doctrine Regarding Faith as Reflected in the 'Kitāb al-Īmān of Abū 'Ubayd al-Qāsim b. Sallām' (1970) 32 *Studia Islamica* 253—as it accurately reflects they way in which Sarakhsī used the term.

[44] Sarakhsī *al-Muḥarrar fī Uṣūl al-Fiqh* (n 14) 1:259.

[45] Ibid 1:244.

[46] Ibid 1:261.

[47] Ibid 1:261.

that when a narrator has concealed exactitude, he or she establishes a relationship between the meaning of a *ḥadīth* and its juridical application when thinking about the transmission and its relation to law. Once so cognized, the narrator then transmits the juridical meaning of the transmission as he or she understood it, though not necessarily with the exact words that he or she heard.

Sarakhsī claimed that strong concealed exactitude was all that was required of a trustworthy narrator.[48] It would be unrealistic to expect narrators to have remembered the exact words of transmissions as they heard them and added that it was unnecessary for them to do so. Sarakhsī said that this was because the words of the Prophet were not inimitable in their wordings nor in their ordering (*naẓm*). Thus, so long as the meaning of his saying was preserved, the transmission should be considered accurately delivered.[49] By extension, he concluded that transmissions by jurists would preserve the juridical meaning better than those of non-jurists, if only because jurists are better able to make the appropriate connections between the inner meanings of transmissions and jurisprudence.[50] Sarakhsī held that transmissions of jurists were superior (*rājiḥ*) in the weight they hold in legal arguments, though he did not repudiate (*muʿāriḍ*) transmissions from non-jurists.[51] Rather, he assumed that single transmissions were trustworthy and communicated the meaning that the Prophet intended to convey, unless the narrator was proven to be an unrepentant sinner. Sarakhsī merely privileged the reports of jurists because they more accurately conveyed the meaning intended by Muḥammad.

Single transmissions were therefore, on the whole, reliable sources for accessing the *sunna*. However, since there was still the possibility that some transmissions might have a measure of fabrication, he conceded that believers could not have indubitable knowledge (*ʿilm al-yaqīn*) of their veracity.[52] This did not pose a problem for Sarakhsī, and he pointed out that there are other types of knowledge than indubitable knowledge. The type of knowledge that the single transmissions impart, he said,

48 Ibid 1:261.
49 Ibid 1:262.
50 Ibid 1:255.
51 Ibid 1:262.
52 Ibid 1:241.

is one that creates peace of mind (*ṭum'anīnat al-qalb*).[53] This peace of mind in the veracity of single transmissions is a type of knowledge that allows a believer to be confident that genuine prophetic imperatives are contained therein. Sarakhsī argued that if a believer is afforded this level of confidence, then receiving an imperative in the form of a single transmission is similar to receiving a direct imperative from the Prophet himself.[54] Since believers are required to obey the Prophet, they are likewise required to obey the content of single transmissions. Though single transmissions were not considered to be in the same category as sources that generated indubitable knowledge, they generated similar practical results.

Still, the fact that single transmissions did not generate indubitable knowledge had a major practical implication for Sarakhsī. He previously argued that the foundations of the religion (*uṣūl al-dīn*) could only be established by sources that generate indubitable knowledge. Consequently, single transmissions were not to be used to discuss the foundations of the religion. Sarakhsī enumerated these foundations, which include God's unity (*tawḥīd*), God's attributes (*ṣifāt Allāh*), and the institution of prophethood (*ithbāt al-nubuwwa*).[55] Nevertheless, Sarakhsī argued that while single transmissions did not generate indubitable knowledge concerning their veracity, they could generate action (*yūjib al-ʿamal lā al-ʿilm*).[56] From this he concluded that all matters other than those related to the foundations of the religion can be decided based upon single transmissions. Hence, the jurist must make use of single transmissions in pronouncing judgment whenever possible, so long as the transmissions do not contradict the Qur'ān or *mutawātir* transmissions.[57] This meant that single transmissions were meant to take precedence over juridical analogy (*qiyās*), the jurist's intellect, or any contextual considerations other than those required by necessity (*ḍarūriyyāt*).[58] Single transmissions were, therefore, authoritative evidence (*ḥujaj*) that could and should be used in the formation of juridical codes in all times and all places.[59]

[53] Ibid 1:247.
[54] Ibid 1:247.
[55] Ibid 1:242.
[56] Ibid 1:241.
[57] Ibid 1:243.
[58] Ibid 1:254.
[59] Ibid 1:261.

Sarakhsī passionately defended his position by placing it within the larger prophetic narrative. He provided two arguments that, he believed, proved that the Prophet intended his message to be spread through single transmissions. First, if the Prophet charged one of his Companions with a task, that Companion was obliged to act without waiting for multiple transmissions from the Prophet. Further, if one Companion told another Companion about a task that the Prophet commanded, they would both be obligated by that command, despite the latter Companion's only hearing of the prophetic command through a single transmission.[60] In his second example, Sarakhsī contended that the very mission of the Prophet required that single transmissions be accepted as authoritative evidence. Failure to authorize them as such would mean that the Prophet failed in his duty. Sarakhsī argued that,

> ...the single transmission generates action [upon it], because the Prophet was raised for all of mankind. [God] the Most High said, 'And We have not sent [Muḥammad] except for all mankind.' There is no dispute that he completed his mission, [and] it is known for certain that he did not come to each person and preach to him directly. Rather, he preached to [his] nation himself and then sent some [people] from his nation out to [preach to] others, and sent some out with letters. That he sent letters to rulers far and wide is well-known and cannot be denied. So if the single transmission were not authoritative evidence, then he [would have been unable to] convey the message of his Lord through these mediums to all of mankind. Furthermore, many far off lands like Yemen and Bahrain were conquered through means of treaties, and [Muḥammad] did not come to them himself, but rather dispatched emissaries to all corners [of the land] to teach those people religious injunctions (*al-aḥkām*).[61]

If single transmissions could not be used as authoritative evidence, then those whom the Prophet did not reach himself would not know religious injunctions with any level of certitude. In his argument, Sarakhsī assumed a necessary link between the injunctions of Islam and the overall message of the Prophet. Individual injunctions were part and parcel of the prophetic mission for Sarakhsī, and failure to preach them to others would result in an incomplete message. Preaching the complete message

[60] Ibid 1:242. [61] Ibid 1:243.

required utilizing single transmissions as legal proofs to reconstruct and imitate the intended message as established in 'Muḥammad's nation.' Sarakhsī essentially argued that single transmissions must be authoritative evidence on the basis of his own conception of the prophetic mission.

BRIEF REVIEW

It is important to remember that the *sunna* of Muḥammad is agreed to be an authoritative source of law; this fact is never in question. The only matter of concern to our discussion is how accessible that *sunna* is to scholars of the 5th/11th century. We now have a taste of Dabūsī and Sarakhsī's assumptions about the accessibility of the *sunna* in their time. For Dabūsī, the single transmissions were a helpful guide for emulating the *sunna*, but one could never be sure about their authenticity. The transmissions were advantageous for justifying a particular injunction, but he did not believe them to be a valid basis for deriving authoritative injunctions. His concern was negative rather than positive; that is, he was not interested in creating law through single transmissions, but ensuring that they not serve as an impediment to context-specific jurisprudence. His regular mention of constraint (*ḥaraj*) as a barrier to applying single transmissions demonstrated a commitment to the application of jurisprudence over the received jurisprudence itself. In this discussion, he reiterated his assertion that the foundations of the religion (*uṣūl al-dīn*) were of paramount importance and that Islamic law was meant for humans in all times and all places as a means of living in fidelity with the *uṣūl al-dīn*. Jurisprudence, therefore, was a potentially creative enterprise that helped move communities toward a realization of the *uṣūl al-dīn* in their own context, not an exercise in replicating law regardless of context.

Sarakhsī concluded almost the exact opposite in his discussion of the topic. He defended the trustworthy nature of narrators and argued that believers were compelled to follow single transmissions. It is interesting to note that for Dabūsī, the *mashhūr aḥādīth* caused peace of mind (*ṭum'anīnat al-qalb*) for the believer such that he could act on them with a degree of confidence, if not certainty.[62] For Sarakhsī, on the other hand, it was single transmissions that gave the believer peace of mind. He held that not only were believers compelled to act on the single transmissions, but that they should be comfortable with these transmissions dictating the bulk of jurisprudence. Furthermore, Sarakhsī explicitly stated that the aim of the prophetic mission was to create juridically uniform societies based on single transmissions. In fact, he said that if these societies were not so created, then the prophetic mission would have been a failure. In contrast to Dabūsī, Sarakhsī saw jurisprudence in relation to single transmissions as a largely applicative enterprise that enacted pre-existing injunctions, potentially despite context.

The issue of single transmissions brings their different conceptions of the *sunna* into particularly sharp relief. Dabūsī spoke of the permissibility of using single transmissions and enumerated instances wherein they should be avoided. That is to say, for Dabūsī, single transmissions generated neither certain knowledge nor action. Sarakhsī resolutely held the position that single transmissions generate action, though not knowledge. This severe divide in their approaches to the subject mirrored an earlier split amongst Ḥanafī scholars, but was expressed by Dabūsī and Sarakhsī in novel ways.[63] The ideas were their own and

[62] Dabūsī's stance reflected an early Ḥanafī opinion that no other major Ḥanafī scholar held after ʿĪsā b. Abān (d. 221/836). Sarakhsī's position was in line with the dominant Ḥanafī opinion from the time of Abū Bakr al-Jaṣṣās and which persists to the modern day. It may have been that the burgeoning popularity of the Shāfiʿī school of thought after ʿĪsā b. Abān's time fundamentally shifted the discussion, which in turn affected Sarakhsī's opinion. The Shāfiʿīs held a deep regard for the single transmissions and questioned the faith of anyone who rejected them. ʿĪsā b. Abān, by contrast, was well-known for saying that one does not become a heretic by rejecting even the *mashhūr aḥādīth*. Dabūsī, however, did not overtly align himself with Ibn Abān, though he mentioned his positions. Perhaps this was because by that time, Ibn Abān had been repudiated by major scholars including the Ḥanafī al-Ṭaḥāwī (d. 323/935), al-Shāfiʿī's main disciple Abū al-ʿAbbās b. Surayj (d. 306/918) and the literalist Dā'ūd b. ʿAlī al-Ẓāhirī (d. 296/909); Bedir, 'An Early Reply to Shāfiʿī' (n 13) 294. Dabūsī must have known that the ideas he was presenting were unpopular and that to align himself with the early Ḥanafīs would earn him rebuke, even within his own legal school. Yet, to assign the single transmissions any higher status would mean compromising the system and the vision of jurisprudence that he was promoting with regard to other topics. Sarakhsī, by contrast, was able to appropriate popular ideas to buttress his overall thesis regarding law and the purpose of prophethood.

[63] There is no doubt that Dabūsī and Sarakhsī were promoting ideas that were articulated before them. However, their positions cannot be reduced to exact conformity with

reflected their particular approaches to the *sunna*. Far from being purely academic, these divergent approaches could palpably influence the way a judge or jurist might apply inherited principles and injunctions. The impact of their positions finds it clearest expression in their respective arguments for the abrogation of the Qurʾān by the *sunna*.

ABROGATION OF THE QURʾĀN THROUGH THE *SUNNA*

The Sunnī schools of thought were unanimous that the Qurʾān could abrogate the Qurʾān and that *sunna* could abrogate *sunna*. There was far less enthusiasm for the Ḥanafī position that the *sunna* may abrogate the Qurʾān and the Qurʾān may abrogate the *sunna*. In practice, most Sunnī scholars abrogated the Qurʾān with the *sunna* and vice versa, but rhetorically they argued for a radical distinction between the Qurʾān and the *sunna* in the realm of abrogation theory. They held that the *sunna* might specify a Qurʾanic imperative (*takhṣīṣ*) or explain it, but the practice of the Prophet could never truly abrogate the Word of God. The Ḥanafīs disagreed and, indeed, they were forced to do so in order to maintain some of the injunctions that they held to be normative in their school; injunctions that could not be defended except by recourse to the *sunna* abrogating the Qurʾān. They were therefore required to demonstrate both why this abrogation was sanctioned and how abrogation functioned in the derivation of jurisprudence.

Dabūsī on the *Sunna* Abrogating the Qurʾān

Following the position of his juridical school, Dabūsī affirmed that the Qurʾān could abrogate the *sunna* and vice versa. To buttress his

any of them. Dabūsī was in congruence with ʿIsā b. Abān with regard to single transmissions, but not with regard to rejecting a *mashhūr ḥadīth* in favor of an analogy. Sarakhsī's position was in agreement with the majority of his contemporary Ḥanafīs, but diverged from the positions of the early Ḥanafīs. It is certain that the two jurists worked within the Ḥanafī paradigm and advocated positions that were attributable in part to eminent Ḥanafī juridical figures. However, the particularities of their thought are evident and appear to have been shaped by their unique perspectives on the function of Islamic law with regard to single transmissions.

position, he appealed to the doctrine of prophetic infallibility (*ʿiṣma*). This doctrine, briefly glossed above, held that God did not allow the Prophet to persist in an error; meaning that He would send revelation to correct the Prophet's actions when they were erroneous. In that case, the Qur'ān would abrogate a *sunna* that was incorrect (*khaṭa'*) and replace it with something better (*akhyar*).[64] Since God was sure to correct the wayward Prophet, the idea that the Qur'ān could abrogate the *sunna* was unproblematic for Ḥanafīs.

Dabūsī recognized that it was harder to argue that the *sunna* could abrogate the Qur'ān, especially since such abrogation might suggest that Muḥammad was correcting God. That, however, was not the major obstacle for Dabūsī when justifying the Ḥanafī position. Rather, the main problem was that the *sunna* was passed down through transmissions, some of which may have contained falsehood. A general principle that Ḥanafī scholars maintained was that whatever is conjectural in nature cannot abrogate something that generates indubitable knowledge.[65] Therefore, the Qur'ān could only be abrogated by something that likewise generated indubitable knowledge. Dabūsī thereby concluded that only the *mutawātir* or the well-established (*mashhūr*) *aḥādīth* that reached the level of *tawātur* could abrogate the Qur'ān, since they were beyond conjecture.[66]

Dabūsī further stipulated that in order for *mutawātir* or *mashhūr* transmissions to abrogate the Qur'ān, the text of the abrogating transmission must be unrecited revelation (*waḥy ghayr matlū*).[67] This additional stipulation stemmed from Dabūsī's stance that the Prophet's personal opinion on a matter was not a binding authority, so his personal opinions could not abrogate a Qur'anic imperative on their own.[68] Hence, the *mutawātir* transmission must not be merely a prophetic opinion, but revelation that was for some reason not included in the official codex. If there were an authentic unrecited revelation that specified or contradicted an imperative contained in the codex, then that Qur'anic

[64] Dabūsī (n 14) 240.
[65] Bedir, 'An Early Reply to Shāfiʿī' (n 13) 310.
[66] Dabūsī (n 14) 246.
[67] Ibid 244.
[68] Ibid 249.

imperative could be considered abrogated by a *waḥy ghayr matlū*.[69] During the Prophet's lifetime, a single transmission of this unrecited revelation would have been enough for the Companions to act upon since they could immediately verify the authenticity of the transmission. Dabūsī argued that after the death of the Prophet, however, the transmission would have to be proven to be beyond reproach before being accepted as an authentic prophetic saying.[70]

These stipulations significantly limited the number of *aḥādīth* that could be used to abrogate the Qur'anic text. This created difficulties for Dabūsī because he was forced to defend several well-known and foundational Ḥanafī injunctions that were based on *aḥādīth* abrogating the Qur'ān. The *aḥādīth* that Ḥanafīs used to justify those injunctions were often of a lesser status than those that Dabūsī allowed to abrogate the Qur'ān. He was thus forced to either abandon those Ḥanafī juridical positions or somehow justify them. Abandoning the positions would have put Dabūsī on a precarious footing amongst the Ḥanafīs. That is because the juridical positions in question were of the most staunchly defended injunctions and were often used to differentiate the Ḥanafīs from other schools of thought. Dabūsī's treatment of three such positions will be examined here: the punishment for adultery, bequests for children and relatives, and wiping over footgear during ritual ablution.

Adultery

The dominant Ḥanafī opinion regarding the punishment for adultery is that the adulterers should both be stoned, despite the Qur'anic imperative to either confine the adulterers to their houses or to lash them one hundred times.[71] The verse calling for confinement, Q. 4:15, states, 'As for those[72] guilty of lewdness from among your women, bring forth

[69] Ibid 232. [70] Ibid 246.

[71] John Burton, 'The Exegesis of Q. 2:106 and the Islamic theories of *naskh*: *mā nansakh min āya aw nansahā na'ti bi khairin minhā aw mithlihā*' (1985) 48:3 *Bulletin of the School of Oriental and African Studies* 452.

[72] Although the relative pronoun used in this verse is feminine, the possibility of the verse addressing lesbians had been roundly rejected by the 5th/11th century. The last reported individual to have raised this possibility was Abū Muslim al-Iṣfahānī (d. ca. 322/934) as reported by Everett Rowson, 'Straight or Gay? The Curious Exegetical

four witnesses from amongst you against them. And if [the witnesses] so testify then confine [the guilty women] in their houses until death reaches them or Allah appoints a way for them.' The verse of lashing, Q. 24:2, states, 'The male fornicator and the female, lash them both with one hundred stripes.' The Ḥanafīs traditionally argued that these verses from the Qur'ān were abrogated by the *ḥadīth*, 'Indeed Allah has appointed a way for [fornicators]: For the virgin [who had intercourse] with a virgin, one hundred lashes. And for the married person [who committed adultery] with a married person, strike them one hundred times and stone them.'[73]

Since Dabūsī did not consider the abrogating *ḥadīth* to be *mutawātir*, he was forced to employ a creative explanation to justify the position of his school. He cited the saying of ʿUmar b. al-Khaṭṭāb, the close companion of the Prophet and the second Caliph, who claimed that there existed a verse that commanded stoning in the Qur'ān, but that at some point it was no longer recited.[74] Dabūsī deduced from this report that the imperative to stone the fornicator was based on unrecited revelation.[75] Thus, the abrogation taking place would be unrecited revelation abrogating recited revelation, not *sunna* abrogating the Qur'ān. This deduction, however, was not enough for Dabūsī to allow for abrogation of the Qur'anic imperative, because the saying of ʿUmar was not *mutawātir*.

Dabūsī was able to maintain both his theory of abrogation and the integrity of the Ḥanafī position by stating that the *ḥadīth* did not actually abrogate the Qur'anic verse, but rather clarified it (*bayyanahu*). He suggested that the *ḥadīth* was the fulfillment of the end of Q. 4:15, '... or Allah appoints a way for them.'[76] The way shown by God was contained in the *ḥadīth* of stoning, which begins, 'Indeed Allah has appointed a way ...' The *ḥadīth*, therefore, did not abrogate but elaborated the verse of the Qur'ān. Dabūsī demonstrated his own discomfort with his explanation by stating that while this argument established the permissibility of

History of Qur'ān 4:15–16' *Annual Meeting of the American Oriental Society*, March 18, 2005.

[73] Yaḥyā b. Sharaf al-Nawawī, *Sharḥ Saḥīḥ al-Muslim* (Wahba al-Zuḥaylī ed, Dār al-Khayr 1998) 11:337.

[74] Ibid 11:338.

[75] Dabūsī (n 14) 242.

[76] Ibid 242.

stoning, it did not mandate it.[77] The punishment stipulated in the Qur'ān is foundational, he said, and the jurist can justifiably choose not to stone by relying on the Qur'anic imperative. In this way, Dabūsī found a way to maintain the dominant Ḥanafī position, but not violate his own theoretical framework by leaving the decision for punishing adulterers up to the discretion of individual judges.

It should be noted here that Dabūsī's discussion is not primarily about the punishment for adulterers, nor the basis for the related Ḥanafī injunction. Rather, Dabūsī is discussing abrogation and its limits through the discourse of adultery. He is not subverting the inherited Ḥanafī tradition by doing so, but he is influencing the way in which a jurist who is concerned about abrogation theory might apply Islamic law. In other words, Dabūsī is not providing a liberal reading of the sources in order to mitigate the Ḥanafī punishment for adultery, he is arguing for a particular method for applying those sources in light of abrogation theory.

Bequests

Dabūsī discussed bequests for children and relatives in a manner similar to his take on adultery. The two major verses that deal with bequests and inheritance law are, respectively, Q. 2:180 and Q. 4:11–12. Q. 2:180, known as the 'bequest verse' (*āyat al-waṣiyya*), discusses leaving a legacy after one's death in broad terms. Q. 4:11–12, known as the 'inheritance verse' (*āyat al-irth*), makes specific stipulations regarding how one should divide an inheritance amongst parents and relatives. The traditional Ḥanafī opinion is that, initially, the inheritance verse expanded upon the bequest verse; but then the bequest verse was abrogated in its entirety by a *ḥadīth* that forbade bequests to parents and relatives.

The bequest verse reads, 'It is prescribed for you that when death approaches that you make a bequest (*waṣiyya*) to parents and relatives (*aqrabīn*).' The inheritance verse was then assumed to expand on the idea of making bequests by stipulating the exact distribution of inheritance that should be included in the bequest. Up until this point, no abrogation

[77] Ibid 135.

has occurred. Abrogation comes into play due to the *ḥadīth* that forbids bequests entirely, which reads, 'Indeed Allah [by His revelation of the inheritance verse] has bestowed rights upon all who have a right [to inheritance, including parents and relatives], so [make] no bequest to the inheritors.'[78] According to the majority of Ḥanafīs, bequests to parents and relatives were nullified by this *ḥadīth* and so the bequest verse was considered abrogated.

To summarize, the Ḥanafī juridical position argued that, to begin with, the inheritance verse only expounded on the bequest verse, but did not necessarily abrogate it. Theoretically, it would still be possible to create a bequest for parents and relatives while abiding by the stipulations of the inheritance verse. The *ḥadīth*, however, clarified that the inheritance verse was meant to nullify all bequests to parents and relatives, thereby abrogating the bequest verse. Without the *ḥadīth*, the bequest verse would not necessarily be abrogated by the inheritance verse.[79]

As with the case of stoning adulterers, the *ḥadīth* nullifying bequests posed a problem for Dabūsī because it did not conform to his definition of a *mutawātir* transmission. Thus, the *ḥadīth* should not be able to abrogate a Qur'anic imperative. In an attempt to maintain the Ḥanafī position that bequests were not to be made to inheritors and also keep non-*mutawātir aḥādīth* from abrogating the Qur'ān, Dabūsī sought to give new meaning to the text of the *ḥadīth*. The Prophet, he said, was not issuing an imperative, but interpreting the relationship between the bequest verse and the inheritance verse.[80] Through his personal interpretation (*tafsīr*), Muḥammad was remarking about how the inheritance verse made the bequest verse unnecessary. The *ḥadīth* should therefore be understood as saying, 'Since God bestowed rights on all who have the right [to inheritance], there is no need to make a bequest to inheritors.' With this new reading, Dabūsī said that Muḥammad was not abrogating the bequest verse, but noting

[78] Muḥammad b. 'Īsā al-Tirmidhī, *Jāmi' al-Tirmidhī* ('Ādil Murshid ed, Dār al-A'lām 2001) 475.

[79] David Powers, 'On the Abrogation of the Bequest Verses' (1982) 29:3 *Arabica* 246, 254.

[80] Dabūsī (n 14) 241.

how 'the right [of inheritance] that was [previously] established by bequests for parents and relatives became clear stipulations in the inheritance [verse].'[81] The Prophet, he said, was merely commenting on how progressive revelation functioned in the case of inheritance. Dabūsī did mention that the majority of Ḥanafī scholars held that the *ḥadīth* under discussion abrogates the bequest verse.[82] Yet, he did not see fit to rebuke them or argue for the superiority of his interpretation. Nor did he need to, since his method of interpretation maintained the conclusion of the Ḥanafīs, if by different means.

The means, however, are quite significant and have results beyond the narrow discussion of bequests and inheritance. For instance, there is an important difference between the dominant reading of the prophetic reports as 'so [make] no bequests to inheritors' and Dabūsī's portrayal of the same *ḥadīth* as 'there is no need to make bequests to inheritors.' In the first reading, if a person were to make a bequest to an inheritor, that person would be in direct violation of a prophetic command. The person would be seen as acquiring sin and, perhaps, necessitating punishment. In the second reading, the same person would be erroneous, but not in contempt of prophetic command. Such a person would not be seen as sinful, but errant, and the situation might require rectification, but not punishment. Again, the justifications provided by Dabūsī for the inherited injunctions related to inheritance concern the way the law is applied, it is not an apology for why the law exists.

[81] Ibid 241.

[82] Ibid 240. Dabūsī acknowledged that the majority of Ḥanafī scholars held that the *ḥadīth* under discussion abrogated the bequest verse. He nonetheless appears undisturbed by this reality since his method of interpretation maintains the conclusion of the Ḥanafīs, even if by different means. Although he cited Abū Bakr al-Jaṣṣāṣ as also denying the abrogation of the bequest verse through the *ḥadīth*, Jaṣṣāṣ' methodology for proving that point was markedly different from Dabūsī's. Jaṣṣāṣ used a legal loophole to argue that the bequest verse was not abrogated, while Dabūsī used reinterpretation. The result was that Dabūsī's argument maintained the Ḥanafī juridical position regarding bequests to parents and relatives, while Jaṣṣāṣ was forced to deviate from the dominant Ḥanafī position slightly. It may have been a commitment to Ḥanafī jurisprudence that led Dabūsī to argue in the manner he did. By contrast, Jaṣṣāṣ was known for occasionally crafting novel jurisprudence that differed from mainstream Ḥanafī opinions, though these novel opinions were often discredited by later Ḥanafīs.

Wiping Over Footgear

The final relevant Ḥanafī position that we will examine concerning the abrogation of the Qur'ān by the *sunna* is the issue of wiping over footgear (*masḥ ʿalā al-khuffayn*). The Qur'ān requires washing feet as a part of ritual ablution in Q. 5:6, 'O you who believe, when you rise up for prayer...wash...your feet up to the ankles.' However, there are reports of Muḥammad and his Companions wiping over their footgear instead of washing their feet,[83] though these reports did not attain Dabūsī's standard of *mutawātir*. In this case, the practice of the Prophet departed from the letter of a Qur'anic imperative in that he wiped over footgear rather than washing his feet up to the ankles. In his section on additions to the text (*ziyāda ʿalā al-naṣṣ*), Dabūsī said that such a departure and reinterpretation was tantamount to abrogation.[84] The only sources of abrogation in this case, however, were transmissions that Dabūsī did not consider *mutawātir*. This posed a problem for Dabūsī, not least because Ḥanafīs in particular were staunch defenders of wiping over footgear and their position on this issue became one of the hallmarks of their school.

A J Wensinck suggested that this attitude was in response to the views of the Khārijīs and Shiʿīs who did not hold wiping over footgear to be permissible.[85] Early on, the Ḥanafīs elevated the matter to a theological level, such that if believers did not uphold the permissibility of wiping over footgear, they were suspect believers, if not unbelievers. The apocryphal creed of Abū Ḥanīfa, the *al-Fiqh al-Akbar II*, which is prefaced with the

[83] See Muḥammad ʿAbd al-Raḥmān Mubārakpūrī, *Tuḥfat al-Aḥwadhī* (al-Maktabah al-Salafiya 1963) 1:277; and for a full treatment of the issue of *masḥ ʿalā al-khuffayn* in the *aḥādīth*, particularly as related to issues of *mashhūr* and *tawātur*, see G H A Juynboll, '(Re) appraisal of Some Technical Terms in Ḥadīth Science' (2001) 8:3 *Islamic Law and Society* 303, 335ff.

[84] Dabūsī (n 14) 233. Dabūsī was neither the first nor the only Ḥanafī to make this observation. Others mentioned that in light of the Qur'anic text alone, wiping was permissible only out of necessity. However, because of the *mashhūr aḥādīth* that testify to the permissibility of wiping, one can make an addition to the text that allows for it; Aḥmad b. Sulaymān ibn Kamāl Pāshā, *al-Īḍāḥ fī Sharḥ al-Iṣlāḥ* (Dār al-Kutub al-ʿIlmiyya 2007) 55–6. Most Ḥanafīs, however, held that wiping was established by *mutawātir* reports, allowing it to abrogate the Qur'ān without any need for further justification; Jaṣṣāṣ, *Aḥkām al-Qur'ān* (ʿAbd al-Salām Shāhīn ed, Dār al-Kutub al-ʿIlmiyya 1994) 2:437; Jaṣṣāṣ, *Sharḥ Mukhtaṣar al-Ṭaḥāwī* (ʿIṣmat Muḥammad ed, Dār al-Sirāj 2010) 1:450.

[85] A J Wensinck, *The Muslim Creed: its Genesis and Historical Development* (Frank Cass 1965) 158.

statement, '[T]he foundation of God's unity and that which is correct conviction consists of [the following],' included the permissibility of wiping over footgear as its ninth tenet.[86] The permissibility of wiping over footgear is lodged in between 'We do not proclaim any Muslim to be an unbeliever on account of any sin, however great, unless he deem [the sin] to be permissible' and 'We do not say that sins will not harm the believer, nor do we say that they will cause him to remain in hell indefinitely, even if he leaves the world in a state of sin.'[87] Moreover, the widely accepted creed of the Ḥanafī scholar al-Ṭaḥāwī included the permissibility of wiping over footgear as its 76th tenet[88] out of 105 'fundamentals of the religion and faith in the Lord of the Worlds.'[89]

Given the emphasis on the permissibility of wiping over the footgear amongst Ḥanafī scholars, it is remarkable that Dabūsī made no mention of it at all. In fact, he did not discuss it in any of his extant works, which include books of *uṣūl al-fiqh*, jurisprudence,[90] and spirituality (*taṣawwuf*). This absence is in stark contrast to the ubiquitous presence of the issue of wiping over footgear in similar works by Dabūsī's contemporaries. It is normally difficult to make conclusions about a jurist's legal position from silence, but in this case the omission is glaring. In several situations Dabūsī alludes to related topics, but never takes a personal stand on this issue which is so central to Ḥanafī jurisprudence. It can be safely surmised that Dabūsī did not hold the opinion of his fellow Ḥanafī juridical scholars, but

[86] Ibid 55. [87] Ibid 55.

[88] Aḥmad b. Muḥammad al-Ṭaḥāwī, *al-'Aqīda al-Ṭaḥāwīya* (Qadīmī Kutub Khāna n.d.) 12. Nor was the importance of the doctrine limited to the Ḥanafī school. The mystic, proto-Malikī Dhu al-Nūn al-Miṣrī (d. 246/861) reportedly stated: 'Three signs [demonstrate one's adherance to] the *sunna*: wiping over footgear, regularly attending congregational prayer, and loving the pious predecessors, may God have mercy on them.' Abū 'Umar Ibn 'Abd al-Barr, *Ṣaḥīḥ Jāmiʿ Bayān al-ʿIlm* (Abū al-Ashbāl al-Zuhayrī ed, Maktabat Ibn Taymiyya 1996) 480.

[89] Ibid 5.

[90] Ahmad Atif Ahmad rightly notes that though Dabūsī's *Ta'sīs al-Naẓar* is a work of jurisprudence, it functions as a work of *takhrīj al-furūʿ 'alā al-uṣūl*; Ahmad, *Structural Interrelations of Theory and Practice in Islamic Law* (Brill 2006) xxi-xxii. Dabūsī does mention the issue of wiping over footgear in this text, but only obliquely, placing the position in the mouth of a previous Ḥanafī authority and does not support the argument; Dabūsī, *Ta'sīs al-Naẓar* (Zakariyā ʿAlī Yūsuf 1972) 99. The non-mention of the issue is particularly stark in his *Kitāb al-Manāsik min al-Asrār* (Nāyif ʿAmrī ed, Dār al-Manār 1991), wherein he mentions wiping over headgear, wiping over bandages, and the like, but never once mentions wiping over footgear.

were he to make that known he would be accused of heresy. Such prudence was well-founded, as Sarakhsī quoted al-Karkhī saying, 'I fear heresy is upon whomsoever rejects wiping over the footgear.'[91] It would be nearly impossible to harmonize the Ḥanafī opinion on the issue—which requires that a non-*mutawātir* transmission abrogate the Qur'ān—with Dabūsī's conception of abrogation. Being so unable to create an accord, we may infer that Dabūsī chose not to discuss the issue at all.

Dabūsī's approach to the *sunna* abrogating the Qur'ān is a curious one. His position does not seem to have any Ḥanafī juridical precedent, yet he maintained the central injunctions advocated by Ḥanafī jurists despite the need to engage in hermeneutical acrobatics to do so. It would seem that straightforward juridical applications of his theory would result in injunctions that he, or his compatriots, would not be comfortable with. Thus, he articulated a position that was unique and in keeping with his overall conception of the role of the *sunna* in Islamic law, but qualified his position so as to remain in fidelity with prominent injunctions in Ḥanafī jurisprudence.

Sarakhsī on the *Sunna* Abrogating the Qur'ān

Sarakhsī closely followed the formula of the Ḥanafī school when he professed that the Qur'ān could abrogate the *sunna* and vice versa.[92] He, like Dabūsī, defended the Qur'ān's ability to abrogate the *sunna* through

[91] Sarakhsī, *Kitāb al-Mabsūṭ* (Kamāl ʿInānī ed, Dār al-Kutub al-ʿIlmiyya 2001) 1:229. This appears to be a common formulation and is most likely a misattribution. The 'I fear…' preface was a common reverse-attribution, especially when arguing a doctrinal point. For instance, ʿAlāʾ al-Dīn al-Bukhārī, while arguing against Ḥanafīs who believed that a person's stated intention was of secondary importance in ritual practice, quoted Abū Ḥanīfa as saying 'I fear for the impermissibility of the prayer [of one who does not make a stated intention].' Bukhārī (n 7) 1:208. Given early reports of Abū Ḥanīfa's position on the matter, this is almost certainly a misattribution, but by using 'I fear…' Bukhārī lends his quotation rhetorical force in what is almost certainly an attempt to distance Abū Ḥanīfa from charges of being a Karrāmī or Murjiʾī; see Aron Zysow 'Two Unrecognized Karrāmī Texts' (1988) 108:4 *Journal of the American Oriental Society* 577, 581, 583. In any case, the 'I fear' prefix became very popular with regard to footgear, as evidenced by the Shāfiʿī jurist Sulaymān b. ʿUmar al-Jamal's statement, 'some Ḥanafīs fear disbelief for whoever denies that [wiping over footgear] is a foundational [matter]'; al-Jamal, *Ḥashiya al-Jamal ʿalā Sharḥ al-Minḥāj* (ʿAbd al-Razzāq Ghālib ed, Dār al-Kutub al-ʿIlmiyya 1996) 1:217.

[92] Sarakhsī, *al-Muḥarrar fī Uṣūl al-Fiqh* (n 14) 2:52.

an appeal to prophetic infallibility (ʿ*iṣma*). The Prophet could not persist in an error, and revelation would correct him when he was wrong, thus the Qurʾān would abrogate any incorrect *sunna*.[93] Sarakhsī reasoned that the *sunna* could also abrogate the Qurʾān precisely because of the implications of prophetic infallibility. He inferred from the doctrine of ʿ*iṣma* that all Prophetic actions and opinions were, in reality, unrecited revelation (*waḥy ghayr matlū*). Since God protected the Prophet from persisting in error, if the Prophet made a statement or held an opinion that was incorrect, then God would correct him through revelation. Hence, if revelation did not come to correct the Prophet, then his opinion had implicit Divine sanction. Sarakhsī thereby defended his position that the *sunna* could abrogate the Qurʾān on the grounds that the *sunna* was merely another type of revelation on par with the Qurʾān.[94]

Still, Sarakhsī recognized that the actual sayings of the Prophet and the *aḥādīth* that reported his sayings were not one and the same.[95] In order for a *ḥadīth* to abrogate the Qurʾān, one would have to have indubitable knowledge of its veracity. This status, according to Sarakhsī, was only conferred upon *aḥādīth* that were either *mutawātir* or well-established (*mashhūr*).[96] As stated earlier, Sarakhsī did not provide details about the difference between *mutawātir* and *mashhūr aḥādīth*, and at times used the terms interchangeably. This led to a collapsing of categories that allowed many *aḥādīth* to function with the legitimacy of the *mutawātir*.

Although Sarakhsī did not state this overtly, he believed that any *ḥadīth* that had more chains of transmission than a *khabar al-wāḥid* could potentially be classified as *mashhūr*. In Sarakhsī's writings, *mashhūr aḥādīth* were not sharply distinct from the *mutawātir*. Hence, any *ḥadīth* that had more than one or two chains of transmission could be considered to have the status of *tawātur*. This gave Sarakhsī a bevy of *aḥādīth* that could be used to abrogate the Qurʾān, especially when compared with Dabūsī. Dabūsī argued that only a subset of the *mashhūr* reached the level of *tawātur*, leaving him with relatively few *aḥādīth* with which to abrogate the Qurʾān. By giving all the *mashḥūr aḥādīth* the power to abrogate the Qurʾān, Sarakhsī made it much easier to defend traditional Ḥanafī

[93] Ibid 2:53. [94] Ibid 2:53. [95] Ibid 2:60. [96] Ibid 2:60.

injunctions that required such abrogation. This becomes manifest in Sarakhsī's straightforward approach to punishing adulterers, bequests and inheritance, and wiping over footgear, especially in light of Dabūsī's hermeneutical acrobatics on the same issues.

Adultery

According to Sarakhsī, the punishment for fornication laid down in the Qur'ān—that of confining the fornicators to their houses—was abrogated by the prophetic practice of stoning.[97] He enumerated some *aḥādīth* that commanded stoning the fornicator, but dismissed them as weak transmissions that cannot abrogate a Qur'anic imperative. Instead, like Dabūsī, he focused on the statement of 'Umar b. al-Khaṭṭāb wherein the latter claimed that the command for stoning was originally found in a verse of the Qur'ān. Though that verse was not included in the codex, Sarakhsī nevertheless accepted its existence as a fact and accorded it the status of *waḥy ghayr matlū*.[98] Thus, the imperative for stoning was actually revelation, albeit unrecited, that abrogated the imperatives of confinement and lashes found in the recited revelation. Unlike Dabūsī, Sarakhsī did not deliberate on the authenticity of 'Umar b. al-Khaṭṭāb's report being either *mutawātir* or *mashhūr*, but rather assumed that the report accurately represented the wording of unrecited revelation. He did not explain his reasons for assuming the report to be true, nor did he consider any possible objection to his methodology. Consequently, Sarakhsī was able to provide a simple theoretical justification for the traditional Ḥanafī injunction that held stoning to abrogate the Qur'anic punishment for fornication, though such simplicity required him to completely ignore the complex issues related to according revelatory status to single transmissions.

Bequests

With regard to the bequest verse and the inheritance verse, Sarakhsī was unambiguous. He said that the *ḥadīth* of the Prophet, '... so make no

[97] Ibid 2:56. [98] Ibid 2:55.

bequest to inheritors' abrogated the bequest verse completely.[99] This was so because Sarakhsī granted the *ḥadīth* the status of *mashhūr*.[100] He did not explain why the *ḥadīth* was considered *mashhūr*, but stated it as fact. Moreover, he repudiated those who would say that the *ḥadīth* only explained the bequest verse rather than completely abrogating it. He was adamant that the verse was forever abrogated and could never be put into practice because of the presence of the *mashhūr ḥadīth* that nullified its application.[101] In this case, Sarakhsī demonstrated the abrogating power of *mashhūr aḥādīth* and maintained the traditional Ḥanafī juridical opinion on the matter.

Wiping Over Footgear

Wiping over the footgear was a seminal matter for Sarakhsī as it was for most Ḥanafī scholars. He mentioned it in several places in his *uṣūl al-fiqh* work as well as in his works on jurisprudence.[102] Sarakhsī said that he considered wiping over footgear to be a practice with self-evident justification. He used the *ḥadīth* permitting wiping over footgear as proof that the *sunna* can abrogate the Qur'ān: 'We hold that it is permissible for the Qur'ān to be abrogated by the *sunna*... because of the example of the *mashhūr* report [that sanctions] wiping over the footgear.'[103] Thus, the permissibility of wiping over the footgear was used as a proof in and of itself for the ability of the *sunna* to abrogate the Qur'ān, even if the proof authenticated the principle that established it. The example of wiping over footgear also highlights the fact that, for Sarakhsī, the line between *mutawātir* and *mashhūr* was nebulous. Whereas in the quote cited above he described the report of wiping over the footgear as *mashhūr*, he described it elsewhere as *mutawātir*.[104] While this could have been a simple writing error, the inexact nomenclature that Sarakhsī utilized lent itself to imprecise categorization of *ḥadīth* reports. There is no instance in which Sarakhsī explained why a *ḥadīth* was considered *mashhūr*; he simply attached the descriptor to *aḥādīth* at his discretion.

[99] Ibid 2:54. [100] Ibid 2:54. [101] Ibid 2:55.
[102] He devoted an entire chapter to the subject in *al-Mabsūṭ* (n 91) 1:227–41.
[103] Sarakhsī, *al-Muḥarrar fī Uṣūl al-Fiqh* (n 14) 2:60. [104] Ibid 1:220.

It is impossible to determine whether this was done by design, but it is an invaluable tactic for expanding the power of the transmitted *sunna* in abrogating the Qurʾān.

CONCLUSION

As with their treatment of the Qurʾān as a source of law, Dabūsī and Sarakhsī utilized almost identical terms and worked within almost identical frameworks to come to disparate conclusions regarding the status and definition of the *sunna*. At this point, one can begin to see some underlying commitments that drive their respective legal theories. In Dabūsī's case, there is a devotion to the recipients of the law as seekers of divine intentionality. He overtly claimed to use law as a creative means for individuals in novel situations to know God. Dabūsī's treatment of the *sunna* typified that claim. In his system, the Prophet was a guide whose example left only a few, but sufficient authoritative and normative standards for future generations. These standards, often doctrinal in nature, restricted the purview of jurisprudence, but were necessary for a society to properly know God.

There is a clear minimalist thrust to Dabūsī's approach to *ḥadīth* such that jurisprudence can adapt to circumstance and was subject to fewer restrictions. The only truly authoritative and normative sources of the *sunna* in Dabūsī's system are the *mutawātir* transmissions and the *mashhūr aḥādīth* that reach the level of *tawātur*. All other *aḥādīth* can be applied or discarded as circumstance requires. Still, it is striking that Dabūsī went to great lengths to defend traditional Ḥanafī positions rather than proffer some novel conclusions that his system affords, and which incidentally would require less interpretive gymnastics. However, given his atypical justifications for these positions, his approach should be seen as a function of his social context as a jurist working within the Ḥanafī framework who wishes to maintain his credibility as a Ḥanafī legal scholar.

While working within the Ḥanafī framework, Dabūsī defined terms such that the normativity of the *sunna* is expressed as a model for emulation. Muḥammad's practice might help explain the dictates of the Qur'ān and may suggest a course of action for the jurist when deriving jurisprudence, but it rarely dictates how a jurist must apply the law. Instead, the *sunna* acts as a guideline, or perhaps a baseline, from which the jurist can come to a decision in relation to context. It is only in the rare case of the *mutawātir* or *mashhūr aḥādīth* when the *sunna* as embodied in *aḥādīth* dictates the only acceptable course of action.

In contrast, for Sarakhsī the normativity of the *sunna* expresses itself as a model for imitation. Muḥammad's practice as captured in *ḥadīth*, and especially in injunctions stemming from those *ḥadīth*, delineates acceptable courses of action in perpetuity, and a desire to enact those injunctions brings one closer to God. The best life for Sarakhsī is one in which the pristine jurisprudence articulated by his Ḥanafī predecessors plays a central role in communal practice. His framework assumed that such a community would set a singular standard for all societies, present and future.

Yet, this seems an impossible task. Dabūsī is right to criticize those who argue that it is necessary to act upon all the single transmissions if only because humans are incapable of the task. To insist that a community as a whole enact all the injunctions found in *aḥādīth* is to set the community up for failure. Sarakhsī's system is intelligible, however, in light of his discussion of the objective (*maqṣad*) of God's laws recounted in the previous chapter. In that discussion, he said that humans do not come closer to God through obedience itself, but through a willingness to be obedient. This preconception of God's purpose is vital for comprehending Sarakhsī's system, and he said as much himself.[105] Without it, his model would seem untenable; it would clearly be impossible to enumerate all the laws found in single transmissions and apply them to all places and all times. Sarakhsī's standards may be unattainably lofty, but they are also highly theoretical. Sarakhsī's perfect community does not need to enact all the injunctions in the *aḥādīth*, it only needs to desire to do so.

What we begin to see is that the two jurists justified the inherited terms and structures of Islamic legal theory to weave separate narratives.

[105] Ibid 1:7.

They are not merely discussing law and legal application, but the nature of the God–human interaction and the function of Islamic law in that relationship. Dabūsī and Sarakhsī both place law at the nexus of knowing God and fulfilling the mission of Muḥammad, but the narratives in which they situate the God–law–human interaction—in which God is testing believers either through their action or faith; in which the Qur'ān either discloses multiple potential meanings or has a single meaning disclosed by jurists; in which Muḥammad was sent to provide either foundations for emulation or injunctions for imitation—require believers to interact with the law to accomplish those tasks in significantly different ways. The way in which believers are to understand their role in the world comes into sharp relief in discussions on considered opinion (*ra'y*), wherein the fallible human enterprise of deriving law comes into direct contact with infallible dictates from God and His prophet.

3

The Limits of Considered Opinion (*Ra'y*): Analogy and Precedent

Early Ḥanafī legal scholars distinguished themselves from other major schools by embracing *ra'y* as a means for deriving Islamic jurisprudence when the Qur'ān, *sunna*, and Consensus of the community (*ijmā'*)—three sources that are hereafter referred to as 'the texts' (*nuṣūṣ*)—were silent on a legal matter.[1] The use of *ra'y*, however, was limited to two major legal concepts: *qiyās* and juristic preference (*istiḥsān*). *Qiyās* is normally translated as 'analogical reasoning' in the sense of 'syllogism' in philosophy and theology, although only a minority of legal scholars, especially those amongst the Mu'tazila, promoted such a view of *qiyās*. Ḥanafīs, by contrast, tended to define *qiyās* in a narrow manner as a comparison of novel legal cases to injunctions established by the texts.[2] In Ḥanafī legal discussions, *qiyās* could not manipulate or establish axioms, as in the case of syllogisms utilized in dialectical theology and philosophy; rather, it could only be used to derive jurisprudence in specific circumstances. *Qiyās* as a technical term of legal theory, therefore, was a legal tool that did not extend in either definition or application beyond the realm of jurisprudence; and even within that realm it played a limited role.

[1] Bernard Weiss, *The Spirit of Islam* (University of Georgia Press 2006) 66. For a complete picture of how theological and metaphysical concerns influenced the way in which Sunnī scholars restricted the use of reason in Islamic law, see Anver Emon, *Islamic Natural Law Theories* (Oxford University Press 2010).

[2] Wael Hallaq, 'Non-Analogical Arguments in Sunni Juridical *Qiyās*' (1989) 36:3 *Arabica* 286, 288.

Early Ḥanafīs allowed for *qiyās* to be abandoned in favor of an injunction that facilitated ease for the laity.[3] If a jurist (*mujtahid*) felt that an injunction resulting from *qiyās* was overly harsh or irrelevant to the case, then he was free to abandon it in favor of passing a more lenient judgment, so long as that judgment did not contradict the texts.[4] In this situation, the *mujtahid* would 'prefer' an injunction that promotes ease over a *qiyās* that causes difficulty, a process known as juristic preference (*istiḥsān*). This position elicited censure from the Shāfiʿīs, who believed that the use of *ra'y* should be limited to *qiyās* alone. They argued that *ra'y* in any form must be used minimally in order for jurisprudence to stay true to the texts and they feared that an over-reliance on human opinion would introduce corrupt interpretations.[5] Many Shāfiʿīs equated the Ḥanafī doctrine with that of the Muʿtazila, which was tantamount to proclaiming the Ḥanafīs to be heretics for promoting *istiḥsān.*[6] In the face of this criticism, the Ḥanafī conception of *istiḥsān* changed drastically.[7] By the end of the 3rd/9th century, the dominant Ḥanafī opinion was that *istiḥsān* did not involve abandoning *qiyās* in favor of a more palatable

[3] Muḥammad b. Aḥmad al-Sarakhsī, *Kitāb al-Mabsūṭ* (Kamāl ʿInānī ed, Dār al-Kutub al-ʿIlmiyya 2001) 10:151.

[4] Wael Hallaq, *A History of Islamic Legal Theories* (University of Cambridge Press 1997) 107.

[5] Ibid 108.

[6] This despite the similarity of *istiḥsān* to the Shāfiʿī theory of *istiṣlāh*. See Hallaq, *A History of Islamic Legal Theories* (n 4) 112ff.

[7] The use of *ra'y* in the derivation of Islamic jurisprudence, which involved applying independent legal reasoning (*ijtihād*) to source texts, was a hotly contested issue in the 5th/11th century; Wael Hallaq, 'Was the Gate of *ijtihād* Closed?' (1984) 16: 1 *International Journal of Middle East Studies* 19. The harshest critique of the use of *ra'y* came from the school of Dā'ūd b. ʿAlī b. Khalaf (d. 270/884). Known as 'the literalists' (*al-Ẓāhiriyya*), these scholars contended that the Qur'ān and the *sunna* provided adequate guidance for the whole of humanity for all times. They advocated strict reliance on a literal reading of the texts and sought to remove any subjectivity from the practice of *fiqh*; J-C Vadet, 'Dawud ibn Khalaf,' *Encyclopedia of Islam* (2nd edn, 1998). The clearest exposition of Ẓāhirī *uṣūl al-fiqh* came in the form of Ibn Ḥazm's (d. 456/1064) *al-Iḥkām fī Uṣūl al-Aḥkām*. In this treatise he condemned the Ḥanafīs, Shāfiʿīs, and the Muʿtazila alike for distorting the application of Islamic jurisprudence through their use of *ra'y*; Ibn Ḥazm, *al-Iḥkām fī Uṣūl al-Aḥkām* (Muḥammad ʿAbd al-ʿAzīz ed, Maktabat ʿĀṭif, 1978) 2:1424, though he also faults these groups for engaging in uncritical adherence (*taqlīd*) to their predecessors; 1:17–18. Ibn Ḥazm provoked many prominent jurists into debates regarding the validity of *ra'y* in legal reasoning, yet his opinions were marginal in the development of Islamic legal theory; R Arnaldez, 'Ibn Ḥazm,' *Encyclopedia of Islam* (2nd edn, 1998). The bulk of the debate surrounding the use of *ra'y* in the 5th/11th century concerned the divergent approaches of the Shāfiʿīs and the Ḥanafīs,

injunction, but actually involved preferring one *qiyās* over another based on circumstance.[8]

The unintended consequence of relegating *istiḥsān* to an arbiter of competing *qiyās'* was that independent legal reasoning (*ijtihād*) as a whole began to be seen amongst Ḥanafī scholars as little more than *qiyās*. Dabūsī, for example, did not reference *ijtihād* outside of *qiyās* and Sarakhsī openly warned against using reasoning apart from *qiyās*.[9] The diminished role of *ijtihād* coincided with a promotion of uncritical adherence (*taqlīd*) to historical precedent.[10] Those who championed the senescence of *ra'y* in legal reasoning argued that uncritically adhering to the findings of legal masters from previous generations made *ra'y* unnecessary. Such attempts to limit the production of new judgments reflected an anxiety about the potential for error that inevitably accompanies the use of reason. The issues of *qiyās, taqlīd,* and error were therefore intertwined, in that the more one is comfortable with the potential for jurists to err, the more space is afforded *ra'y*, and vice versa. The relationship among these concepts has a direct bearing on broader conceptions of Islamic law. If jurisprudence is an exact science that allows little or no margin for error, then *ra'y* should rightly be limited in favor of more indubitable sources of law. If, however, jurisprudence is more malleable and contingent on circumstance, then *ra'y* must play a more significant role in order to appropriately respond to context.

THE BEDROCK OF *QIYĀS*: DETERMINING THE RATIO LEGIS (*'ILLA*)

The classical Ḥanafī conception of *qiyās* has four major constitutive elements. The first is the legal injunction (*ḥukm*) taken directly from

[8] For the evolution of the idea of *istiḥsān* and related concepts amongst Ḥanafīs of the time, see Baber Johansen, 'Coutumes Locales et Coutumes Universelles' in *Contingency in a Sacred Law* (Brill 1999) 166–8.

[9] Muḥammad b. Aḥmad al-Sarakhsī, *al-Muḥarrar fī Uṣūl al-Fiqh* (Ṣalāḥ b. Muḥammad ed, Dār al-Kutub al-'Ilmiyya 1996) 2:95.

[10] Muhammad Fadel, 'The Social Logic of Taqlīd and the Rise of the Mukhtaṣar' (1996) 3:2 *Islamic Law and Society* 193, 194.

a text—meaning the Qur'ān, *sunna*, or *ijmā'*—which functions as the major premise (*kubrā*), that which is 'known.' The *mujtahid* examines the injunction and then tries to determine a *ratio legis* (*'illa*) that reveals the logic that grounds the injunction.[11] This *'illa* is the second element of *qiyās*, although exactly how to determine the *'illa* is a matter of dispute, as will be seen below. Regardless, once the *'illa* is determined, it is applied to the third element of *qiyās*: a novel legal case that the text does not directly address. This novel case functions as the minor premise (*ṣughrā*)—the 'unknown.' Finally, the *mujtahid* is charged with deriving an injunction that addresses the novel case. So he examines the novel case and tries to identify the underlying *'illa*, and then links it to an already established injunction that shares the same *'illa*. Once that shared *'illa* is determined, the *mujtahid* can argue that it should apply to the novel case just as it does to the established injunction.[12] The *'illa* is then applied to the novel case to produce a new injunction. This new injunction is the fourth element of *qiyās* and functions as the conclusion (*natīja*) of the syllogism. The process is then repeated for all novel cases that the texts either address only implicitly or do not address at all.[13]

The most controversial and imprecise element in this process of *qiyās* is determining a divine *'illa* behind the legal injunctions in the texts. Ḥanafī theorists historically differed on how to determine the *'illa*, and whether the extrapolated *'illa* was an accurate reflection of the divine intention, and the extent to which believers were bound to accept and follow new injunctions derived from that *'illa* through *qiyās*.[14] These arguments concerned the status of new laws derived through *qiyās* compared to those laws that are explicitly stated in the texts (*nuṣūṣ*). The extent to which scholars viewed the *'illa* as an accurate reflection of the divine intention influenced the status that they accorded *qiyās* as a source of Islamic jurisprudence.

[11] Nebil Shehaby, ''Illa and Qiyās in Early Islamic Legal Theory' (1982) 102:1 *Journal of the American Oriental Society* 27, 34.
[12] Wael Hallaq, 'The Logic of Legal Reasoning in Religious and Non-Religious Cultures: The Case of Islamic Law and the Common Law' (1985–86) 34 *Cleveland State Law Review* 79, 88.
[13] Wael Hallaq, 'Non-Analogical Reasoning' (n 2) 287.
[14] Aron Zysow, 'Mu'tazilism and Māturīdism in Ḥanafī Legal Theory' in Bernard Weiss (ed), *Studies in Islamic Legal Theory* (Brill 2002) 248.

Dabūsī on Determining the *Ratio Legis*

Dabūsī defined *qiyās*, at its most basic level, as positing a link between two apparently disconnected items.[15] He recognized the importance of *qiyās* to dialectical theology and philosophy in the form of categorical syllogisms, but stated that *qiyās* plays a different role and has different rules when applied to religious practice (*ʿibādāt*). The first major difference between the two concerns the application of *qiyās* to theology. Dabūsī prohibited the use of *qiyās* to any matters pertaining to God or His attributes,[16] meaning that one could not make conclusions about God by positing analogies about His attributes. Rather, *qiyās* could only pertain to matters that had practical ramifications for personal and societal laws (*muʿāmalāt*).[17] Another point of distinction between categorical syllogism and *qiyās* as utilized in jurisprudence was that categorical syllogisms were based either on axioms that theologians viewed as self-evident or on corollaries derived from other syllogisms that were themselves based on axioms. In contrast, Dabūsī held that *qiyās* in Islamic jurisprudence could only use as its source (*aṣl*) a text from the Qurʾān or *sunna* or the *ijmāʿ* of the Companions of the Prophet,[18] not on any kind of 'self-evident axiom.' To use any non-textual source as a foundation would invalidate a *qiyās*' juridical application.

Moreover, Dabūsī restricted *qiyās* to only one iteration—the injunction resulting from a *qiyās*, no matter how valid, could not be used as a basis for a subsequent *qiyās*.[19] All analogies had to stem from the texts (*nuṣūṣ*) and an injunction resulting from *qiyās* did not itself become a source on par with the texts. The one exception to this rule was when the contemporaneous community agreed to the validity of a *qiyās* by Consensus (*ijmāʿ*). In that case, Dabūsī said that the *qiyās* changes its status as a source of law from considered opinion (*raʾy*) to Consensus (*ijmāʿ*) with regard to its application in jurisprudence. Since *ijmāʿ* was one

[15] Abū Zayd al-Dabūsī, *Taqwīm al-Adilla* (Khalīl al-Mays ed, Dār al-Kutub al-ʿIlmiyya 2001) 278.
[16] Ibid 190.
[17] Nebil Shahaby (n 11) 44.
[18] Dabūsī (n 15) 279.
[19] Ibid 279.

of the foundational texts, it could then be used as the basis for a future *qiyās*.

The major premises upon which *qiyās* should be based must be found in the Qur'ān, *sunna*, or *ijmā*ʿ because all injunctions contained within those sources were considered to be indubitable expressions of the divine will. As such, each injunction contained therein was sure to have a divinely-ordained underlying *ratio legis* (*ʿilla*). Dabūsī contended that the *ʿilla* is a divinely sanctioned rationale, of which particular injunctions (*aḥkām*) are mere instantiations.[20] Theoretically, then, if one could ascertain the divine *ʿilla* behind a particular injunction, then that *ʿilla* could be brought to bear on novel legal cases concerning which a *mujtahid* could not find explicit legal prescriptions in the texts. By connecting the *ʿilla* to the novel case, the *mujtahid* could produce a new injunction through *qiyās*.

Dabūsī proposed that the *ʿilla* be determined by examining the revealed texts (*nuṣūṣ*) and finding within them attributes (*awṣāf*, sing. *waṣf*) characterizing their injunctions.[21] The *waṣf* found in a particular legal verse of the Qur'ān or a *ḥadīth* of the Prophet would invariably point to the *ʿilla* behind the injunction contained in the text. Dabūsī acknowledged that determining the *ʿilla*, despite identifying the *waṣf*, is inherently an inexact science. For any particular injunction and its *waṣf* there is indeed one divine *ʿilla* that generates indubitable knowledge in its veracity (*ʿilla huwa wāḥid ʿinda Allāh taʿālā mūjib lil-ʿilm qaṭʿan*).[22] However, humans can only conjecture through their understanding of the *waṣf* as to the *ʿilla*, and they run the risk of being incorrect.

By way of illustration, Dabūsī compared the *waṣf* to a report (*khabar*) that relates a saying of the Prophet, and compared the *ʿilla* to the original prophetic saying that the *khabar* purports to relate.[23] The original prophetic saying generates indubitable knowledge as to its veracity and if one were to hear it first-hand then they would be bound to accept it and act upon its injunctions. However, when the reports of this original prophetic saying are passed down from generation to generation, they admit an element of conjecture due to the vagaries of the transmission

[20] Ibid 272. In its application to legal cases, the *ratio legis* is not bound by the instantiation, just as a *ratio decidendi* is not bound by the judgment it determines.
[21] Ibid 270. [22] Ibid 273. [23] Ibid 273.

process. Thus, the transmitted report cannot require action (*lam yajib al-ʿamal bi-hā*)[24] because of its conjectural nature unless it is externally authenticated.

In the same way, Dabūsī said that one could never be certain that the *ʿilla* one has determined through reflection (*taʾammul*) on the *waṣf* is the true *ʿilla* because discursive reasoning is not an indubitable source of knowledge. Since *qiyās* is always based upon an *ʿilla*, and the *ʿilla* is always conjectural, Dabūsī concluded that the *qiyās* of one jurist did not have binding authority on any other jurist.[25] Rather, *qiyās* can provide the jurist with peace of mind (*ṭumʾanīnat al-qalb*) that he is living in fidelity with the divine law.[26] To demonstrate his sincerity, a *mujtahid* who formulates a *qiyās* must follow the injunctions resulting from that *qiyās*, as must his followers. But the *qiyās* determined by one *mujtahid* is not authoritative for the community at large, and its resulting injunction need not be followed by other *mujtahid*s or their followers.

Dabūsī's conclusions about the applicability of an injunction derived from *qiyās* rest on his belief that the *ʿilla* cannot be known with perfect certainty. In the absence of a method for ascertaining certainty, Dabūsī provided rules for determining the relative veracity of a possible *ʿilla*. He instructed *mujtahids* to rely on the *waṣf* in the body of the text to determine the *ʿilla* whenever possible.[27] Sometimes the *waṣf* provided in the text points to the *ʿilla* in an obvious manner, requiring minimal reflection (*aqall al-taʾammul*) to determine the *ʿilla* that establishes the injunction.

According to Dabūsī, this was the case with the text that establishes the need for ritual ablution due to bleeding. In the relevant text, ʿĀʾishah, the wife of Muḥammad reported,

> Fāṭima bint Abī Ḥubaysh approached the Prophet and said, 'O Messenger of God, I am a woman with a prolonged menstrual period, so I am [regularly] in a state of ritual impurity. Should I leave off prayer?' The Prophet responded, 'No, surely that [blood is from a ruptured] vein, not from menstruation, so

[24] Ibid 273. [25] Ibid 272. [26] Ibid 272. [27] Ibid 304.

> when you complete your menstrual cycle, perform your prayers. And whenever blood comes out [thereafter], wash it off and pray.[28]

Dabūsī said that the clear *waṣf* in this case was bleeding due to a ruptured vein that caused the flow of blood. This flow of blood from the ruptured vein was therefore the *ʿilla* for the Prophet's command to 'wash it off,' which Dabūsī interpreted to mean 'perform ritual ablution.'[29] Having determined the *ʿilla*, a jurist can use *qiyās* to formulate judgments in cases involving the need for ritual ablution due to bleeding from a ruptured vein in other parts of the body. For example, if a vein in one's nose ruptured and resulted in bleeding, one could use *qiyās* based on the *ʿilla* of the ruptured vein found in the *hadīth* to say that ritual ablution would be necessary. However, the *qiyās* would not extend to a woman on her menses because the *ʿilla* of the ruptured vein is not present. To determine whether or not a woman on her menses was required to make ritual ablution, the *mujtahid* would have to find some other text or make a different *qiyās*. Despite the fact that the *waṣf* found in the text above clearly delineated the *ʿilla*, Dabūsī stated that the *ʿilla* is still not known with absolute certainty because determining the *ʿilla* involved reflection and thought upon the *waṣf*.[30] Nevertheless, he said that extrapolating the *ʿilla* from the text was the only means available to the *mujtahid*.

Dabūsī recognized that the *waṣf* rarely appears in the text itself and that the *ʿilla* usually has to be extracted through discursive reasoning (*naẓar*). He likened the process of extracting the *ʿilla* under such circumstances to determining the intended referent (*waḍʿ*) in a metaphor (*istiʿāra*).[31] Just as the referent of a metaphor can only be inferred by someone with an intimate knowledge of language, so can the *ʿilla* only be inferred by a scholar of law (*ṣāḥib al-sharīʿa*). Further, just as one cannot have absolute

[28] Muḥammad b. ʿĪsā al-Tirmidhī, *Jāmiʿ al-Tirmidhī* (ʿĀdil Murshid ed, Dār al-Aʿlām 2001) 34–5. Dabūsī was not given to paraphrasing *aḥādīth*, but in this case he paraphrased the above *ḥadīth* twice, both times adding terms. Whereas in the *ḥadīth*, Muḥammad is reported as saying, 'No, surely that is [from a] vein (*ʿirq*),' Dabūsī quotes Muḥammad once saying, 'Surely it is veinal blood (*damm ʿirq*), [so] perform ablution for each prayer' (p 133) and once saying, 'Surely it is blood from a ruptured vein (*damm ʿirq infajar*), [so] perform ablution for each prayer.' (p 292) Dabūsī clearly meant to highlight the veinal origin of the bleeding, and so I included that intention in brackets in the translation of the *ḥadīth* cited above.

[29] Dabūsī (n 15) 292. [30] Ibid 272. [31] Ibid 268.

certainty regarding the intended referent in a metaphor, according to Dabūsī, so can the *mujtahid* never have certainty in his having identified the correct *ʿilla*.[32] Consequently, *qiyās* based on an *ʿilla* that is derived through tedious deliberation is far removed from generating either indubitable knowledge or action. To the contrary, Dabūsī argued that this *qiyās* is relegated to the level of verses of the Qur'ān that admit multiple interpretations (*mu'awwalāt*) and single transmissions from the Prophet (*khabar al-wāḥid*).[33] Thus, a *mujtahid* can only argue for the strong likelihood (*ghalabat al-ra'y*) of having identified the correct *ʿilla* upon which to base his *qiyās*.[34] In effect, the jurist can only reach a conjectural conclusion based on *qiyās*, unlike the certainty generated by injunctions found in the revealed texts (*nuṣūṣ*).

With regard to determining the likelihood of the *ʿilla*'s veracity, Dabūsī believed that the most reliable measure of an *ʿilla*'s likelihood is its effect (*ta'thīr*) on jurisprudence.[35] This effect is evaluated based on two criteria. First, the resulting injunction must not contradict an explicit text (*naṣṣ*) from the Qur'ān, *sunna*, or *ijmāʿ*. Since determining the *ʿilla* requires the use of human intellect, the injunction derived therefrom is seen as inferior to that found in the texts.[36] Therefore, if *qiyās* contradicts a text, then that contradiction is proof that the *ʿilla*—and by extension the *qiyās*—is invalid (*fāsid*). Second, the *ʿilla* must serve as a transitive (*mutaʿaddī*) cause for all other related cases in Islamic jurisprudence.[37] That is, once an *ʿilla* has been extracted from an injunction, it must serve as an *ʿilla* to all comparable injunctions. The principle of concomitance (*iṭṭirād*) encapsulated this idea by holding that when the *ʿilla* for an injunction was known then all similar injunctions would possess the same *ʿilla*.[38]

Dabūsī used the example of ritual fasting, in particular that which causes a fast to be invalid, to illustrate transitivity and concomitance. Q. 2:186 states that, when fasting, one is allowed to eat until dawn, after which one must fast until dusk. Given the *waṣf* in the text, it is easy to

[32] Ibid 286.
[33] Ibid 269.
[34] Ibid 269.
[35] Ibid 270.
[36] Ibid 280.
[37] Ibid 271.
[38] Ibid 312.

conclude that the *ʿilla* for invalidating the fast is ingestion of some foodstuff between dawn and dusk. Once that *ʿilla* is determined, any and all ingestion of foodstuff in daylight hours must, in all circumstances, invalidate the fast without exception. Failure for the *ʿilla* to serve as a transitive cause to all related cases would invalidate the *ʿilla* and would prove that the *mujtahid* derived the wrong *ʿilla* from the text.[39]

The *ʿilla* derived from the above Qur'anic text tests the principle of concomitance because it potentially contradicts an injunction in a different text taken from the *sunna*. Specifically, if the fasting individual ate during the day out of forgetfulness, then his fast would not be invalid according to the *ḥadīth*, 'Whoever forgets he is fasting and eats and drinks [out of forgetfulness] is to complete his fast, for it is Allah who fed him and gave him drink.'[40] If the *ʿilla* of invalidating the fast as derived from the Qurʾān were applied to the case of the unmindful, then the text of the *ḥadīth* would be violated. Normally, this would signal that the *ʿilla* derived from the Qurʾanic text was invalid.

Dabūsī attempted an important, and ultimately controversial, reconciliation by arguing that the *ʿilla* of ingestion does indeed invalidate the fast and, at the same time, eating out of forgetfulness does not invalidate the fast.[41] He defended this apparent violation of the principle of concomitance by first affirming that the *ʿilla* of ingestion invalidating the fast was correctly determined because it was derived directly from the *waṣf* in the text. He then suggested that the contradiction that arises when a person eats out of forgetfulness is not due to an incorrectly derived *ʿilla*, but rather due to an impediment (*mānīʿ*) that inhibited the application of an otherwise sound *ʿilla*.[42] The impediment in the above case is the forgetfulness of the faster. The *ʿilla* remained operative because ingestion does indeed violate the fast, but that *ʿilla* could not be applied because of the impediment of forgetfulness on the part of the faster. Dabūsī explained that many jurists erroneously assumed that concomitance meant that a soundly derived *ʿilla* would always

[39] Ibid 294.
[40] Yaḥyā b. Sharaf al-Nawawī, *Sharḥ Saḥīḥ al-Muslim* (Wahbah al-Zuḥaylī ed, Dār al-Khayr 1998) 8:222.
[41] Dabūsī (n 15) 314.
[42] Ibid 310.

produce a related injunction whenever the cause obtained, regardless of circumstance. He countered that, due to an impediment, the *ʿilla* may obtain though not its injunction (*mawjūd ʿilla wa-lā ḥukm*).[43] The impediment does not invalidate the *ʿilla* because the *ʿilla* is determined without concern for impediments or deficient[44] circumstances (*al-ʿilla tūjad ṣaḥīḥa dūn al-ḥukm li-māniʿ aw nuqṣān shayʾ*).[45]

For example, ownership of taxable property is an *ʿilla* for the payment of tax. Hence, ownership of property that is valued above the exemption limit (*al-niṣāb*) obliges one to pay tax on that property.[46] However, the *ʿilla* requiring the payment of taxes is present even before the tax year concludes. Therefore, the remaining time until the tax year concludes is an impediment to paying taxes although the *ʿilla* is present due to the ownership of taxable property.[47] In this case, as with the case of fasting, Dabūsī argued that impediments and deficient circumstances do not affect the soundness of the *ʿilla*. If the impediment were removed, then the *ʿilla* would be applicable.[48] In other words, the *ʿilla* is determined and serves as a transitive cause only in ideal cases. Dabūsī said that it should not be supposed that the *ʿilla* is unsound or was improperly derived because of impediments, but rather that it has been limited (*takhaṣṣa*) due to circumstance. Dabūsī concluded that circumstance could cause a limitation of the *ʿilla* (*taskhṣīṣ al-ʿilla*) that does not invalidate the *ʿilla* itself.[49]

Determining the *ʿilla* may seem like a convoluted enterprise dominated by technicalities. But once the technical terms are understood, the substantive argument is quite simple. Dabūsī held that for every injunction there is an *ʿilla* that is known by God. *Mujtahids* can try to determine the *ʿilla*, preferably through a *waṣf* in the text. Failing that, they can attempt to derive the *ʿilla* by engaging in independent reasoning (*ijtihād*). The veridical probability of an *ʿilla* derived through *ijtihād* is judged by its concordance with injunctions found in the Qurʾān, *sunna*,

[43] Ibid 312.
[44] I have translated *nuqṣan* as 'deficient' based on the *fiqhī* principle of the *nuqṣān* of property, which Baber Johansen's translates as 'deterioration' in Johansen, 'A Response to Ann Elizabeth Mayer' (1992) 24 *International Journal of Middle East Studies* 553, 554.
[45] Dabūsī (n 15) 310. [46] Ibid 310. [47] Ibid 310.
[48] Ibid 315. [49] Ibid 312.

and *ijmāʿ*, as well as its legal effect (*taʾthīr*), most notably in its ability to serve as a transitive cause to all analogous injunctions. Though the *ʿilla* must serve as a transitive cause, its injunction might be exanimate if circumstantial impediments prevent the application of the *ʿilla*. This situation, known as 'limitation of the *ratio legis*' (*takhṣīṣ al-ʿilla*), does not invalidate the *ʿilla* because the *ʿilla* is independent from circumstantial concerns.

This conception of the *ʿilla*, with its relative likelihood and contextual caveats, suggests a disconnect between God's divinely ordained law and jurisprudence as practiced in society. Dabūsī held that God knows the *ʿilla*s that underlie all injunctions, but jurists can never know those *ʿilla*s with certainty. Furthermore, even after conjecturing about the *ʿilla* and proving that it applies to all analogous cases, circumstance may prevent its application. Dabūsī did not view this disconnect with the original divine intention as problematic, instead taking for granted that the jurisprudence that *mujtahid*s articulate is largely conjectural. Far from being a dilemma, he viewed the resulting imperfect jurisprudence as meritorious in the sight of God, as will be seen.

Sarakhsī on Determining the *Ratio Legis*

In his discourse on determining the *ʿilla*, Sarakhsī mirrored Dabūsī almost step-by-step. He, too, posited that behind every legal injunction in the Qurʾān, *sunna* and *ijmāʿ* was a divine *ratio legis* that provided the underlying logic for the injunction. This *ʿilla* could not be known with certainty, but could be derived from the *waṣf* present in the text through a *mujtahid*'s reflection (*taʾammul*). Though the *ʿilla* thus determined could not generate indubitable knowledge in its veracity, a jurist could have peace of mind (*ṭumʾanīnat al-qalb*) that it was correct. The *ʿilla* could then be applied to all analogous cases through *qiyās*. Though the true *ʿilla* for any single case cannot be known with certainty, its likelihood can be measured through its effect (*taʾthīr*). The effect of an *ʿilla* is measured based on its non-contradiction of the texts (*nuṣūṣ*) and in its serving as a transitive (*mutaʿaddī*) cause to all analogous cases. Sarakhsī was a staunch proponent of the doctrine of concomitance (*iṭṭirād*) and argued that whenever the *ʿilla* is known, all analogous injunctions (*aḥkām*) must be operative.

On the face of it, Sarakhsī's conception of determining the *ʿilla* appears to mimic Dabūsī's. However, there is a subtle difference that proves to be a crucial point of departure. Whereas Dabūsī spoke of a jurist having peace of mind in the soundness of the *qiyās* he derives, Sarakhsī says that a *mujtahid* can have peace of mind in the *ʿilla* he determines. The implications of this seemingly minor difference are far-reaching.

For Sarakhsī, the process of determining the *ʿilla* from the *waṣf* was spiritual and transformative. The *waṣf* itself was apparent (*ẓāhir*) in a legal text and rather easy to identify, but the *ʿilla* was concealed (*ghāʾib*) from the senses (*maḥsūs*). That meant that the *mujtahid* would have to access the unseen in order to determine the *ʿilla*. Dabūsī would argue that trying to access the unseen introduces conjecture into the process, which directly undermines the authoritativeness of the resulting injunction. Sarakhsī, in contrast, argued that 'the mind is able to perceive the unseen through reflection (*taʾammul*).'[50] He believed that reflection could ultimately lead a jurist to 'perceive' the *ʿilla* with a level of certainty that grants him peace of mind. This method begins with a sincere *mujtahid* who reflects on the text in search of the *ʿilla*. He continues this reflection on the inner meanings of the text until his bosom achieves a state of repose (*taʾammul fī al-maʿnā al-manṣūṣ ḥattā waqif ʿalayhi inshirāḥ ṣadrihi*). This repose arrives because 'the light that God placed in the bosom of every Muslim' perceives by reflecting the light that 'God placed [within] the *sharīʿa*.'[51] Once the *mujtahid* uses the light in his bosom to perceive the light in the *sharīʿa*, he can have peace of mind regarding the *ʿilla* he determines. Since the *ʿilla* will then be articulated only through the aid of reflection, its veracity cannot be known with indubitable knowledge. Yet, according to Sarakhsī, that which gives peace of mind requires action upon its dictates, as was seen in his treatment of the *khabar al-wāḥid*. Therefore, the legal injunctions derived from the *ʿilla*s determined by sincere *mujtahid*s through *qiyās* require action from believers.[52]

[50] Sarakhsī, *al-Muḥarrar fī Uṣūl al-Fiqh* (n 9) 2:100. [51] Ibid 2:100.
[52] Ibid 2:122.

The manner in which Sarakhsī described the derivation of the *ʿilla*—through a connection forged by reflection between the internal light of the scholar and the light in the *sharīʿa*—indicates that he believed that the *sharīʿa* could always provide the one, true answer to any novel case by disclosing to pious *mujtahid*s the one, true *ʿilla* intended by God. As a result, Sarakhsī was deeply suspicious of anything that suggested that the derived *ʿilla* was somehow dissolute in its effect (*taʾthīr*) of serving as a transitive cause. If God intended the *ʿilla* both in the texts and in the bosom of the *mujtahid*, then any restriction on that effective cause in serving as a transitive cause would impugn God's ability to provide universal ideals. In that spirit, Sarakhsī railed against proponents of the doctrine of 'limitation of the *ratio legis*' (*takhṣīs al-ʿilla*). He argued that if deficient circumstances (*nuqṣān*) limit the *ʿilla*, then those circumstances are in fact limiting God's ability to legislate. For Sarakhsī, the ability of the *ʿilla* to serve as a transitive cause was a reflection of divine ability and so must not be limited in any way.

To ensure that God's ability is not limited, Sarakhsī argued for strict adherence to the doctrine of concomitance. He repeatedly asserted that 'the absence (*inʿidām*) of the injunction (*ḥukm*) [is in fact evidence of] the absence of the *ʿilla*'[53] and vice versa. This, he said, was because the *ʿilla* is latent in the *sharīʿa* itself; therefore, saying that the *ʿilla* cannot be applied to an analogous injunction due to some impediment suggests that the *sharīʿa* itself is deficient and did not account for the impediment.[54] According to Sarakhsī, limiting the *ʿilla* was a practice of the Muʾtazila and 'those who oppose the *ahl al-sunna*.'[55]

[53] Ibid 2:157. This became something of a catchphrase amongst opponents of *takhṣīṣ al-ʿilla*; Muḥammad b. ʿAlī al-Ḥaṣkafī, *Ifāḍat al-Anwār* (Muḥammad Saʿīd Burhānī ed, n.p. 1992) 271; Muḥammad b. Walī al-Dīn al-Farfūr, *Mukhtaṣar al-Afkār* (Walī al-Dīn al-Farfūr ed, Dār al-Farfūr 2001) 205; al-Qāsim b. ʿAbd Allāh b. Quṭlubughā, *Khulāṣat al-Afkār* (Thanāʾ Allāh Zāhidī ed, Dār Ibn Ḥazm 2003) 170; Muḥammad b. ʿAbd Allāh al-Tamartāshī, *al-Wuṣūl ilā Qawāʿid al-Uṣūl* (Muḥammad Sharīf ed, Dār al-Kutub al-ʿIlmiyya 2000) 276.

[54] Sarakhsī, *al-Muḥarrar fī Uṣūl al-Fiqh* (n 9) 2:156.

[55] Ibid 2:153. Al-Farfūr made this link explicit by linking the issue of *takhṣīṣ* to *iṭṭirād* and the *taṣwīb* of the *mujtahid*. He reasoned that the Muʿtazila believed that every *mujtahid* was *muṣīb*. He denounced this as an erroneous position; rather the *mujtahid* should be seen as correct in the beginning, but not in the end. If *takhṣīṣ al-ʿilla* were permissible, then it would mean that the *mujtahid* who first determined that the *ʿilla* was legitimate because it produced concomitant injunctions as well as the later *mujtahid* who limited the *ʿilla* were both correct; Farfūr (n 53) 205. If this were the case, then two *mujtahids*

Sarakhsī explained that situations might appear to require *takhṣīṣ al-ʿilla*, but are actually cases that require the use of juristic preference (*istiḥsān*). In the case of fasting, for example, the *ʿilla* for invalidating the fast taken from the Qur'anic text is the ingestion of food. Sarakhsī agreed that the action of eating enacted by the faster invalidates the fast in all cases. However, he pointed out that the *ḥadīth* regarding forgetful eating says that eating out of forgetfulness does not invalidate the fast because God is doing the feeding. In the *ḥadīth*, Sarakhsī explained, a separate *ʿilla* of forgetful eating results in an injunction (*ḥukm*) that affirms the validity of the fast. He said that this was because the action (*fiʿl*) of feeding was enacted by God, not the faster. Thus, by arguing that this second *ʿilla* is operative in the case of the forgetful faster, Sarakhsī was able to argue that the first, Qur'anic *ʿilla* was not limited, but rather misidentified as the operative *ʿilla* in the case of forgetful eating. He placed the onus on the *mujthaid* for choosing the correct *ʿilla* over all other possible *ʿilla*s that could be applicable in any given situation. Through certain criteria, including promoting ease (*yusr*) and ensuring that derived injunctions do not contradict the texts (*iṭṭirād*), the jurist is to use *istiḥsān* to determine which *ʿilla* should be used in relevant cases.

To understand the import of Sarakhsī's departure from Dabūsī's conception of determining the *ʿilla*, it is helpful to focus on two issues. The first concerns the relationship of the *mujtahid* to the *ʿilla*. In Dabūsī's system, the *mujtahid* conjectures concerning the possible *ʿilla* given his intellectual capabilities and reflection on the *waṣf* in the text. For Sarakhsī, the jurist determines the *ʿilla* through reflection upon the texts such that he perceives the unseen with a level of certainty that generates peace of mind. The former system creates a radical indeterminacy regarding the *ʿilla* while the latter promotes an intimate certainty that the *mujtahid* attempts to capture in legal language. For Dabūsī, then, the *ʿilla* articulated by a *mujtahid* is a possibility amongst possibilities and the resulting injunctions derived from that *ʿilla* are irremediably conjectural, yet can give one peace of mind. Sarakhsī, on the other hand, promoted

arguing disparate positions would be *muṣīb*, which is the doctrine of the Mu'tazila. This explains Sarakhsī's equating those who argue for *takhṣīṣ al-ʿilla* with the Mu'tazila.

a conception of the *ʿilla* as intimately known by the *mujtahid* who has peace of mind in its validity, a peace of mind that can border on certainty if the *ʿilla* demonstrates transitivity. In that case, the jurisprudence that results is considered a close expression of God's will. This may explain why, for Dabūsī, the *qiyās* that is based upon the *ʿilla* does not require action, whereas the opposite is true for Sarakhsī.

The issue of the intimacy and knowledge of the *ʿilla* helps explain the second major point of divergence between the two scholars, that of limiting the *ʿilla* (*takhṣīṣ al-ʿilla*). Dabūsī viewed *takhṣīs al-ʿilla* as unproblematic and did not think it was in conflict with *istiḥsān*, the latter to which he devoted very little discussion. He mentioned that the principle of *istiḥsān* allowed a *mujtahid* to abandon a particular *qiyās* when circumstances demand a more relevant, competing *qiyās*. He saw *istiḥsān* working in tandem with *takhṣīṣ al-ʿilla* based on the particularities of a given situation. Sarakhsī, on the other hand, viewed *takhṣīṣ al-ʿilla* as heresy. Though he nevertheless promoted the same injunctions resulting from *qiyās* as did Dabūsī, Sarakhsī's repudiation of *takhṣīṣ al-ʿilla* and championing of *istiḥsān* discloses a deeper trend in his thought. He regularly argued for the integrity of the *sharīʿa* as a consistent and consistently applicable extension of the divine will. Failure to enact it in its entirety represented a failing of the *mujtahid* rather than a failing of the *sharīʿa*. Sarakhsī, therefore, could not abide any institutionalized limitation of any aspect of the *sharīʿa*. Dabūsī did not share Sarakhsī's concern about the universal applicability of the *sharīʿa* and thus was not similarly constrained. Both Dabūsī and Sarakhsī believed that the laws of the *sharīʿa* were underpinned by a divine logic, but their views on the ability of the *mujtahid* to grasp and apply that divine logic set their broader visions of Islamic law apart.[56]

[56] Neither Dabūsī nor Sarakhsī can be said to have upheld traditional Ḥanafī positions regarding *takhṣīṣ al-ʿilla*. Although Abū Bakr al-Jaṣṣāṣ did not deny the validity of limiting the effective cause, he mentioned that the early Ḥanafīs and some of his contemporaries (*aṣḥābinā*) held it to be an important and unproblematic legal device—indeed, Pazdawī suggested that it was a mainstay of Abū Ḥanīfa himself; Abū al-Yusr Muḥammad al-Bazdawī, *Kitāb fīhi Maʿrifat al-Ḥujaj al-Sharʿiyya* (Marie Bernand and Éric Chaumont ed, Institut Français d'archéologie Orientale 2003) 45. For his part, Jaṣṣāṣ argued that limitation of the effective cause was an unnecessary theory; Aḥmad b. ʿAlī al-Jaṣṣāṣ, *Uṣūl al-Jaṣṣāṣ* (Muḥammad Tāmir ed, Dār al-Kutub al-ʿIlmiyya 2003) 2:356. He, like Sarakhsī,

TAQLĪD OF THE *MUJTAHID*

Taqlīd can be loosely translated as 'uncritical adherence'[57] and concerns the level of fidelity that one might demonstrate to historical juridical opinions formulated by jurists engaging in *qiyās* or independent legal reasoning (*ijtihād*). A hallmark of Imāmī Shīʿīs[58] and certain Sufī groups,[59] *taqlīd* was heavily debated amongst Sunnīs. Some argued that believers needed to engage in *taqlīd* of major legal personalities,[60] others argued that one could only engage in *taqlīd* of the Companions of the Prophet,[61] and yet others argued that *taqlīd* should not be engaged in at all.[62] Of interest in the present discussion of *taqlīd* is the extent to which *mujtahids* are required to follow the opinions of their forbears, since *mujtahids* were the intended audience of legal theory manuals. The extent to which a *mujtahid* is bound by legal precedent or the positions of eminent legal personalities corresponds to his freedom to formulate novel legal injunctions. Encouraging a *mujtahid* to engage in *taqlīd* is to promote a view of Islamic law as more static, in that once a juridical injunction has been promoted by an eminent legal personality, that ruling achieves a normative status for all succeeding generations. Restricting *taqlīd*, by contrast, affords the *mujtahid* greater latitude in formulating

maintained that a proper understanding of *istiḥsān* mediated all problems otherwise requiring limitation of the cause. Māturīdī, likewise, repudiated any use of *takhṣīṣ al-ʿilla* as ascribing incoherence (*tanāquḍ*) to God; Aron Zysow, 'Muʿtazilism and Māturīdism' (n 14) 249. Interestingly, Māturīdī cited the same example of the unmindful faster, but defended his position with an argument different from Sarakhsī's. Māturīdī argued that the *ʿilla* was actually 'eating out of mindfulness' that invalidates the fast, and that 'eating out of unmindfulness' is a separate situation requiring a separate injunction, so that unmindful eating has no formal relation to invalidating the fast; Bazdawī, *Kitāb fīhi Maʿrifat al-Ḥujaj al-Sharʿiyya* (n 56) 45–6. It would therefore be impossible to say that they were either promoting or departing from Ḥanafī precedent in this issue, or that they were affirming or negating a consensus. Rather, it can be said that they each agreed with historical positions that affirmed their particular approaches to Islamic jurisprudence.

57 Sherman Jackson, 'Taqlid, Legal Scaffolding and the Scope of Legal Injunctions in Post-Formative Theory' (1996) 3:2 *Islamic Law and Society* 165, 170.

58 Abdulaziz Sachedina, *The Just Ruler in Shīʿite Islam: The Comprehensive Authority of the Jurist in Imamite Jurisprudence* (Oxford University Press 1988) 236.

59 Margaret Malamud, 'Sufi Organizations and Structures of Authority in Medieval Nishapur' (1994) 26:3 *International Journal of Middle East Studies* 427, 435.

60 Abū Ḥāmid al-Ghazālī, *al-Mustaṣfā fī ʿIlm al-Uṣūl* (Muḥammad ʿAbd al-Shāfī ed, Dār al-Kutub al-ʿIlmiyya 2000) 368.

61 Fadel, 'The Social Logic of Taqlīd and the Rise of the Mukhtaṣar' (n 10) 20.

62 Fazlur Rahman, *Islam* (University of Chicago Press 1979) 196.

legal injunctions, and suggests that Islamic law may look different depending on the context in which it is applied.

Dabūsī on *Taqlīd*

Dabūsī prefaced his discussion of *taqlīd* by differentiating between the *taqlīd* of laypersons and jurists. He encouraged laypersons to identify a jurist to follow in matters of dispute and uncritically adhere to his judgments.[63] Dabūsī did not detail the characteristics of an archetypal *mujtahid* whom the laity should seek out, but simply said that they should follow one who is just (*ʿādil*).[64] Laypersons are then bound by the *ijtihād* of the *mujtahid* whom they follow, if only because they are not equipped to weigh the merits of competing juridical opinions. However, when discussing the need for *mujtahid*s themselves to engage in *taqlīd*, Dabūsī contended that the *ijtihād* of any jurist living in a generation after the Companions was not binding upon any other jurist.[65] Hence, *mujtahids* were actually forbidden from uncritically adhering to the juridical opinions of any personality who lived after the generation of the Companions.

Dabūsī acknowledged that his position ran counter to those of some of the Ḥanafī legal masters who held that, at the very least, a jurist should engage in *taqlīd* of the generation after that of the Companions of the Prophet, known as the Successors, in addition to *taqlīd* of the Companions themselves.[66] Some argued further that the views of eminent Ḥanafī jurists warranted uncritical adherence. Dabūsī responded that the revealed texts (*nuṣūṣ*) did not give the generation of the Successors any special status,[67] and so there was no reason to uncritically adhere to their opinions. By extension, the texts did not merit the founders of legal schools and eminent legal figures any special status and therefore their opinions do not warrant uncritical adherence, even by jurists who identify with their school. This meant that self-identified members of a school of law were not bound by the juridical opinions of their school

[63] Dabūsī (n 15) 413. [64] Ibid 413. [65] Ibid 256.
[66] Ibid 256. [67] Ibid 257.

and could either promote the opinions of a past authority or construct a novel opinion in response.[68] Thus, the jurist was not constrained by conformity to the thought of personalities or loyalty to a legal school when articulating jurisprudence.

If we expand this logic, legal schools are not set apart based on their adherence to eminent legal figures. Rather, a legal school is defined by the methodology that it utilizes to derive that jurisprudence. This echoes Dabūsī's opinion regarding interpretation of the Qur'ān; namely, that it is not as important to arrive at the correct interpretation as it is to utilize a sound hermeneutical method. It is important to remember here that even though Dabūsī's rhetoric argued for possible non-conformity to historical injunctions, he rarely deviated from the received Ḥanafī jurisprudential tradition.

Dabūsī made an exception, however, for the generation of the Companions regarding *taqlīd*. He acknowledged that amongst Ḥanafī jurists there was much debate surrounding the status of individual opinions from the Companions as authoritative evidence for extrapolating juridical opinions. The debating parties agreed that when the Companions were in Consensus on a matter, that Consensus was a *ḥujja* for all times. But there was a multiplicity of views regarding the authoritativeness of individual opinions about which the Companions disagreed. Dabūsī took a nuanced approach to this subject that addressed the debates and concerns of his predecessors, but was not identical to any of them.

Dabūsī argued that the Companions were a special generation for two reasons. First, they enjoyed the company of Muhammad, the conduit of revelation (*ṣāḥib al-waḥy*), and received their religious instruction directly from him.[69] Secondly, Muhammad himself reportedly described the Companions as 'stars: whomsoever you follow, you will be guided.'[70] Since the texts conferred a special status upon the Companions, they were considered independent sources of guidance for the rest of humanity. Dabūsī cautioned, however, that the ability to guide does not imply infallibility. The Companions, he emphasized, were fallible and were not

[68] Ibid 257. [69] Ibid 257. [70] Ibid 256.

to be followed in every matter.[71] The frequent disagreements amongst the Companions attested to their fallibility and thus it would be difficult, if not impossible, for later jurists to determine the preponderance (*tarjīḥ*) of one Companion's opinion over another.[72] Hence, a *mujtahid* could not uncritically adhere to an opinion of a Companion or base authoritative judgments upon it alone.

Nevertheless, given their special status, the opinions of the Companions were superior to the opinions of *mujtahid*s who succeeded them. Since the opinion of a Companion is accorded unqualified preponderance over an opinion of a later *mujtahid*, Dabūsī concluded that the juridical opinions of Companions for which no conflicting opinion of another Companion could be found should refute (*radd*) a *qiyās* reached by a jurist in a succeeding generation.[73] When conflicting opinions amongst the Companions could be found, that was considered evidence that their generation did not come to an authoritative conclusion and thus their views do not exhaust the possibilities of judgment. Therefore, if the Companions were in disagreement about a juridical opinion, then the *mujtahid* was free to either follow any of their opinions or suggest a different course of action through the use of *qiyās*.[74]

Dabūsī conceded that it would be difficult to determine whether a juridical opinion of a Companion did or did not conflict with the opinion of another.[75] In order to know if there were a conflicting opinion, one would have to know all of the sayings of the Companions regarding that particular issue. Furthermore, one would have to determine whether or not the Companion changed his or her mind after issuing an opinion. Finally, the report containing the opinion of the Companion would have to have been reliably transmitted so as to mitigate concerns about the authenticity of the report. Dabūsī did not suggest that this was an impossible task, but rather stressed the need for jurists to be well versed in the opinions of the Companions in order to properly conduct *qiyās*.

[71] Ibid 258. [72] Ibid 259.

[73] This was the case because of Dabūsī's position on *ijmāʿ* wherein silence does not indicate consent. If that were the case, then a Companion's opinion for which no conflicting opinion could be found would be considered *ijmāʿ*; Rumee Ahmed, *Constructing an Islamic Legal Narrative* (PhD Diss, University of Virginia 2008) 122–9.

[74] Dabūsī (n 15) 258. [75] Ibid 257.

Failure to engage in such research might result in a *qiyās* that would be refuted by a conflicting opinion of a Companion about which the jurist was unaware. Alternatively, poor research might lead a jurist to erroneously refute a *qiyās* using a Companion's opinion, not knowing that the Companion later reversed his or her opinion, or that the position was contested by other Companions.[76]

By pointing out these possibilities for error, Dabūsī set a high standard for aspiring *mujtahids* when issuing juridical opinions. There is no reason to believe that he was suggesting that this level was unattainable because the tone of Dabūsī's argument is one of encouragement and reverence for sacred knowledge and legal scholarship. In any case, the strictures for which he advocated bound the *mujtahid* to the opinion of a Companion only in instances wherein either the Companions formed a Consensus regarding a juridical opinion or there existed only one opinion from a Companion on the subject.

Sarakhsī on *Taqlīd*

Sarakhsī agreed with Dabūsī that the Companions comprised a special generation that was blessed by God and His Prophet. No one in any subsequent generation could hope to attain their status, either as spiritual leaders or as legal guides. Sarakhsī also cited the tradition of the Prophet comparing his Companions to stars and said that the Companions were the ultimate source of guidance after the texts (*nuṣūṣ*) themselves.[77] This did not, however, mean that one could choose any Companion as an object of *taqlīd*, since the Companions often disagreed on issues. Moreover, there was an internal stratification of Companions so that some would consult others in matters of jurisprudence and some Companions would serve as judges over others. Sarakhsī said that the most obvious example of this stratification was the case of the first four caliphs of the early community serving as arbiters and judges for the rest of the Companions.[78] He said that all Muslims should uncritically adhere to the

[76] Ibid 258.
[77] Sarakhsī, *al-Muḥarrar fī Uṣūl al-Fiqh* (n 9) 2:83.
[78] Ibid 2:82.

juridical opinions of these caliphs, known as the 'Rightly-Guided' caliphs (*al-khulafā' al-rāshidūn*) on account of a prophetic tradition to that effect. Their opinions should be followed in all times and in any circumstance, except when necessity (*ḍarūra*) precludes that possibility.[79]

Sarakhsī added that all other Companions, though not objects for *taqlīd*, should nonetheless be seen as guides for later generations. Their opinions should always outweigh the opinions of later jurists. In the same vein, Sarakhsī held that the juridical opinion of any Companion should refute (*radd*) the *qiyās* of a later *mujtahid* that addresses a similar issue.[80] Whether or not the Companions agreed or disagreed on any issue, the fact that the Prophet likened them to stars meant that following any of them should result in being properly guided. Therefore, valid judgments could be reliably produced by recourse to a statement of any Companion and this method was more dependable than using independent legal reasoning through *qiyās*. *Qiyās* could only be engaged in if the relevant injunction was not previously addressed by a juridical opinion from a Companion. If there were multiple opinions on a subject from the Companions, then the *mujtahid* was free to choose one and be confident that he would be properly guided by legislating upon the ensuing injunction.[81]

Extending the logic concerning opinions of the Companions, Sarakhsī argued that *mursal aḥādīth* were also preferable to *qiyās* when deriving jurisprudence.[82] A *mursal* transmission is a report attributed to Muḥammad, but in which the name of the narrating Companion was omitted. A Successor might have misattributed the *ḥadīth* either out of simple neglect or a concerted effort to strengthen a report by placing it in the mouth of the Prophet.[83] This misattribution led many jurists to disallow *mursal aḥādīth* from contributing to the articulation of jurisprudence because either the Successor misremembered the chain of transmission or intentionally sought to falsify it. In either case, the dubiousness of the narrator led the content of the *ḥadīth* to be viewed with suspicion. Sarakhsī nevertheless embraced *mursal aḥādīth* as, if not an actual saying of the Prophet at least the opinion of a Companion as

[79] Ibid 2:82. [80] Ibid 2:85. [81] Ibid 2:83. [82] Ibid 2:87.
[83] G H A Juynboll, 'Some Notes of Islam's First Fuqahā' Distilled From Early Ḥadīth Literature' (1992) 39:3 *Arabica* 287.

narrated by a Successor. He concluded that since the purported *hadīth* was, minimally, a saying of a Companion, it was therefore preferable to the *qiyās* of a later jurist.[84] The opinions of the Companions were to be sought out and adhered to, even if the narrators who transmitted the reports were not reliable transmitters.

Sarakhsī's approach to *mursal aḥādīth* discloses a larger ethos to which he was beholden. He argued that, because of their proximity to Muḥammad, the opinions of the Companions and Successors were 'furthest removed from containing error' (*abʿad ʿan iḥtimāl al-khaṭa'*) when compared to individuals from subsequent generations.[85] This suggests that chronological distance from the time of the Prophet is causally related to degenerate reasoning and thus a higher probability of error. Sarakhsī championed this principle, arguing that jurists should defer not only to the opinions of the Companions, but also to the opinions of jurists before them.[86] If opinions from jurists of previous generations were available, then the subsequent jurists should not deviate from the possibilities already proffered. The jurist may select from amongst the previous opinions, but should not offer a new injunction unless out of necessity (*ḍarūra*).[87] Again, the ethos that underlies this thought is that historically established juridical opinions are further from error than more contemporary ideas—a view that will be explored further below. Sarakhsī captured this frame of mind by saying, 'the best thing is imitation; the worst is invention.'[88]

Sarakhsī institutionalized the power of historical juridical opinions in his treatment of *majhūl aḥādīth*. *Majhūl aḥādīth* are reports attributed to Muḥammad wherein at least one of the narrators in the chain of transmission is an unknown individual. As a result, it is impossible to conduct thorough narrator-criticism to determine whether or not the *ḥadīth* is authentic.[89] Yet, Sarakhsī preferred even these transmissions

[84] Sarakhsī, *al-Muḥarrar fī Uṣūl al-Fiqh* (n 9) 2:83.
[85] Ibid 2:85.
[86] Ibid 2:84.
[87] Sarakhsī, *Kitāb al-Mabsūṭ* (Kamāl ʿInānī ed, Dār al-Kutub al-ʿIlmiyya 2001) 16:82.
[88] Sarakhsī, *al-Muḥarrar fī Uṣūl al-Fiqh* (n 9) 1:10.
[89] Muhammad Hashim Kamali, *A Textbook of Hadith Studies* (The Islamic Foundation 2005) 186.

to the use of *qiyās* in any given situation.[90] That is because even though a narrator in the chain of transmission is unknown, it is certain that the unknown narrator lived in a previous generation, else they would be known. For Sarakhsī, the fact that the narrator lived in a previous generation seems to have been the only necessary qualification for his or her narration to be preferred over the *qiyās* of a qualified *mujtahid* of a later generation.

Sarakhsī held a deep suspicion of the intellectual capabilities of his contemporary *mujtahids*, and also a general misgiving about individuals chronologically removed from the time of the Prophet. Proximity to the Prophet is a self-sustaining check on deviance for Sarakhsī, and the march of history is only a degeneration of the pristine example set forth by the Prophet and his Companions. He exhorted later jurists to, whenever possible, recreate the pristine example by uncritically adhering to the opinions of the Companions. If the pristine early example cannot be replicated exactly, the jurist should try to replicate the example of jurists chronologically closest to the pristine example. If the early jurists did not address the matter explicitly, the jurist may engage, again out of necessity, in *istiḥsān* and, if need be, formulate a *qiyās* that results in a new injunction.[91] This, however, is the last resort; one should try not to use *ijtihād* when deriving jurisprudence if at all possible.

The issue of *taqlīd* in these discussions had direct bearing on the role of history not just in Islamic law, but also in understanding contemporary society. If a *mujtahid* subcribes to Sarakhsī's theory, then his generation is, *de facto*, degenerate, and the next generation is sure to be more degenerate than the last. Proponents of *taqlīd* often cite the decadence of the contemporary community as justification for uncritically adhering to the injunctions of the past. Uncritical adherence in this case means that one can be sure that previous injunctions, whether they are relevant or not, *should* be relevant. That is, if a previous injunction is no longer relevant, that is most likely a sign that the community has gone astray, not that a new injunction should be derived. In that conception, the

90 Ibid 2:87.
91 Sarakhsī, *al-Mabsūṭ* (n 88) 16:98.

contemporary community should strive to imitate the community that preceded it, or at least not evolve so that the injunctions of the past can no longer apply. Dabūsī's conception of *taqlīd* may appear to differ from Sarakhsī's only in that the former does not require *mujtahids* to engage in *taqlīd* of other *mujtahids* coming after the generation of the Companions.[92] But his attitude toward history is a distinction that has far more import to a *mujtahid*'s approach to the overall project of articulating Islamic law.

TAṢWĪB OF THE *MUJTAHID*

The doctrine of *taṣwīb* of the *mujtahid* was one of the rare topics about which Ḥanafī jurists explicitly argued for diverse positions. Whereas most debates were coded so as to present a veneer of uniformity within the legal school, this issue was openly debated with little regard for unanimity. *Taṣwīb* has been translated as 'imputing correctness' and 'infallibility,'[93] and describes the complex issue that concerns both the unicity of religious truth and the ability for a jurist to err. The Muʿtazila, whom the Ḥanafīs regularly set up as a straw man in this debate, are reported to have held that for any one legal issue there existed multiple truths. For them, two *mujtahids* formulating disparate legal opinions (*fatāwā*) could both be correct, or, *muṣīb* in their judgments.[94] In contrast, some Iraqi Ḥanafīs and early Ashʿarīs held that the Divine Truth is singular, yet since a *mujtahid* cannot know the Divine Truth with certainty, no one can be sure if he is correct or not. Therefore, *mujtahids* should be considered correct in all of their judgments, even if their conclusions differ, because those conclusions cannot be verified.[95] Other Ḥanafīs, like al-Māturīdī (d. 333/944), argued that a *mujtahid* who articulates an incorrect opinion is wrong 'both in the beginning and in

[92] It is noteworthy that Dabusī did not at any point identify Ḥanafī jurisprudence as authoritative. It is also noteworthy that Dabūsī did not mention that his view coincides almost exactly with that of Abū Bakr al-Jaṣṣāṣ; Jaṣṣāṣ, *al-Fuṣūl fī ʿIlm al Uṣūl* (n 56) 1:174, despite mentioning competing historical positions in Ḥanafī scholarship on the subject. This omission may have been because he was trying to align his view primarily with the early founders of the school, whom he said endorsed his position.

[93] Zysow, 'Muʿtazilism and Mīturidīsm in Ḥanafī Legal Theory' (n 14) 239ff.

[94] Ibid 244. [95] Ibid 240.

the end,'[96] suggesting that acting upon an incorrectly formulated legal opinion elicits no reward from God, and may even elicit punishment. Other Ḥanafīs held positions that fell in between the ones enumerated above. The conclusions of these jurists disclosed their outlook on the link between articulating jurisprudence and divine retribution. In the case of the Muʿtazila, different laws may reflect multiple truths, and so all the various opinions on a single issue may be meritorious. In the case of al-Māturīdī, by contrast, the *mujtahid* would only be rewarded if he articulated and followed a particular, correct legal opinion on an issue. The issue of *taṣwīb* was a medium for discussions on whether obedience to God lay in enacting specific legal injunctions or in attempting to articulate a Truth that may be instantiated through multiple channels.

Dabūsī on *Taṣwīb*

Dabūsī described his position regarding the *taṣwīb* of the *mujtahid* as mediating two extremes. The first, championed by 'a group of theologians,' held that every *mujtahid* is *muṣīb* in attaining the truth.[97] This meant that, despite differences in opinion, all *mujtahids* articulated Divine Truth in their attempts to formulate Islamic jurisprudence. The conclusion that these theologians came to was that Divine Truth was composed of diverse, equally valid truths (*al-ḥaqq ʿinda Allāh ḥuqūq al-tasāwī*) that could be expressed by context-specific injunctions.[98] Dabūsī rejected this position and said that, to the contrary, there is a singular Divine Truth that *mujtahids* are constantly attempting to articulate through jurisprudence. The second extreme that Dabūsī attempted to moderate held that since the Divine Truth is singular there can be only one true articulation of Islamic jurisprudence.[99] Those who held this opinion argued that any articulation of jurisprudence that does not reflect the singular Divine Truth must be erroneous (*khaṭa'*) and action upon such erroneous jurisprudence is, by definition, erroneous.

[96] Muḥammad b. Aḥmad al-Samarqandī, *Mizān al-Uṣūl fī Natā'ij al-ʿUqūl* ('Abd al-Mālik Saʿdī ed, Wizārat al-Awqāf 1987) 2:1051.
[97] Dabūsī (n 15) 407.
[98] Ibid 408. [99] Ibid 407.

Dabūsī faulted both of the above positions for creating false expectations of the *mujtahid*. Both assume that the *mujtahid* is expected to articulate the Divine Truth when formulating a juridical opinion. Dabūsī countered that the *mujtahid* is instead only expected to use the tools of *uṣūl al-fiqh* to provide an opinion that has a strong probability (*ghalabat al-ra'y*) of reflecting the Divine Truth.[100]

Dabūsī suggested that the erroneous logic that governed the two extreme positions was based on a misunderstanding of a *mujtahid*'s responsibility (*taklīf*). God, he said, had sole knowledge of Divine Truth, which no human can grasp in its entirety. Thus, it would be outside of the capacity (*wus'*) of the *mujtahid* to know and articulate the Divine Truth with certainty. Dabūsī concluded, therefore, that the *mujtahid* was never expected to articulate the Divine Truth in the first place (*lā yukallifuhum iṣābat al-ḥaqq 'inda Allāh*).[101] Rather, the *mujtahid* was responsible for engaging in *ijtihād* to approximate the Divine Truth.

Approximating the Truth meant that God would not judge the *mujtahid* based on his ability to articulate the Divine Truth, but based on the proper execution of a sound process of deriving injunctions.[102] Whether the injunction accurately reflected the Divine Truth was a secondary matter for Dabūsī. He cited a Prophetic tradition to argue that if an injunction that a *mujtahid* derived were incorrect (*khaṭa'*) then he would nevertheless receive a reward (*ajr*) from God for his effort, and if he were correct (*aṣāba*) then he would receive double-reward (*ajrān*) from God.[103] He further argued that only God can assess the validity of a legal opinion (*fatwā*) and so humans should be concerned with the process rather than with the injunctions themselves.[104] Dabūsī attempted to mediate the two extreme positions by affirming that there is only one Divine Truth concerning a legal matter, but that the Divine Truth can never be known with certainty.

Dabūsī defended his proposed mediation by appealing to the logical consequences for the layperson (*'āmmī*). If there were multiple truths, then laypersons would have license to pick and choose injunctions in

[100] Ibid 408.
[101] Ibid 410.
[102] Ibid 412.
[103] Ibid 409.
[104] Ibid 412.

accordance with their whims (*hawā*) and would have no incentive to follow learned jurists. Even if they were to look to jurists for direction, it is likely that the laity would actively seek out positions that accord with their whims and would pressure *mujtahid*s to forgo executing a sound methodology in favor of deriving propitious injunctions. To prevent a deluge of poorly-reasoned, yet popular juridical opinions, Dabūsī said that the laity must have confidence that *mujtahid*s are *muṣīb* in their judgments and that the business of approximating the Divine Truth should be left to them. Recall that though Dabūsī discouraged *mujtahid*s from engaging in *taqlīd*, he insisted that the laity uncritically adhere to the opinions of a jurist or a group of jurists. His exhortation was driven by a fear of legal anarchy if the laity were freed from *taqlīd*. To some extent, then, the jurists were expected to provide a kind of ordered authoritative community to which the laity could have recourse when they had questions or disputes. This was of necessity, since *mujtahids* were the only means for the laity to know the Divine Truth in matters of jurisprudence, even if *mujtahid*s did not always succeed in articulating that Truth.

It was necessary for Dabūsī to emphasize that *mujtahid*s do not always articulate the Divine Truth itself in order for him to avoid the pitfalls of the other extreme he was mediating. If *mujtahid*s were expected to produce only the Divine Truth, then the laity would have to determine which juridical opinion actually reflected that Divine Truth whenever *mujtahid*s argued for multiple, disparate opinions on an issue. Once the laity determined to correct opinion, all competing opinions would be seen as false (*bāṭil*) and contrary to the Divine Truth. This would not only place a burden on the laity beyond their capacity, but would result in a rigid and polarized juridical environment. For the purposes of upholding the reality of a singular Divine Truth, alleviating the *mujtahids* and the laity alike from exceeding their capacity, and maintaining a functioning social hierarchy, Dabūsī argued that a well-intentioned *mujtahid* must always be viewed as *muṣīb*.

Since the juridical opinions of a *mujtahid* do not necessarily correspond to the Divine Truth and are thus irremediably conjectural, it might be concluded that juridical opinions should not be authoritative.

Dabūsī gave some credence to this, if only because he could not defend the authoritativeness of something that did not generate indubitable knowledge in its veracity without violating principles he laid out earlier. He did, however, present a practical argument concerning the authoritativeness of juridical opinions that made them effective legal tools. The *mujtahid*, he said, was only *muṣīb* if he truly believed that the juridical opinions that he was promoting were the result of sound reasoning and was convinced that they had a strong probability of reflecting the Divine Truth. The *mujtahid*, once convinced of the probity of his own opinion, is then required to act upon his own *qiyās*. Since the process of reaching a *qiyās* was of paramount importance, Dabūsī insisted that the *mujtahid* must act upon his own *qiyās* despite knowing that it might not directly correlate to the Divine Truth. By extension, an uncritical follower (*muqallid*) of a *mujtahid* who believes the latter to be a competent jurist is, due to his affiliation, bound by the *mujtahid*'s *qiyās*, if only because the *muqallid* cannot produce a competing argument.

Dabūsī followed this line of argumentation to question the retributive consequences of incorrect actions. Many of his contemporaries and predecessors argued that if the *qiyās* of a jurist were correct, then acting upon it would be meritorious (*ma'jūr*). However, if the *qiyās* were incorrect (*khaṭa'*) then individuals would be blameless (*ma'dhūr*) for acting upon it, since they thought it was the correct course of action. Dabūsī said that if an action turned out to be incorrect (*yatabayyin al-khaṭa'*), then one must leave that action upon learning of the error and repent properly. Yet, whether the action was actually correct or not, the individual was presumably acting with the intention of pleasing God. If reward and punishment are based on enacting a process that attempts to approximate Divine Truth rather than on acting according to the Divine Truth, then those who are enacting that process should be subject to reward, regardless of being correct or incorrect. Therefore, Dabūsī concluded that believers who are unaware of their errors—a situation that he termed 'veiled error' *(al-khaṭa' al-khafā')*—should not be considered blameless but rather meritorious for their actions.[105] Thus,

[105] Ibid 415.

Dabūsī argued for two major points that flow from his position on *taṣwīb*. First, despite the existence of a singular Divine Truth, human attempts to articulate Islamic jurisprudence need only approximate that Truth. Secondly, if the attempt itself is the basis for reward, then the results of a well-intentioned approximation of the Divine Truth in the form of a legal opinion is not only of secondary concern, but largely irrelevant.

Sarakhsī on *Taṣwīb*

Sarakhsī agreed with many eminent Ḥanafī legal scholars by stating that the *mujtahid* must be considered *muṣīb* concerning his *ijtihād.*[106] He acknowledged that when a *mujtahid* produces a legal opinion he thinks to be valid (*ṣaḥīḥ*), it might in fact be invalid (*fāsid*).[107] The issue of validity for Sarakhsī concerned the correlation between a juridical opinion and the Divine Truth. He argued that the Divine Truth is singular and only action that reflects that truth can be considered valid. The role of the *mujtahid* and his ultimate aim, then, is to disclose the Truth (*aẓhar al-ḥaqq*) and formulate judgments based upon it.[108] Although the aim is to disclose the Truth, Sarakhsī granted that *mujtahid*s sometimes fall short. Despite this unfortunate reality, he maintained that properly executing the rules and methodology of *uṣūl al-fiqh* will invariably lead one to the Truth, and that failure to reach the Truth would reflect faulty reasoning.[109] Faulty reasoning results from a lack of knowledge (*ʿilm*) regarding the sources of law, the presence of which will always produce injunctions that accurately reflect the Truth.[110]

Sarakhsī justified his position by describing the contemporary *mujtahid* as an historical being. Specifically, he argued that the juridical history that preceded contemporary *mujtahid*s provides them with almost all the necessary tools for articulating the Truth with accuracy and precision. As mentioned earlier in his discussion of *taqlīd*, Sarakhsī believed that the Companions of the Prophet were *muṣīb* and provided a

[106] Sarakhsī, *al-Mabsūṭ* (n 87) 16:87.
[107] Sarakhsī, *al-Muḥarrar fī Uṣūl al-Fiqh* (n 9) 2:87.
[108] Sarakhsi, al-*Mabsūṭ* (n 87) 16:82.
[109] Ibid 16:82.
[110] Sarakhsī, *al-Muḥarrar fī Uṣūl al-Fiqh* (n 9) 2:87.

wealth of juridical opinions from which a *mujtahid* could select for legal application and which he could not contradict. Interestingly, Sarakhsī argued that the Companions were *muṣīb* by appealing to the impossibility of persisting in error (*qarra ʿalā khaṭa'*) with which he described the infallibility of the Prophet.[111] The Prophet, he said, could not persist in an error of judgment because God would eventually send him revelation correcting his actions. Similarly, the Companions were unable to persist in error because if they erred then Muhammad would correct them. After Muhammad's death, if they erred then the Rightly-Guided Caliphs whom the Prophet blessed as models for *taqlīd*, would correct their error.[112] For these reasons, the Companions were *muṣīb* in all of their juridical opinions. The contemporary *mujtahid* can choose from any of the statements of the Companions as a basis for law and be assured of being *muṣīb*.

Also in his discussion of *taqlīd*, Sarakhsī held that contemporary *mujtahids* are not allowed to contradict the juridical opinions of righteous *mujtahids* who preceded them (*lā yadaʿa al-mujtahid fī zamāninā ra'yihi li-ra'y man huwa muqaddim ʿalayhi*).[113] This was because of the degenerate nature of later generations and also because of the workings of the Divine in history. Sarakhsī, in his discussion on the blessed nature of the faith community, claimed that God would not let the community agree upon error and so minority opinions should be disregarded.[114] Thus, only majority opinions would survive through the generations. These majority opinions were accorded the status of *ijmāʿ* in Sarakhsī's system, and so were considered to have divine sanction. History thereby serves as a vetting process by which minority—and therefore incorrect—opinions are cast off and only the Truth remains. Sarakhsī explained that the process of *taqlīd* gave contemporary *mujtahids* a bonanza of juridical opinions, all of which are *muṣīb*, from which they can choose for application.[115] In sum, *taqlīd* of transmitted texts, the opinions of the Companions, and the opinions of the majority of jurists provide the *mujtahid* with enough knowledge (*ʿilm*) to produce correct judgments

[111] Ibid 2:83. [112] Ibid 2:83. [113] Ibid 2:84.
[114] Ahmed (n 73), 143–7. [115] Sarakhsī, *al-Muḥarrar fī Uṣūl al-Fiqh* (n 9) 2:84.

that are accurate reflections of Divine Truth. The fruit of *taqlīd*, then, is that the *mujtahid* need never judge without knowledge (*lā ḍarūra lahu ilā qaḍā' bi-ghayr ʿilm*).[116] As seen earlier, Sarakhsī held that a judgment based on knowledge always produces an injunction that discloses the Truth.[117] Therefore, if a *mujtahid* properly engages in *taqlīd*, he can be assured that he will always be *muṣīb* in his legal pronouncements.

This last conclusion warrants some attention. In Sarakhsī's system, a *mujtahid* is *muṣīb* in his personal judgments, but not because one can never know Divine Truth and so any attempt to approximate it will always be conjectural. Rather, an uncritical devotion to the Islamic tradition in the form of texts and historical opinions make it so that the *mujtahid* need never conjecture. So long as the *mujtahid* does not use his own intellect to formulate an injunction, he can never be wrong. Hence, 'correctness' is not imputed to the contemporary *mujtahid*'s independent legal reasoning, but to his *taqlīd* of historical jurisprudence.

This conception becomes problematic when one cannot arrive at an answer to a problem through *taqlīd*. For example, in order to pray while traveling one must determine the location of Mecca and orient oneself in that direction. In that case, the *mujtahid* would have to use his best judgment utilizing the tools at his disposal, and would be unable to rely on *taqlīd*.[118] Sarakhsī permitted the *mujtahid* to make an informed independent judgment when *taqlīd* is not possible, but urged him to use every possible means to come to the correct judgment. When determining the proper orientation in which to pray, the *mujtahid* should use the sun or the stars or wind patterns to calculate the correct direction. After such deliberations, prayer in the calculated direction is permissible (*jā'iz*).[119] Upon returning from the journey, Sarakhsī said that one should try to determine whether the direction in which he prayed was indeed correct. If it is proven that he prayed in the wrong direction, then the prayer is invalid (*fāsid*) and must be repeated.[120] However, since the incorrect decision resulted from a dearth of resources and knowledge, the *mujtahid* is blameless (*maʿdhūr*) for his incorrect judgment.[121] The

[116] Sarakhsī, *al-Mabsūṭ* (n 87) 16:82.
[117] Ibid 16:82; the exact words are: *alladhī qaḍā' bi-ʿilmihi aẓhar al-haqq bi-ḥukmihi.*
[118] Ibid 10:197. [119] Ibid 10:199. [120] Ibid 10:200. [121] Ibid 16:87.

mujtahid's intention to pray in the correct direction is irrelevant for Sarakhsī. The action itself was incorrect and thus no reward is granted. Far from holding that the incorrect action could be rewarded, as per Dabūsī, Sarakhsī feared that someone who prayed in the wrong direction might be guilty of disbelief (*kufr*) because he prayed in a direction other than that in which he was commanded.[122] Sarakhsī was hopeful that God would deem the prayer merely defective (*khalal*), warranting repetition upon learning of the defect but not warranting a charge of disbelief.[123]

For Sarakhsī, the reward for *ijtihād* comes only from either maintaining the dominant opinions of the past or producing the correct opinion when the past cannot provide a precedent, so long as that opinion does not differ from the legal opinions of jurists from a previous generation of believers. In both these cases, the opinion must disclose the Truth and action upon that Truth is the only basis for reward.

CONCLUSION

Once again, the positions of Dabūsī and Sarakhsī regarding *ra'y* disclose an underlying ethos to which they subscribed regarding the role and function of Islamic jurisprudence. Dabūsī depicted Islamic jurisprudence as an attempt to reflect a Divine Truth that is radically detached from the jurist. The Divine Truth can never be known and jurists are merely trying to approximate it. With the exception of the generation of the Companions, the insurmountable distance between a jurist and the Divine Truth meant that no articulation of the Divine Truth through *qiyās* by a *mujtahid* could be authoritative for another *mujtahid*. However, because the *mujtahid* can never know if he has accurately articulated the Divine Truth or not, his effort of independent legal reasoning (*ijtihād*) is rewarded regardless of the correspondence between the resulting injunction and the Divine Truth. The articulation of Islamic jurisprudence, then, is a creative process that creates non-linear solutions based on the relationship among the texts, the *mujtahid*, and prevailing circumstances.

[122] Ibid 10:200. [123] Ibid 10:201.

Sarakhsī presented a markedly different conception of Islamic jurisprudence wherein the Divine Truth is intimately known by the *mujtahid*. The *mujtahid* reflects on the *sharīʿa* until such time as the divine light within it becomes clear to him. He can thereafter articulate injunctions that are accurate reflections of the Divine Truth. Yet, this was more of a description of how *mujtahid*s in the past derived jurisprudence. Contemporary *mujtahid*s were, by dint of their chronological distance from the pristine community, suspect in their ability to articulate Islamic jurisprudence. This suspicion served a dual purpose: it bound the *mujtahid* to the inherited injunctions of his legal school and also legitimated those same injunctions. If contemporary *mujtahid*s did not understand the inherited injunctions or thought them to be irrelevant, that was due to their own degeneracy. One was required to uncritically adhere to the opinions of the past except in dire circumstances in which there was no precedent upon which to rely. For Sarakhsī, *ra'y* was a tool that retained little function in the derivation of Islamic law, so that the opinions of contemporary *mujtahid*s were best kept to themselves.

These strikingly different conceptions of Islamic law are found in the slightest changes in definition. Whereas Dabūsī said that the jurist can have peace of mind in his *qiyās*, Sarakhsī held that the jurist can have peace of mind in the *ʿilla* he determines. Sarakhsī expanded on Dabūsī's position on *taqlīd* of the Companions, using the same principle to argue for *taqlīd* of *mursal* and *majhūl aḥādīth*, as well as *taqlīd* of eminent historical personalities. Both insisted that the *mujtahid* was *muṣīb*, but for very different reasons and with very different outcomes. The subtle differences in the way that Dabūsī and Sarakhsī justified these terms have far-reaching consequences; they present divergent and incommensurable worldviews in which Islamic law might be situated. A jurist relying on the justifications provided by these legal theorists might be led to abduce completely different applications of inherited jurisprudence.

This is especially true when a jurist thinks of Dabūsī and Sarakhsī's conceptions of *ra'y* in light of the justifications provided for inherited principles and injunctions related to the Qur'ān and the *sunna*. When we look at these justifications in the aggregate, we find that Dabūsī and Sarakhsī both worked within the existing Ḥanafī framework of legal theory texts to construct two possible worlds. Whether or not that was their intent, they were quite clearly justifying jurisprudence along particular trajectories. Dabūsī was consistently concerned with the context and circumstance that accompanies the application of Islamic law, presenting applicative jurisprudence as an inherently fallible project and touting method as paramount. Sarakhsī regularly appealed to God's transcendence and human incapacity to argue for a less critical application of inherited injunctions in pursuit of perfection. A jurist reading these texts would be presented with two different and competing worlds in which Islamic law should function. These by no means exhaust the possible worlds that can be created within the inherited legal theory structure, since new and creative justifications of shared terms and concepts are the prerogative and charge of every legal theorist.

Conclusion

It is quite clear that our two jurists—Dabūsī and Sarakhsī—worked within the inherited genre of Ḥanafī legal theory, with its inherited principles and injunctions, to posit very different, and at times opposing, conceptions of Islamic law. These conceptions are only realized through a careful reading of the texts with an eye toward the way in which they justify technical terms and historical positions. These justifications might lead a jurist to make abductions about how the inherited principles and injunctions should be applied, and those abductions might look very different. When taken together, the justifications that Dabūsī and Sarakhsī provided for inherited jurisprudence promote unique and competing conceptions of Islamic law as an applicative enterprise.

The purpose of this book was to describe the creative logic that pervades works of legal theory, but the presence of such logic raises several questions. Foremost of these is whether this phenomenon extends beyond our two jurists; that is, whether a careful reading of other legal theory texts would uncover other, unique conceptions of Islamic law. If so, what are we to make of these discrete views? Did they have any impact on the lived community or were they wholly academic expressions?

As to the first question of prevalence, there is little doubt that the practice of abducing cases from principles and injunctions was widespread and self-conscious amongst legal theorists. Within the Ḥanafī school alone there was great divergence in the justifications offered in legal theory manuals, despite structural uniformity. A contemporary of Dabūsī and Sarakhsī, Abū al-Ḥasan al-Pazdawī, wrote a legal theory work that effectively made communal precedent the ultimate arbiter of Islamic law. His brother, Abū al-Yusr (d. 493/1100), authored a legal theory that gave *ḥadīth* critics greater power in determining law. Their Iraqi predecessor, Abū Bakr al-Jaṣṣāṣ, was suspicious of majority opinions and of the government, so in his legal theory he accorded a privileged place to the independent thought of an educated elite. One of their Central Asian successors, Maḥmūd b. Zayd al-Lāmishī (d. ca early 6th/12th century), used his legal theory work to repudiate Iraqi Ḥanafī positions in favor of Samarqandi Ḥanafī positions. Another successor, ʿAlāʾ al-Dīn al-Samarqandī (d. 539/1144) wrote a legal theory work that erased what he saw as some of the more controversial positions of both Iraqi and Samarqandi Ḥanafīs and effectively made Ḥanafīs appear more in line with Shāfiʿīs. Despite all of these variations, the one feature that remains constant throughout all of these works is a shared structure that more or less upholds inherited Ḥanafī principles and injunctions. Though there are significant differences in their nuanced definitions of terms and justifications that dramatically alter the way that Islamic law is to be conceived and applied, a dogged loyalty to the inherited tradition is found throughout.

Nor was this phenomenon limited to the Ḥanafī school of jurisprudence. One can just as easily find similar disparities between legal theories of jurists in other legal schools. Whether a jurist is arguing the status of reason as a source of law, the assimilation of dialectical theology (*kalām*) into legal argumentation, or the literal application of law, the mode of argumentation is similar: they provide justifications that diverge from their predecessors while paying homage to their legal pedigree and leaving inherited principles and injunctions mostly intact. Though this may have been a function of the social reality of legal schools after the 3rd/9th century, one has to wonder, what was the point? Did different legal theories reflect social history or actually effect change? Put another way, why did these jurists go through the trouble of arguing for disparate conceptions of Islamic law through technical arguments about things like the nature of metaphor in a way that minimally disturbed inherited principles and injunctions?

There are two possible answers to this question. The first is a little easier to digest, but is ultimately less nutritious; and that is that legal theory works were intended to influence the elite religious authorities of the Muslim world in a bid to affect the application of Islamic law. These authorities included scholars, jurists, and judges; all of whom relied on some conceptual framework when articulating Islamic positions, doctrines, and rulings. Thus, legal theories could color the way in which these individuals would apply the law and teach it to others. Legal theory, then, could provide an overarching narrative through which the more practical emissaries of Islamic law could derive law and justify their rulings to the masses.

This explanation, despite its rather straightforward ability to connect legal theory with multiple strata of Muslim society, assumes a fluid relationship between Islamic texts and practitioners that almost certainly did not exist.[1] It was not the case that jurists were intimately connected with the affairs of the populace, nor that jurists directly informed the decisions of judges, nor that judges were all accomplished jurists.[2] In all fairness, it is unreasonable to expect jurists, scholars, and judges in any society to be in direct conversation with one another or intimately connected to the populace, whether through their texts or otherwise. More importantly, there is simply no evidence to suggest that normative Islamic texts had any correlation to lived reality in the Muslim community.[3] Social reality may have been on the jurists' minds, but it did not enjoy a direct dialectical relationship with normative texts.

[1] Which is not to say that there was no correspondence between normative texts and social practice, especially with regard to genres outside of legal theory, see in particular Wael Hallaq, 'Model Shurūṭ Works and the Dialectic of Doctrine and Practice' (1995) 2:2 *Islamic Law and Society* 109ff; Baber Johansen, 'Causuistry: Between Legal Concept and Social Praxis' 1995 2:2 *Islamic Law and Society* 135ff.

[2] The link between the judiciary and religious scholarship began to atrophy as early as the mid-9th century, as caliphs appointed judges who would keep state policy as a primary directive; Muhammad Khalid Masud, Rudolph Peters, and David S Powers, *Dispensing Justice in Islam: Qadis and the Judgments* (Brill 2006) 12–13. Despite this shift, legal theory texts insisted that *muftīs* be skilled *mujtahids*, even if that was not observed in practice; see Wael B Hallaq, 'Ifta' and Ijtihad in Sunni Legal Theory: A Developmental Account' in Muhammad Khalid Masud, Brinkley Messick, and David S Powers (eds), *Islamic Legal Interpretations: Muftis and the Fatwas* (Harvard University Press 1996) 33–43.

[3] Quite the opposite, Johansen noted that a *muftī*'s recounting of a *qadī*'s decision often deviated from the actual ruling inside the courtroom. In that sense, the normative text of the *muftī* represented only the ideal version of the court proceedings; Baber Johansen, 'Coutumes Locales et Coutumes Universalles' in *Contingency in a Sacred Law* (Brill 1999) 170–1. It should be noted that even amongst normative texts, there is a discrepancy between stated principles and practical dictates; Éric Chaumont, '*Ijtihād et Histoire en islam sunnite classique selon quelques jurists et théologiens*' in Robert Gleave (ed), *Islamic Law Theory and Practice* (I.B. Tauris 1997) 7–24. This is not to say that normative texts had nothing to do with court practice. Certainly, *shurūṭ* and *ḥiyal* texts, which were often part of larger normative works, were designed to be used in courts and were most probably used by judges, witnesses, and lawyers alike, if only to be used as a record of an already concluded contract; Jeanette Wakin *The Function of Documents in Islamic Law* (SUNY Press 1972) 30ff.

Islamic legal texts, and especially works of legal theory, should not be judged in light of their practical application. That is a difficult task since we tend to think of law in terms of the secular and quasi-secular legal systems of the modern day, in which law is associated with governance.[4] And yet it is necessary to expand our conception of Islamic law in order to understand the function of Islamic legal theory given the findings of the present work. This requires us to put emphasis on the 'Islamic' part of Islamic legal theory. That is, we may be tempted to make conclusions about how judges might enact Islamic law based on the texts under study, but we must bear in mind that the texts themselves are primarily products of religious devotion, not of policy-making. As Robert Gleave rightly notes, '... in classical Muslim jurisprudence, the motives for an individual scholar's involvement may be hazy, but the discipline as a whole is designed to serve a primarily religious and/or aesthetic purpose.'[5] To understand what Dabūsī and Sarakhsī were trying to accomplish requires us first to understand legal theory texts in the context of religious obligation and devotion.

It is religious obligation that underpins our legal theorists' loyalty to the legal tradition to which they adhered, because enacting religious obligation within a community requires an inherited template that identifies the boundaries of proper execution of the obligation. It is religious devotion that best describes the logic of the justifications provided by legal theorists that might serve as the foundations for abuductive arguments for how the law is applied. These justifications described the way the legal world *should* work as opposed to describing or apologizing for the way the system already works. Such forward-looking statements require a tacit disconnect from observed reality; the fact that legal theorists are arguing for the way that law should be applied implies a recognition that the law is not currently being applied correctly. Thus,

[4] Christian Müller has demonstrated that even the *fatwā*, long considered the most reliable measure of the application of Islamic law in society, did not always capture the ruling of a judge. As a result, he notes that 'if...an effective *qaḍī* jurisdiction did not need to issue a *ḥukm* in every case, our perspective on the *ḥukm* as an indicator of historical facts changes.' Müller, 'Settling Litigation without Judgment' in *Dispensing Justice in Islam* (n 1) 67–8.

[5] Norman Calder, *Islamic Jurisprudence in the Classical Era* (Cambridge University Press 2010) 17.

as a performative work,[6] the legal theory manual is an attempt to remedy the failure of the Muslim community to properly apply law. Since the application of law is an extension and manifestation of the divine-human relationship, the legal theory manual endeavors to create a stronger bond between God and man, if not to repair the rupture between the two caused by the improper application of Islamic law.

In that light, it is helpful to think of legal theory texts not so much as delineating a system that underpins the derivation of positive law, but as a religious ritual enacted by pious practitioners. This is not ritual in a restrictive sense, with a connotation of repeating an action without consideration for its internal logic or external effects. Rather, the term 'ritual' here is meant in a very rich and enriching sense. Seligman et al describe ritual as the creation of subjunctive worlds, such that the very enactment of a ritual is to engage in a social practice predicated on an 'as-if' reality.[7] This 'as-if' reality does not exist without the ritual, and the ritual itself requires practitioners who adhere to social conventions that reflect values and beliefs that may not be observed in—or are perhaps even contrary to—social practice outside of the ritual.

When one engages in a ritual, one enters into a history of religious action that must reconstruct an original, pristine example of that religious action. Even when rituals depart from their historical instantiations in important ways, they retain the character of their historical precedent enough to make the ritual recognizable. To engage in an action that is so historically rooted is to break away from the ever-changing nature of lived reality and to posit a religiously-inflected world that one might not

[6] Here I mean the term 'performative' in the way that J L Austin used the term. The writing of a legal theory manual was, no doubt, a locutionary and illocutionary act that followed particular conventional guidelines. This book was an attempt to describe how the legal theory manual should be read as an illocutionary act. But, as religious devotion, the writing of such texts was also a perlocutionary act in the sense that the writing itself was meant to serve a performative function in the community, especially with regard to the community's relationship to the divine. For Austin on illocutionary and perlocutionary acts, see J L Austin, *How to Do Things With* Words (Oxford University Press 1962) 94ff. I am grateful to Ebrahim Moosa for directing my attention to Austin.

[7] Adam B Seligman, Robert P Weller, Michael J Puett, and Bennett Simon, *Ritual and Its Consequences: Essays on the Limits of Sincerity* (Oxford University Press, 2008), see especially Chapter 1.

find outside of the ritual itself.[8] The creation of this subjunctive, 'as-if' world is the fruit of ritual practice, and it provides religious devotion with meaning and power.

Legal theory texts are to a large extent exercises in such ritual practice. They recreate texts of old and re-instantiate the boundaries of legal theory enumerated by their predecessors. If legal theorists were to work outside of these boundaries, they would lose the character of the ritual and thereby break from the religious community in which they claim membership. The resulting legal theory might be more effective in conveying a unique practical legal system envisioned by the author, but since the fundamental thrust behind writing the text is devotional, circumventing the received tradition would compromise the ritual aspect of normative texts.

Yet, constructing an 'as-if,' subjunctive world does not merely involve entering into a received tradition despite one's lived reality. It is also a statement about how the world can be, or perhaps how the world should be.[9] Each individual ritual act may be bound by received tradition, but it is still personal to the one enacting the ritual. It might mean something unique, or have a unique shape based on the particularities of the practitioner. As Seligman et al point out, if a ritual is to have meaning, it must be engaged in with sincerity. This sincerity concerning the relevance of ritual to one's lived reality is in tension with the received tradition:

[8] The obvious parallel is with Jonathan Z Smith's description of the hunting ritual in 'The Bare Facts of Ritual' in *Imagining Religion: From Babylon to Jonestown* (University of Chicago Press 1982) 53–65. Seligman et al's conception of ritual is more fruitful here because Smith assumes that the practitioners are self-conscious about the disconnect between ritual and practice, and further that ritual's power comes from 'the perceived fact that, in actuality, such possibilities cannot be realized.' Whereas Smith may be justified in psychologizing his subjects due to his intimate relations with them, we cannot do the same with medieval texts from which we have irremediable distance. As Ricouer states, 'The text is mute. An asymmetric relation obtains between text and reader, in which only one partner speaks for the two.' Paul Ricouer, *Interpretation Theory: Discourse and the Surplus of Meaning* (Texas Christian University Press 1976) 75. Thus we are forced to make a more modest claim about the purpose and method of creating and enacting ritual by positing ritual's relation to sincerity.

[9] Here it is important to remember that the world being posited is subjunctive, not optative. That is, though sincerity demands that one hope that the world will one day be aligned with ritual, the subjunctive nature of the world being posited acknowledges that the world is not according to ritual. I am grateful to Bob Gibbs for pointing out this important distinction.

the former informing the world through ritual, the latter conforming the world to ritual.

So, while we cannot honestly say that legal theory texts had a direct impact on social reality, we must still account for the stark differences observed in the theories of Dabūsī and Sarakhsī concerning the correct application of Islamic law. The marked tension between their deference to the structure provided by the tradition and their creative use of the tradition to put forward discrete conceptions of Islamic law suggests that the two jurists were interested in some external result from their legal theories. That Dabūsī consistently argued for law to be an emulative enterprise, giving jurists the ability to factor context into their decisions, cannot be accidental. That Sarakhsī defined law as an imitative enterprise, requiring jurists to adhere to inherited injunctions whenever possible, is not insignificant. Though we cannot definitively say why these jurists argued as they did, nor can we speak to their intended impact, we can observe that their engagement with the ritual of legal theory was directed toward some larger end.

This larger end is seen most clearly in the aggregate justifications made in the text. Dabūsī and Sarakhsī's arguments, when taken together, form a composite that explains how and why Islamic law should function in the way they suggest. These are grand narratives that explain the underlying logic of Islamic law; what was referred to as the 'why' of Islamic law in the Introduction. This is not to say that our jurists were reading a narrative into their works of legal theory; that would require us to read-in a caprice that is not forthcoming from the texts. In the absence of evidence to the contrary, we assume that our jurists were sincere in their readings of the text. We must conclude that their project, at its most basic level, was simply to explain the literal, or, 'plain-sense' meaning of received Islamic legal theory, as they understood it, in the language of their community of interpreters.

The term 'literal reading' is used here in the sense of Hans Frei's *sensus literalis*. When one reads religious texts in this sense, the religious texts map onto the world of the reader. When that reader explains the details of the text, he is only describing how the text works in his world. For the jurist, the literal sense of the text directly reflects the experiences and the world of the jurist such that the grammatical and syntactical meaning(s) of the text correspond to the jurist's own narrative conception of the text's relationship to his practice.[10] The result of a literal reading of the text is that the world of the text and the world of the jurist are unified in a harmonious narrative. This narrative is particular to the jurist and informs how he reads the text and the relationship he envisions between the text and formal practice.[11] There is no reason to suggest otherwise, or to argue that the jurist is somehow surreptitiously trying to undermine historical precedent through his justifications in legal theory. More likely, the justifications in the text are the result of the jurist explaining his reading of the *sensus literalis* of legal theory.

To have discursive weight, this *sensus literalis* needs to be explicated in the language of one's sociolinguistic context; in the case of Dabūsī and Sarakhsī, the Ḥanafī legal tradition. Seen in light of Frei's theory, the jurists are trying to convey 'the sense of the text in its sociolinguistic context—liturgical, pedagogical, polemical, and so on.'[12] Frei cites Charles M Wood to explain this contextual reading:

> The literal sense—this 'natural,' 'plain,' obvious meaning which the community of faith has normally acknowledged as basic, regardless of whatever other constructions might also be properly put upon the text—is grounded in the community's own experience with the text. As those adjectives suggest, it is the sense whose discernment has become second nature to the members of the community.[13]

The community of interpreters thus provides a common discourse within which the literal sense is understood and debated. This discourse is not determinate, but it sets the parameters for acceptable debate. Despite the differences between the jurists in this study regarding the use of foundational sources, none questioned the status of the Ḥanafī discourse

[10] Seligman et al (n 5) 103.

[11] Hans Frei, 'The 'Literal Reading' of Biblical Narrative in the Christian Tradition: Will it Stretch or Will it Break?' in George Hunsinger (ed), *Theology and Narrative: Selected Essays* (Oxford University Press 1993) 146.

[12] Hans Frei, 'Theology and the Interpretation of Narrative: Some Hermeneutical Considerations' in George Hunsinger (ed), *Theology and Narrative: Selected Essays* (Oxford University Press 1993) 104.

[13] Charles M Wood, *The Formation of Christian Understanding* (Westminster Press 1981) 43.

as normative and exclusive. Moreover, they all used the terminologies indigenous to Ḥanafī discussions on jurisprudence to promote their particular understandings.

At a deeper level, the Ḥanafī discourse established that the study of legal texts was *about* the application of law. When the jurists approached the texts, they did not overtly engage hermeneutical theories or conjecture about the meaning 'behind' the text. Even when Sarakhsī brought in his considerable doctrinal concerns, they were used to either expand or, more likely, restrict the application of law. Their central concern was the application of legal texts to communal life—regardless of whether or not their legal theories actually effected practical change. As a product of religious ritual, legal theories could be primarily concerned with social application and fulfill their ritual function even if their arguments were never realized. This concern with application was itself the *sensus literalis* of legal texts provided by their sociolinguistic context. It was within this context that the jurists debated about the proper use of the sources of law and through which competing legal theories emerged. Regardless of the particularities of these legal theories, the primary concern of the discourse itself—one could even say the motivation behind the debate—was about the application of Islamic law. In sum, the debates regarding the derivation of jurisprudence from normative texts were in service to a particular narrative conception of legal applicability. This concern with the legal applicability of normative texts serves as a 'starting point' for the study of Ḥanafī legal theories that informs why they were written and how they should be read.[14]

The sociolinguistic aspect of the *sensus literalis* provides the parameters of the dialogue, the *about-ness* of the legal interpretive project. Meanwhile, the syntactical and grammatical meanings gleaned from literal readings by individual jurists express discrete narratives that situate the *why-ness* of the legal interpretive project. Working backwards, then, a legal theory

[14] When mediating between formalist and objectivist conceptions of the law, the 'starting point' is central, but notoriously difficult to posit; see Roberto Unger, *The Critical Legal Studies Movement* (Harvard University Press 1986) 5–18; Drucilla Cornell, *Tranformations: Recollective Imagination and Sexual Difference* (Routledge 1993) 22.

is the ritual expression of a jurist's narrative understanding of normative texts and their legal application in his sociolinguistic context.

This conception of legal theory, however, leaves some gaps in our understanding of the genre as a whole. The most conspicuous shortcoming of explaining legal theory as narrative interpretation of the *sensus literalis* is the ambiguity it renders onto the composition of the actual narrative of the jurist itself. Certainly, a jurist's personal narrative will be influenced by doctrine, locale, politics, history, temperament, and innumerable other concerns. Simply positing the presence of a narrative understanding of legal sources does not address the level and import of these influences in the articulation of any particular legal theory. The reader is left to hypothesize about the relative strength of external influences on a case-by-case basis. Since the results of such hypothesizing can never be verified, the idea of a 'narrative understanding of the *sensus literalis*' cannot be viewed as describing a state-of-being of the jurist that can be phenomenologically uncovered. Rather it is simply a description of the project and process of jurists articulating legal theories.

This, whether fortunately or unfortunately, is the most we can say about why jurists wrote works of legal theory and what they intended to accomplish. Still, to view a legal theory text as a ritual enacted by a jurist to explicate a narrative of law that flows from his literal reading of the text is itself a powerful idea. If we shed concerns about the social application of legal theory, we can be transported into a world created by the legal theorist in which the possible conceptions of Islamic law are limited only by the possible justifications for terms used in abductive syllogisms. In this way, legal theory has a literary aspect that moves the reader to consider a world that does not exist, but could, and should. It is perhaps therefore a strength that legal theory is somewhat divorced from social application, because it allows for legal theorist and reader alike to transcend the strictures of lived reality into a world of possibility while keeping one foot grounded in the communal discourse and inherited jurisprudence of the world as it is. Revisiting legal theory texts with this background in mind will allow scholars to uncover myriad conceptions of Islam and Islamic law that are as diverse as the legal theorists who articulate them.

APPENDIX

The Ḥanafī Scholars

For those who are interested in the lives of the scholars under study, what follows is a brief synopsis of their lives, times, and influences. Both Dabūsī and Sarakhsī were self-professed acolytes of the Baghdad Ḥanafī tradition, which, as the name suggests, has its roots in the historical Ḥanafī school of jurisprudence. The eponym of the Ḥanafī school, Abū Ḥanīfa Nuʿmān b. Thābit (d. 150/767), was a jurist whose positions, both legal and doctrinal, have been disputed throughout Muslim history. His works are not extant, but his views were captured and recounted by his most prominent students, Muḥammad al-Shaybānī and Abū Yūsuf, though the three were often at odds with one another. Scholars from various regions of the Muslim world at the time came to identify with the views of these three jurists, usually promoting the views of one over another. Muḥammad al-Shaybānī, in particular, found favor amongst Ḥanafī scholars of Baghdad and Central Asia, but these scholars produced multiple commentaries and occasionally offered conflicting accounts of his opinions. Thus, by the 4th/10th century there were multiple conceptions of Ḥanafī thought that were being promulgated by Ḥanafī scholars. The scholarship produced by Ḥanafīs from Baghdad proved to be the most influential in shaping classical Ḥanafī thought.

Baghdad Ḥanafīs

The Baghdad Ḥanafīs originally coalesced around the Muʿtazilī jurist Abū al-Ḥasan al-Karkhī. Karkhī authored several works of law, most of them commentaries on the works of Muḥammad al-Shaybānī. He authored one short treatise on legal theory, which was largely a collection of *responsa*.[1] One of his more significant contributions to the development of Ḥanafī thought concerns the status of singular narrations vis-à-vis Considered Opinion (*raʾy*) and is discussed in Chapter 3 of this book. Karkhī taught many prominent students, though undeniably the most prominent was Abū Bakr al-Jaṣṣāṣ. Jaṣṣāṣ, in turn, taught many students who are considered by contemporary Ḥanafī scholars to be seminal figures in Ḥanafī jurisprudence,[2] and his influence spread far beyond

[1] This is found as an appendix to Dabūsī's *Kitāb Taʾsis al-Nazar* (Cairo: Zakariyā ʿAlī Yūsuf 1972). It is, however, supplied by Abū Ḥafṣ ʿUmar al-Nasafī (d. 537/1142) and no doubt represents some anachronistic conceptions of Karkhī's work.

[2] A Kevin Reinhart, *Before Revelation: The Boundaries of Muslim Moral Thought* (SUNY Press 1995) 54.

Baghdad. Non-Ḥanafī historians branded Jaṣṣāṣ a Muʿtazilī, though recent scholarship has questioned this ascription.[3] A cursory study of his work quickly reveals that he cannot be easily categorized in doctrinal terms. It has been argued that his greatest contribution was in systematizing Ḥanafī legal theory into an analytical science independent from detailed reflections on *responsa*.[4] Central Asian Ḥanafīs, like Dabūsī and Sarakhsī, were particularly beholden to Jaṣṣāṣ and produced works that acknowledged his influence.

Abū Zayd ʿUbayd Allāh b. ʿUmar b. ʿĪsā al-Dabūsī

Little is known about Abū Zayd al-Dabūsī's life and studies.[5] His birth is reported to have been around 367/987[6] and his date of death is disputed, though most place the year at 430/1038.[7] He spent the majority of his life in Transoxiana and though the extent of his travels is unknown, he is presumed to have studied and worked in Transoxiana, particularly in Bukhara,[8] all his life.[9] Although many of his teachers are unknown, he almost certainly studied in the school of Abū Jaʿfar Muḥammad b. ʿAbd Allāh al-Hinduwānī (d. 362/973). Hinduwānī himself studied in Iraq with Jaṣṣāṣ, though the former settled in Central Asia. Hinduwānī wrote a commentary on Muḥammad al-Shaybānī's *al-Jāmiʿ al-Ṣaghīr* and was reported to have promoted the views of Karkhī and Jaṣṣāṣ. Dabūsī also studied under Abū Bakr Jaʿfar al-Astarūshinī (d. unknown),[10] who also received his education from Jaṣṣāṣ.[11] As a teacher and a colleague, Dabūsī was known to be warm and jovial, with a penchant for boisterous laughter.[12]

Dabūsī produced several works on various Islamic sciences,[13] most of which are not extant, including a commentary on Shaybānī's *al-Jāmiʿ al-Kabīr*. His other lost works include *al-Anwār fī Uṣūl al-Fiqh*, *al-Nudhum fī al-Fatāwā*, and *Khizānat*

[3] Christopher Melchert, *The Formation of the Sunni Schools of Law, 9th-10th Centuries C.E.* (Brill 1997) 59.

[4] Reinhart (n 2) 45.

[5] In Sezgin's words, 'Uber sein Leben wissen wir so gut wie gar nichts.' Fuat Sezgin, *Geschichte Des Arabīshcen Schrifttums* (Brill 1967) I: 456.

[6] Yusuf Kavacki, *Fiqh, Islāmic Law and Usul al-Fiqh*, (unpublished, accessible at <http://www.iant.com/imam/book.txt>, last accessed January 15, 2011), 126.

[7] Ibn Abī Wafā al-Qurashī, *al-Jawāhir al-Muḍīyah* (al-Maʿrifa al-ʿUthmaniyya 1988) 499; Sezgin (n 5) I:456.

[8] As for Dabus itself, Ibn Kathīr claimed that it was village in one of the districts of Bukhara; Ismāʿīl b. ʿUmar ibn Kathīr, *al-Bidāyah wa-al-Nihāyah* (ʿAlī Muʿawwad, Dār al-Kutub al-ʿIlmiyya 1993) 12:42. Ibn al-Athīr believed it to be between Bukhara and Samarqand; ʿAlī b. Muḥammad ibn al-Athīr, *al-Lubāb fī Tahdhīb al-Ansāb* (ʿAbd al-Karīm Sam'ānī ed, Dār Ṣādir 1972) 490.

[9] al-Qāsim b. ʿAbd Allāh b. Quṭlubughā, *Tāj al-Tarājim* (Muḥammad Yūsuf ed, Dār al-Qalam 1992) 192.

[10] See Khalīl al-Mays' *'Tarjumat al-Mu'allif'* in Dabūsī, *Taqwim al-Adilla* (Beirut: Dār al-Kutub al-ʿIlmiyya 2001) 7.

[11] Kavacki (n 6) 56.

[12] Ibn Kathīr (n 8) 12:42.

[13] For a full list see Khalīl al-Mays (n 10) 7–8.

al-Hudā. The extant works of Dabūsī include: *Ta'sīs al-Naẓar*,[14] which surveys differences of opinion amongst the founders of the Ḥanafī school; *al-Amad al-Aqṣā*, a treatise on spirituality (*taṣawwuf*); *Kitāb al-Nikāḥ min al-Asrār*, a text on the law of marriage; and the treatise that is the foundation of the present study, *Taqwīm al-Adilla fī Uṣūl al-Fiqh*.[15] This last text is a detailed exposition of legal theory with the explicit aim of identifying valid indicants (*dalā'il*) in Islamic law so as to delineate authoritative evidence (*ḥujaj*) for extrapolating juridical decisions.

Dabūsī was considered one of the leaders of the Ḥanafīs in the 5th/11th century;[16] he was also well-known amongst his contemporaries and he taught several high-profile students in Central Asia. However, his influence waned by the 7th/13th century and thereafter references to him were mostly relegated to biographical dictionaries.

Muḥammad b. Aḥmad b. Abī Sahl al-Sarakhsī[17]

There is no credible date of birth ascribed to Sarakhsī and thus no way to gauge his lifespan.[18] The date of his death is also disputed, though a survey of the rulers with whom he interacted suggests that he died in the final decade of the 11th century C.E.[19] Sarakhsī was born in Transoxiana, all his teachers were Central

[14] For a description of the structure and function of *Ta'sīs al-Naẓar* see Ahmad Atif Ahmad, *Structural Interrelations of Theory and Practice in Islamic Law: A Study of Six Works of Medieval Jurisprudence* (Brill 2006) 50–6.

[15] Sezgin notes another extant manuscript in the Taimūr library titled, '*Kitāb Ta'liqa fī masā'il al-khilāif bayn al-a'imma*'; this is most probably an alternative title for the aforementioned *Ta'sīs al-Naẓar*. See Sezgin (n 5) I: 456. Likewise, Ibn Khaldūn refers to the *Kitāb al-Ta'liqa* of Dabūsī, which is no doubt the *Taqwīm al-Adilla*; Franz Rosenthal (trs), *al-Muqaddimah: An Introduction to History* (Princeton University Press 1967) 3:31.

[16] al-Qurashī (n 7) 500; Ibn al-Athīr (n 8) 1:490. Ibn Khālliqān considered him the founder of the science of legal dialectics; as quoted in Ibn Kathīr (n 8) 12:42 and William Slane, *Ibn Khallikan's Biographical Dictionary, Vol. II* (Cosimo 2010) 28. Ibn Khadūn wrote that Dabūsī 'wrote more widely on analogical reasoning than any other (Hanefite)...'; Rosenthal (n 15) 3:27.

[17] For a comprehensive treatment of Sarakhsī see the forthcoming book by Baber Johansen, *Sarakhsī* (Oxford: Oneworld).

[18] Although Osman Tastan and Muhammad Hamidullah hazard his date of birth to be 400/1010; Osman Tastan, *The Jurisprudence of Sarakhsī* (Ph.D Diss, University of Exeter 1993) 19; I find this unlikely because that would both place him at an advanced age during Ḥulwānī's ascendancy and have him jailed between the ages of 66 and 80. If indeed he were imprisoned in an underground dungeon, then it is unlikely that his health would endure not only during his 14-year imprisonment, but for 3 years beyond.

[19] Though Meron argued that Sarakhsī traveled to Aleppo to teach in the *Ḥalāwiyya*, this argument is untenable given that Nūr al-Dīn al-Zangī did not establish the school as a center for Shāfi'ī study until 543/1149; Ya'akov Meron, 'The Development of Hanafi Legal Thought' (1969) 30 *Studia Islamica* 73, 86–7. It is possible that Meron actually meant to reference the Sadiriyya in Damascus, a Ḥanafī center of learning dedicated in 491/1098, but there is no evidence to suggest that Sarakhsī taught in that school. Most likely, Meron conflated Abū Bakr al-Sarakhsī with Raḍī al-Dīn Muḥammad b. Muḥammad al-Sarakhsī (d. 544/1149–50). See Osman Tastan's discussion on the topic in Tastan (n 18) 21ff.

Asian, and his final days were spent in Central Asia. There is no evidence to suggest that he left for any appreciable time in between his study and his death.

Sarakhsī was most deeply influenced by "his Shaykh," ʿAbd al-ʿAzīz b. Aḥmad al-Ḥulwānī (d. 448–9/1056–8),[20] who was known by the title *Shams al-Aʾimmah* (splendor of the religious authorities). Ḥulwānī lived and taught in the Central Asian city of Bukhara where he produced a commentary of Muḥammad al-Shaybānī's legal positions entitled *al-Mabsūṭ*. While in Bukhara, he met and taught Sarakhsī, who soon became his star pupil. Upon Ḥulwānī's death, the title of *Shams al-Aʿimmah* was transferred to Sarakhsī, who settled in Uzjand, a town near Farghana in Transoxiana.[21]

Sarakhsī had a formal relationship with the ruling Qarā-Khānids, which was not surprising since they regularly sought counsel with religious scholars.[22] In 466/1074, Sarakhsī was imprisoned by the local Khan, Shams al-Mulk, in an underground dungeon.[23] The circumstances surrounding this imprisonment are disputed; it has been argued that it was due to Sarakhsī espousing ideas thought to be heretical,[24] or his encouraging the non-payment of a tax,[25] or the most popular explanation, Sarakhsī's offering the Khan unwelcome advice (*naṣīḥā*) in the form of a juridical opinion that censured the Khan for the manner in which he married a woman.[26] For whatever reason, Sarakhsī was confined to his prison until 480/1088. While in prison, it is reported that he dictated several books to his students who were listening to his teachings from aboveground.[27] These books included the bulk of his expansive legal commentary, *al-Mabsūṭ*, and the beginning of his book on legal theory, *al-Muḥarrar fī Uṣūl al-Fiqh*, commonly known as *Uṣūl al-Sarakhsī*.[28] Upon his release from prison, Sarakhsī moved to Marghinan and completed *al-Muḥarrar fī Uṣūl al-Fiqh*, which, for the present study, serves as the wellspring for his thoughts on legal theory. Sarakhsī continued to teach and write in Marghinan until his death, most probably around 483/1090.[29]

[20] A minority opinion holds his death to be in 448 or 9/1056 or 7; al-Qurashī (n 7) 189.

[21] Tastan (n 18) 20.

[22] Ibid 16.

[23] Though Tastan and Schacht doubt that the jail was an underground dungeon (*jubb*), I see no reason to doubt that, particularly given the level of detail provided by students of Sarakhsī regarding the placement and dimensions of the dungeon.

[24] Joseph Schacht, 'Notes on Sarakhsī's Life and Works' in *900. Ölum Yilönümü Münasebetiyle Büyük İslâm Hukukcusu Şemsu'l-E'imme* (Ankara Universitesi Basimevi 1965) 3–4.

[25] Tastan (n 18) 22.

[26] Al-Qurashī (n 7) 234–5. Schacht doubts this last, popular rendition of events because the story involves the Khan accepting Sarakhsī's advice and also because the incident was reported to have happened after Sarakhsī was released from prison; Schacht (n 24) 3.

[27] Al-Qurashī (n 7) 235.

[28] For a full list of Sarakhsī's works, see Kamāl ʿAbd al-ʿAzīz al-ʿInānī's "*Muqaddima*" in Sarakhsī, *al-Mabsūṭ* (Dār al-Kutub al-ʿIlmiyya 2001) 1:48.

[29] Al-Qurashī (n 7) 234.

Sarakhsī was celebrated in his own time, sometimes overshadowing his contemporaries whose works have been overlooked as a result.[30] Sarakhsī remains one of the most celebrated Ḥanafī jurists and his thought was foundational for the development of post-classical Ḥanafī law.[31]

[30] Abū al-Yusr Muḥammad al-Bazdawī, *Kitāb fīhī Maʿrifat al-Ḥujaj al-Sharʿiya* (Marie Bernand and Éric Chaumont ed., Institut français d'archéologie orientale 2003) 6.
[31] N Calder, 'al-Sarakhsī' *Encyclopedia of Islam* (2nd edn, 1998).

Bibliography of Arabic Sources

Al-Aḥsā'ī, Abū Bakr b. Muḥammad, *Zawāhir al-Qalā'id 'alā Mahammāt al-Qawā'id* (Yaḥyā b. Abī Bakr ed, Dār al-Nu'mān lil-'Ulūm 2002).

Ibn al-Athīr, 'Alī b. Muḥammad, *al-Lubāb fī Tahdhīb al-Ansāb* ('Abd al-Karīm Sam'ānī ed, Dār Ṣādir 1972).

Ibn 'Abd al-Barr, Abū 'Umar Yūsuf, *Ṣaḥīḥ Jāmi' Bayān al-'Ilm wa Faḍlihi* (Abū al-Ashbāl al-Zuhayrī ed, Maktabat Ibn Taymiya 1996).

Al-Bazdawī, Abū al-Yusr Muḥammad, *Kitāb fīhī Ma'rifat al-Ḥujaj al-Shar'iyah* (Marie Bernand and Éric Chaumont ed, Institut français d'archéologie orientale 2003).

Al-Bukhārī, 'Abd al-'Azīz b. Aḥmad, *Kashf al-Asrār 'an Fakhr al-Islām al-Bazdawī* (Muḥammad Baghdādī ed, Dār al-Kitāb al-'Arabī 1997).

Al-Dabūsī, 'Ubayd Allāh b. 'Umar, *Ta'sīs al-Naẓar* (Zakariyā 'Alī Yūsuf 1972).

——*Kitāb al-Manāsik min al-Asrār* (Nāyif 'Amrī ed, Dār al-Manār 1991).

——*Kitāb al-Nikāḥ min al-Asrār* (Nāyif 'Amrī ed, Dār al-Manār 1993).

——*Taqwīm al-Adilla* (Khalīl al-Mays ed, Dār al-Kutub al-'Ilmiyya 2001).

——*al-Amad al-Aqṣā* ('Abd al-Ghanī Mastū ed, al-Maktabat al-'Aṣriya 2008).

Al-Farfūr, Muḥammad b. Walī al-Dīn, *Mukhtaṣar al-Afkār* (Walī al-Dīn al-Farfūr ed, Dār al-Farfūr 2001).

Al-Ghazālī, Muḥammad b. Muḥammad, *al-Mustaṣfā fī 'Ilm al-Uṣūl* (Muḥammad 'Abd al-Shāfī ed, Dār al-Kutub al-'Ilmiyya 2000).

Al-Ḥaṣkafī, Muḥammad b. 'Alī, *Ifāḍat al-Anwār* (Muḥammad Sa'īd Burhānī ed, n.p. 1992).

Ibn Ḥazm, 'Alī b. Aḥmad, *al-Iḥkām fī Uṣūl al-Aḥkām* (Muḥammad 'Abd al-'Azīz ed, Maktabat 'Āṭif 1978).

Al-Jamal, Sulaymān b. 'Umar, *Ḥashiyat al-Jamal 'alā Sharḥ al-Manhaj* ('Abd al-Razzāq Ghālib ed, Dār al-Kutub al-'Ilmiyya 1996).

Al-Jaṣṣāṣ, Aḥmad b. 'Alī, *Aḥkām al-Qur'ān* ('Abd al-Salām Shāhīn ed, Dār al-Kutub al-'Ilmiyya 1994).

——*Mukhtaṣar Ikhtilāf al-'Ulamā'* ('Abd Allāh Aḥmad ed, Dār al-Bashā'ir Islamiyyah 1995).

——*Uṣūl al-Jaṣṣāṣ* (Muḥammad Tāmir ed, Dār al-Kutub al-'Ilmiyya 2003).

——*Sharḥ Mukhtaṣar al-Ṭaḥāwī* ('Iṣmat Muḥammad ed, Dār al-Sirāj 2010).

Ibn Kamāl Pāshā, Aḥmad b. Sulaymān, *al-Īḍāḥ fī Sharḥ al-Iṣlāḥ* ('Abd Allāh Dā'ūd ed, Dār al-Kutub al-'Ilmiyya 2007).

Ibn Kathīr, Ismā'īl b. 'Umar, *al-Bidāyah wa al-Nihāyah* ('Alī Mu'awwaḍ ed, Dār al-Kutub al-'Ilmiyya, 1994).

Al-Lāmishī, Muḥammad b. Zayd, *Kitāb fī Uṣūl al-Fiqh* ('Abd al-Majīd Turkī ed, Dār al-Gharb al-Islāmī 1995).

Mubārakpūrī, Muḥammad 'Abd al-Raḥmān, *Tuḥfat al-Aḥwadhī* (al-Maktabah al-Salafiya 1963).

Al-Nawawī, Yaḥyā b. Sharaf, *Sharḥ Saḥīḥ al-Muslim* (Wahba al-Zuḥaylī ed, Dār al-Khayr 1998).

Qāḍīkhān, al-Ḥasan b. Manṣūr, *Fatāwā Qāḍīkhān* (Sālim Muṣṭafā ed, Dār al-Kutub al-ʿIlmiyya 2009).

Al-Qurashī, Ibn Abī Wafā, *al-Jawāhir al-Muḍīyah* (Majlis Dāʾirat al-Maʿārif al-ʿuthmānīya 1988).

Ibn Quṭlubughā, al-Qāsim b. ʿAbd Allāh, *Tāj al-Tarājim* (Muḥammad Yūsuf ed, Dār al-Qalam 1992).

—— *Khulāṣat al-Afkār* (Thanāʾ Allāh Zāhidī ed, Dār Ibn Ḥazm 2003).

Al-Saghnāqī, al-Ḥusayn b. ʿAlī, *Kitāb al-Wāfī fī Uṣūl al-Fiqh* (Muḥammad Akhsīkathī ed, Dār al-Qāhira 2003).

Al-Samarqandī, Muḥammad b. Aḥmad, *Mizān al-Uṣūl fī Natāʾij al-ʿUqūl* (ʿAbd al-Mālik Saʿdī ed, Wizārat al-Awqāf 1987).

Al-Sarakhsī, Muḥammad b. Aḥmad, *al-Muḥarrar fī Uṣūl al-Fiqh* (Ṣalāḥ b. Muḥammad ed, Dār al-Kutub al-ʿIlmiyya 1996).

——*Kitāb al-Mabsūṭ* (Kamāl ʿInānī ed, Dār al-Kutub al-ʿIlmiyya 2001).

——*Uṣūl al-Sarakhsī* (Abū al-Wafāʿ ed, Dār al-Kutub al-ʿIlmiyya 2005).

Al-Ṣuyūṭī, ʿAbd al-Raḥmān b. Abī Bakr, *al-Itqān fī ʿUlūm al-Qurʾān* (Muṣṭafá Dīb ed, Dār Ibn Kathīr 2000).

Al-Ṭaḥāwī, Aḥmad b. Muḥammad, *al-ʿAqīda al-Ṭaḥāwīya* (Qadīmī Kutub Khāna n.d.).

Al-Tamartāshī, Muḥammad b. ʿAbd Allāh, *al-Wuṣūl ilā Qawāʿid al-Uṣūl* (Muḥammad Sharīf ed, Dār al-Kutub al-ʿIlmiyya 2000).

Al-Tirmidhī, Muḥammad b. ʿĪsā, *Jāmiʿ al-Tirmidhī* (ʿĀdil Murshid ed, Dār al-Aʿlām, 2001).

Walīullāh, Shāh, *al-Fawz al-Kabīr fī Uṣūl al-Tafsīr* (Salmān al-Ḥusaynī ed, Dār al-Bashāʾir n.d.).

Abū Zahra, Muḥammad, *Uṣūl al-Fiqh* (Dār al-Thiqāfat al-ʿArabiyya 1957).

Bibliography of Non-Arabic Sources

Ahmad, A, *Structural Interrelations of Theory and Practice in Islamic Law* (Brill 2006).

Ahmed, R, *Constructing an Islamic Legal Narrative* (PhD Diss, University of Virginia 2008).

——'The Ethics of Prophetic Disobedience: Qur'ān 8:67 at the Crossroads of the Islamic Sciences' (2011) 39:3 *Journal of Religious Ethics*.

Ahmed, S, 'Ibn Taymiyyah and The Satanic Verses' (1998) 2 *Studia Islamica*.

Austin, J L, *How to Do Things With Words* (Oxford University Press 1962).

Bearman, P, Bianquis, T, Bosworth, C, van Donzel, E, and Heinrichs, W (eds), *Encyclopedia of Islam* (2nd edition, Brill 2005).

Bedir, M, 'An Early Response to Shāfiʿī: ʿĪsā b. Abān on the Prophetic Report' (2002) 9:3 *Islamic Law and Society*.

——'Reason and Revelation: Abū Zayd al-Dabbūsī on Rational Proofs' (2004) 43:2 *Islamic Studies*.

Brown, J, *Hadith: Muhammad's Legacy in the Medieval and Modern World* (Oneworld 2009).

Burton, J, 'The Exegesis of Q. 2:106 and the Islamic theories of *naskh*: *mā nansakh min āya aw nansahā na'ti bi khairin minhā aw mithlihā*ʿ (1985) 48:3 *Bulletin of the School of Oriental and African Studies*.

Calder, N, *Islamic Jurisprudence in the Classical Era* (Cambridge University Press 2010).

Carré, O, *Mysticism and Politics: A Critical Reading of Fī Ẓilāl al-Qur'ān by Sayyid Qutb* (Carol Artigues tr, Brill 2003).

Colapietro, V and Olshewsky, T (eds), *Peirce's Doctrine of Signs* (Mouton de Gruyter 1996).

Cornell, D, *Tranformations: Recollective Imagination and Sexual Difference* (Routledge 1993).

Dien, M W, *Islamic Law: From Historical Foundations to Contemporary Practice* (Edinburgh University Press 2004).

Donaldson, W J, *Sharecropping in the Yemen: A Study of Islamic Legal Theory, Custom and Pragmatism* (Brill 2000).

Dutton, Y, '*Amal* v. *Hadith* in Islamic Law: The Case of *Sadl al-Yadayn* (Holding One's Hands by One's Sides) When Doing the Prayer' (1996) 3:1 *Islamic Law and Society*.

Emon, A, *Islamic Natural Law Theories* (Oxford University Press 2010).

van Ess, J, *Die Erkenntnislehre des ʿAdudaddin al-Içi* (Weisbaden 1966).

—— 'Ḍirār b. ʿAmr und die "Cahmiya": Biographie einer vergessenen Schule' (1967) 43 *Der Islam*.

Fadel, M, 'The Social Logic of Taqlīd and the Rise of the Mukhtasar' (1996) 3:2 *Islamic Law and Society*.

Frei, H, *The Eclipse of Biblical Narrative: A Study in Eighteenth and Nineteenth Century Hermeneutics* (Yale University Press 1974).

Ghazali, M, *A Thematic Commentary on the Qur'ān* (International Institute of Islamic Thought 2000).

Gleave, R (ed), *Islamic Law Theory and Practive* (I.B. Tauris 1997).

Griffel, F, *al-Ghazālī's Dialectical Theology* (Oxford University Press 2009).

Hallaq, W, 'Was the Gate of *ijtihād* Closed?' (1984) 16: 1 *International Journal of Middle East Studies*.

—— 'The Logic of Legal Reasoning in Religious and Non-Religious Cultures: The Case of Islamic Law and the Common Law' (1985–1986) 34 *Cleveland State Law Review*.

—— 'On the Authoritativeness of Sunni Consensus' (1986) 18 *International Journal of Middle East Studies* 427, 444.

—— 'Non-Analogical Arguments in Sunni Juridical *Qiyās*' (1989) 36:3 *Arabica*.

—— 'Model Shurūṭ Works and the Dialectic of Doctrine and Practice' (1995) 2:2 *Islamic Law and Society*.

—— *A History of Islamic Legal Theories* (University of Cambridge Press 1997).

—— 'The Authenticity of Prophetic Ḥadīth: A Pseudo-Problem' (1999) 89 *Studia Islamica*.

Hallaq, W and Little, D (eds), *Islamic Studies Presented to Charles Adams* (Brill 1991).

Heemskerk, M, *Suffering in the Mu'tazilite Theology* (Brill, 2000).

Heinrichs, W, 'On the Genesis of the *Haqîqa-Majâz* Dichotomy' (1984) 59 *Studia Islamica*.

Hunsinger, G (ed), *Theology and Narrative: Selected Essays* (Oxford University Press 1993).

Istanbul University (ed), *900. Ölum Yilönümü Münasebetiyle Büyük İslâm Hukukcusu Şemsu'l-E'imme* (Ankara Universitesi Basimevi 1965).

Jackson, S, 'Taqlid, Legal Scaffolding and the Scope of Legal Injunctions in Post-Formative Theory' (1996) 3:2 *Islamic Law and Society*.

Johansen, B, 'A Response to Ann Elizabeth Mayer's Review of *The Islamic Law on Land Tax and Rent: The Peasant's Loss of Property Rights as Interpreted in the Hanafite Legal Literature of the Mamluk and Ottoman Periods*' (1992) 24 *International Journal of Middle East Studies*.

—— 'Casuistry: Between Legal Concept and Social Praxis' (1995) 2:2 *Islamic Law and Society*.

—— 'Coutumes Locales et Coutumes Universelles' in *Contingency is a Sacred Law* (Brill 1999).

Juynboll, G, *Muslim Traditions* (Cambridge University Press 1983) 58.

—— 'Some Notes of Islam's First Fuqahā' Distilled From early Ḥadīth Literature' (1992) 39:3 *Arabica*.

—— '(Re)appraisal of Some Technical Terms in Ḥadīth Science' (2001) 8:3 *Islamic Law and Society*.

Kamali, M, *Principles of Islāmic Jurisprudence* (Islamic Texts Society 1991).

—— *A Textbook of Hadīth Studies* (Islamic Foundation 2005).

Kavacki, Y, *Fiqh, Islāmic Law and Uṣūl al-Fiqh*, (unpublished, accessible at <http://www.iant.com/imam/book.txt>, last accessed January 15, 2011).

Keuny, K, *The Rhetoric of Sobriety: Wine in Early Islam* (SUNY Press 2001).

Knysh, A (trs), *al-Qushayri's Epistle on Sufism* (Garnet Publishing 2007).

Koskenniemi, M, *From Apology to Utopia: The Structure of International Legal Argument* (Cambridge University Press 2005).
Landau-Tesseron, E (trs), *The History of al-Ṭabarī Vol. XXXIX* (SUNY Press 1998).
Larkin, M, *The Theology of Meaning* (The American Oriental Society 1995).
Lowry, J, *Early Islamic Legal Theory: the Risala of Muḥammad ibn Idrīs al-Shāfiʿī* (Brill 2007).
MacCormack, N, *Legal Reasoning and Legal Theory* (Oxford University Press 1978).
Madelung, W, 'Early Muslim Doctrine Regarding Faith as Reflecting in the 'Kitāb al-Īmān of Abū 'Ubayd al-Qāsim b. Sallām' (1970) 32 *Studia Islamica.*
Madigan, D, *The Qur'ān's Self-Image: Writing and Authority in Islam's Scripture* (Princeton University Press 2001).
Makdisi, G, 'The Juridical Theology of Shāfi'ī: Origins and Significance of Uṣūl al-Fiqh' (1984) 59 *Studia Islamica.*
—— *Ibn Aqil: Religion and Culture in Classical Islam* (Edinburgh Press 1997).
Malamud, M, 'Sufi Organizations and Structures of Authority in Medieval Nishapur' (1994) 26:3 *International Journal of Middle East Studies.*
Masud, M, Messick, B, and Powers, D (eds), *Islamic Legal Interpretations: Muftis and the Fatwas* (Harvard University Press 1996).
Masud, M, Peters, R, and Powers, D, *Dispensing Justice in Islam: Qadis and the Judgments* (Brill 2006).
Melchert, C, *The Formation of the Sunni Schools of Law: 9th-10th Centuries C.E.* (Brill 1997).
—— 'Traditionist-Jurisprudents and the Framing of Islāmic Law' (2001) 8:3 *Islamic Law and Society.*
—— 'Qur'ānic Abrogation Across the Ninth Century' in Bernard Weiss (ed), *Studies in Islāmic Legal Theory* (Brill 2002).
Meron, Y, 'The Development of Hanafi Legal Thought' (1969) 30 *Studia Islamica.*
—— 'Marghinānī, His Method and His Legacy' (2002) 9:3 *Islamic Law and Society.*
Modarressi, H, 'Early Debates on the Integrity of the Qur'ān' (1993) 77 *Studia Islamica.*
Na'im, A, *Toward an Islāmic Reformation: Civil liberties, human rights and international law* (Syracuse University Press 1990).
Peirce, C, *Reasoning and the Logic of Things* (Kenneth Ketner ed, Harvard University Press 1992).
—— *Pragmatism as a Principle and Method of Right Thinking* (SUNY Press 1997).
Pencak, W, 'Charles Peirce's Understanding of the Four Ages and of his Own Place in the History of Human Thought' (1991) 179 *Semiotica.*
Powers, D, 'On the Abrogation of the Bequest Verses' (1982) 29:3 *Arabica.*
Rahman, F, *Islam* (University of Chicago Press 1979).
Reinhart, A, *Before Revelation: The Boundaries of Muslim Moral Thought* (SUNY Press 1995).
Ricouer, P, *Interpretation Theory: Discourse and the Surplus of Meaning* (Texas Christian University Press 1976).

Rosenthal, F (trs), *al-Muqaddimah: An Introduction to History* (Princeton University Press 1967).
Sachedina, A, *The Just Ruler in Shī'īte Islām: The Comprehensive Authority of the Jurist in Imamite Jurisprudence* (Oxford University Press 1988).
—— (tr), *Prolegomena to the Qur'ān* (Oxford University Press 1998).
Seligman, A, Weller, R, Puett, M, and Simon, B, *Ritual and Its Consequences: Essays on the Limits of Sincerity* (Oxford University Press, 2008).
Sezgin, F, *Geschichte Des Arabishcen Schrifttums* (Brill 1967) I: 456.
Shehaby, N, 'Illa and Qiyās in Early Islamic Legal Theory' (1982) 102:1 *Journal of the American Oriental Society.*
Slane, W, *Ibn Khallikan's Biographical Dictionary, Vol. II* (Cosimo 2010).
Smith, J, *Imagining Religion: From Babylon to Jonestown* (University of Chicago Press 1982).
Sperl, S and Shackle, C (eds), *Qasida Poetry in Islamic Asia and Africa: Eulogy's Bounty, Meaning's Abundance* (Brill 1996).
Tastan, O, *The Jurisprudence of Sarakhsī* (PhD Diss, University of Exeter 1993).
Unger, R, *The Critical Legal Studies Movement* (Harvard University Press 1986).
Vishanoff, D, *Early Islamic Hermeneutics: Language, speech and meaning in preclassical legal theory* (PhD Diss, Emory University 2004).
—— *The Formation of Islamic Hermeneutics: How Sunni Legal Theorists Imagined a Revealed Law* (American Oriental Society 2011).
Vogel, F, *Islamic Law and Legal System: Studies of Saudi Arabi* (Brill 200).
Wakin, J, *The Function of Documents in Islamic Law* (SUNY Press 1972).
Weiss, B, *In Search of God's Law: Islamic Jurisprudence in the Writings of Sayf al-Dīn al-Āmidī* (University of Utah Press 1992).
—— *The Spirit of Islam* (University of Georgia Press 1998).
—— (ed), *Studies in Islamic Legal Theory* (Brill 2002).
Wensinck, A, *The Muslim Creed: its Genesis and Historical Development* (Frank Cass 1965).
Wheeler, B, *Applying the Canon in Islam: the Authorization and Maintenance of Interpretive Reasoning in Ḥanafī Scholarship* (SUNY Press 1996).
Wood, C, *The Formation of Christian Understanding* (Westminster Press 1981).
Zadeh, T, *Translation, Geography and the Divine Word* (PhD Diss, Harvard University 2007).
—— 'Touching and Ingesting: Early Debates over the Material Qur'an' (2009) 129:3 *Journal of the American Oriental Society* 443.
Zysow A, *The Economy of Certainty: An Introduction to the Typology of Islamic Legal Theory* (PhD Diss, Harvard University 1984).
—— 'Two Unrecognized Karrāmī Texts' (1988) 108:4 *Journal of the American Oriental Society.*
—— 'Muʿtazilism and Māturīdism in Ḥanafī Legal Theory' in Bernard Weiss (ed), *Studies in Islamic Legal Theory* (Brill 2002).

Index

The manufacturer's authorised representative in the EU for product safety is Oxford University Press España S.A. of El Parque Empresarial San Fernando de Henares, Avenida de Castilla, 2 - 28830 Madrid (www.oup.es/en or product.safety@oup.com). OUP España S.A. also acts as importer into Spain of products made by the manufacturer.
Printed and bound by CPI Group (UK) Ltd, Croydon, CR0 4YY
14/09/2026
02216307-0004